WILLIAM FAULKNER,

LIFE GLIMPSES

"A biographer fashions a man or woman out of seemingly intractable materials of archives, diaries, documents, dreams, a glimpse, a series of memories."
          —Leon Edel, "The Figure under the Carpet"

WILLIAM FAULKNER, LIFE GLIMPSES

Louis Daniel Brodsky

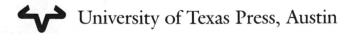 University of Texas Press, Austin

First Edition, 1990

Requests for permission to reproduce material from this work should be
sent to Permissions, University of Texas Press, Box 7819, Austin, Texas
78713-7819.

⊗ The paper used in this publication meets the minimum requirements
of American National Standard for Information Sciences—Permanence of
Paper for Printed Library Materials, ANSI Z39.48-1984.

Library of Congress Cataloging-in-Publication Data

Brodsky, Louis Daniel.
    William Faulkner, life glimpses / by Louis Daniel Brodsky. — 1st ed.
      p.   cm.
    Includes bibliographical references (p.).
    ISBN 0-292-79048-1 (alk. paper)
      1. Faulkner, William, 1897–1962—Biography.   2. Novelists,
    American—20th century—Biography.   I. Title.
    PS3511.A86Z6355   1990
    813'.52—dc20
      [B]   89-28368
                                                          CIP

For

Jan, Trilogy, and Troika,
my family,

Charlotte and Saul,
my parents,

Robert W. Hamblin,
my friend

CONTENTS

Photo section following page 181.
   All photographs courtesy Brodsky Faulkner Collection,
   Southeast Missouri State University, Cape Girardeau, Missouri.

ACKNOWLEDGMENTS

This book has been evolving for eight years. During this evolution, a few of these chapters have appeared in substantially or somewhat different form in *The Faulkner Journal, Studies in Bibliography,* and *Southern Review.* To James B. Carothers, Fredson T. Bowers, and Lewis P. Simpson and Fred Hobson, editors of these respective publications, I wish to extend my enormous appreciation. Their cogent and insightful suggestions encouraged me to keep probing and weaving additional materials into the mix that ultimately rendered this full-blown treatment of William Faulkner's life.

Rita Stam, of Farmington, Missouri, deserves more than passing praise for the patience, competence, and friendliness with which she always approached and accomplished the requests I asked of her in typesetting and advancing on the word processor the developing revisionary drafts of this book.

Linda Hermelin has spent considerable labors trying to protect me from myself by isolating and suggesting corrections I might make in spelling, punctuation, grammar, and style.

Also, I would like to use this occasion to make the following recognitions:

To Dr. Bill W. Stacy, President of Southeast Missouri State University, who, "no strings attached," initially made his institutional facilities available to me as a repository for the Brodsky Faulkner Collection and as a center of operations from which I might focus my scholarly energies on the task of writing this book;

To Edwin Jay Baum, who, during the time I was writing this book, served as President of Biltwell Company, Inc., of St. Louis, Missouri, a men's clothing manufacturer for whom I worked. He sanctioned and indulged my "research" leaves;

To Evans Harrington and Ann Abadie, Co-directors of the Faulkner and Yoknapatawpha Conference series held annually at the University of Mississippi in Oxford. Their invitations to me to participate in four programs and their many kindnesses have helped nurture my interests in Faulkner studies;

To William R. Ferris, Director of the Center for the Study of Southern Culture at Ole Miss, who is responsible for sponsoring the full-scale series, *Faulkner: A Comprehensive Guide to the Brodsky Collection,* published since 1982 by the University Press of Mississippi and which I have frequently cited as a major source of primary materials upon which I have relied to substantiate the conclusions this book draws;

To Frankie Westbrook, Sponsoring Editor of the University of Texas Press, who has championed this book from the day we first discussed it by phone to the last entry in the index.

To James B. Colvert, Professor Emeritus, University of Georgia, whose constructive, appreciative reading of this book in manuscript led to many unexpected enhancements;

To Barbara Spielman, Managing Editor of the University of Texas Press, who refined the manuscript for this book with the deftness of a magician, and to Sarah Buttrey, her copyeditor assigned the task of refining the manuscript;

To Jane Goldberg, who not only created the index for this book but also put the final, magical touches to it—thank you, Janie;

And to Rolla Gordon, of Farmington, Missouri, who as friend was always available for supportive discussion and who as President of the Mercantile Bank of Farmington was always willing to lend to me his institution's unequivocal financial backing for so many of the valuable artifacts that form the significant core of the Brodsky Faulkner Collection.

Victoria Fielden Johnson has been patient with and sympathetic toward my obsession to "get to know" William Faulkner. With her daughter, Gillian, she has made me a very welcome guest in their home and in their lives, and she has become a very dear friend of mine.

I feel compelled to make special mention of the fact that for eleven years Robert W. Hamblin and I have shared a mutual respect for each other's professional work, and, more important, we have been trusted, best friends. Borrowing from Faulkner's dedication to Saxe Commins in *Big Woods,* I offer this salvo: "We've not only been looking at the same thing, but we've always seen it eye to eye."

Charlotte and Saul Brodsky have made funds available to me for numerous Faulkner acquisitions I have purchased over nearly three decades, many of which have strengthened the evidentiary foundations upon which myriad conclusions in this book have been based. For their financial support and their abiding, manifest love, I am, and always will be, their devoted, loving son.

Finally, to my wife, Jan, I express my love; she has witnessed the edifice being constructed, *almost* from the ground up. And to our children, Trilogy and Troika, I extend my deepest, widest, highest love, always.

INTRODUCTION

This book of "biographical glimpses" into the life of William Faulkner is intended to give, through random impressions, a collective cohesiveness to an eclectically lived life. In no way does it pretend to approximate a fully embodied intimate portrait or to encourage the reader to superimpose on the subject's life a gratuitous or arbitrary sense of completeness. In writing it, I have been guided by one overriding assumption: namely, that Faulkner lived his life by fits and starts, not always by disciplined and predictably discernible patterns implemented by conscious volition. Unlike previous biographers who have panned Faulkner's lifesweep with meticulous attention to data, details, continuities and patterns of behavior, and/or psycho-biographically oriented literary developments, I have chosen to hold the camera steady on selected events and time frames, hoping to arrest and fix certain essences, then present them chapter by chapter in a cubistic montage.

Ultimately, this approach does not derive just from a fundamental belief in the discontinuous and illogical quality of human history and perspectives, or merely from my hope to make essences stand for and explain entire movements or dramatic passages in a person's life, but rather from an unslakable desire to present original information in as unique a way possible. I would like to think that this book of "biographical glimpses" *is* original in inferences it promulgates and conclusions it nudges the reader to make and share with its author.

The actual composition of this book consists of a main section, "Glimpses," containing seven chapters arranged in approximate chronological fashion, and a secondary four-part appendix section, "Glimpses within Glimpses." Three chapters in the main body of the book, "Life Masks," "Bill and Buzz: Fellow Scenarists," and "'White Beaches,'" are intended as overviews of Faulkner's entire life and literary career. These chapters open, close, and give the middle of this work integrity, almost in the way covers of a book tightly fitted to the spine binding strip give a volume internal strength. Of these three, Chapters 4 and 7 appear in the form of interviews that I conducted, respectively, with Faulkner's Hollywood friend from the forties, Albert I. "Buzz" Bezzerides and with his granddaughter Victoria Fielden Johnson.

My chief motive for employing interviews, arresting living voices and mingling them with my own, has been not only to listen for new interpretations but to look out from the eye while seeing in from the edges of the storm, to capture a certain dynamic resonance and to experience a "recreation," thereby closing some of the distance the years have put between Faulkner and us, a double distancing, really, since most of us never knew William Faulkner in the first place.

The opening chapter, "Life Masks," is the fullest expression of my own voice trying to blend previously unwoven strands into a new crazy quilt. Much of the unique material introduced in this chapter surfaced as a result of friendships I made with Emily Whitehurst Stone, widow of Phil Stone, Faulkner's early literary mentor and lifelong lawyer from Oxford, Mississippi; Dorothy Berliner Commins, widow of Faulkner's trusted editor Saxe; Victoria Fielden Johnson, Faulkner's granddaughter and a contemporary of mine who lived sporadically over a twenty-year period at Rowan Oak, the Faulkners' Oxford home; Joan Williams, the youthful "protégée" Faulkner took for a companion in 1949 when he was fifty-two; Ruth Ford, a Hollywood "friend" to whom Faulkner gave his play, *Requiem for a Nun;* and Malcolm Cowley, one of America's foremost critics and early champion of Faulkner's one-time neglected literary reputation.

Between Chapters 1 and 4 I have interspersed two more-narrowly focused units based on materials from personal discoveries I have made over the last decade. Specifically, Chapters 2 and 3 concentrate on bringing to light previously unknown information about the origins of two poems Faulkner wrote in the early twenties, "Elder Watson in Heaven" and "Pregnacy" [*sic*], and in doing so give insight into Faulkner's developing literary and personal aesthetics during the twenties and thirties.

Located pivotally between Chapters 4 and 7, which are devoted to full-scale biographical overviews, Chapters 5 and 6 concentrate on a singularly catalytic time frame in Faulkner's life and literary career: the decades of the forties and fifties. They describe the transformation or metamorphosis that occurred when Faulkner's Hollywood experience as a scenarist at Warner Bros. (1942–1945) collided with his old notions of artistic integrity, then converged on his growing public recognition and celebrity at decade's end. These companion-piece chapters pinpoint and analyze Faulkner's emergence from a fiction writer enjoying relative insularity into a polemicist with an urgent compulsion to make controversial political protests addressing the issues of social and racial injustice in America and the threat of atomic Armageddon as symptoms of hatred and misunderstanding between people of similar as well as different nationalities.

These chapters assess this metamorphosis by examining its origins and the effects it had upon Faulkner's personality and on his art. In doing so, they rely on many previously unavailable materials, most notably the 3,500-page Warner Bros. Story File of scripts Faulkner wrote while under contract during his early-to-mid-forties sojourn in Hollywood and manuscripts Faulkner left with A. I. Bezzerides when he made his final "flight" from Burbank. Also, letters formerly belonging to Faulkner's stepdaughter, Victoria Franklin Fielden, sent to Faulkner during the mid-fifties in response to a crucial civil rights essay he contributed to *Life* magazine and items that were in the possession of Cleanth Brooks, the distinguished literary scholar and Faulknerian, help inform and shape the substance of these two chapters. They should provide a new perspective on and fuller understanding of the changing dynamics of the man who, in the late twenties and early thirties, could write with the bleakest of outlooks such novels as *Sanctuary* and *The Sound and the Fury,* yet who by 1950 in his Nobel Prize speech would deliver one of the most impassioned and eloquently expressed affirmations of the collective human spirit's durability and capacity for hope ever written.

Also, I have included in this book a secondary, somewhat more bibliographically oriented appendix consisting of four sections, A–D. These "Glimpses within Glimpses" highlight very specific material—a handmade booklet containing Faulkner's only story for children, an instruction sheet on curing pork, two public speeches, and a document recording Faulkner's "impressions" of a musical entertainment performed in his honor in a foreign country. At various points within the main text, I have directed the reader's attention, by means of a note, to a corresponding section in the appendix where I focus at a much higher power on specific artifacts to give deeper insight into tendencies and attitudes unique even when measured against Faulkner's own idiosyncratic standards. Since the chief purpose of these sections is to reinforce existing contentions with more specialized scholarly apparatus, they need not be considered obligatory for the general reader. However, they should be accorded far more respect than merely extended notes might command.

William Faulkner, Life Glimpses is my attempt to distill almost thirty years of reflection, strategizing, brooding, and second-guessing convincingly, with insight and compassion. I would like to hope that during the time you spend reading this book, William Faulkner "comes alive" before your very eyes. Even more, I hope that when you have finished it, you will have derived a similar experience to that which Barry K. Wade, Chief Editor of W. W. Norton & Company, Publishers, described to me when he wrote, "I have now read *William Faulkner, Life Glimpses* and I feel a little as if I have spent a week or two at Rowan Oak with the man himself."

GLIMPSES

ONE

LIFE MASKS

"Beginning with Sartoris *I discovered that my own little postage stamp of native soil was worth writing about and that I would never live long enough to exhaust it, and by sublimating the actual into apocryphal I would have complete liberty to use whatever talent I might have to its absolute top."*
—William Faulkner, interview with Jean Stein, 1956 [1]

"Bud, you're an animal, but I'm just a vegetable!"
—William Faulkner to A. I. Bezzerides, ca. 1944 [2]

William Faulkner was essentially a passive person who not only privately condemned himself for his passivity but also at times disparaged his own character publicly. In fact, not only as a youth but also as an adult he repeatedly adopted as personae figures who represented the life of courage and action. Furthermore, he would spend the better part of his adulthood attempting to sublimate the myriad active elements he considered as constituting his "vegetable" life into the apocryphal matter of his fantasies. If in reality Faulkner's "own little postage stamp of native soil" would be "worth writing about," provide the stuff of fiction, then fiction itself would engender in him the stuff of living. His existence would be that of a double agent's disguised conspiracy against reality itself.

A graphic illustration of Faulkner's dissatisfaction with himself as a physically inactive individual and with his role as writer appears through implication at the outset of *Absalom, Absalom!,* in which Miss Rosa Coldfield makes Quentin Compson a willing conspirator in the fall of the house of Sutpen:

> So I dont imagine you will ever come back here and settle down as a country
> lawyer in a little town like Jefferson, since Northern people have already seen

to it that there is little left in the South for a young man. So maybe you will
enter the literary profession as so many Southern gentlemen and gentlewomen
too are doing now and maybe some day you will remember this and write
about it. You will be married then I expect and perhaps your wife will want a
new gown or a new chair for the house and you can write this and submit it
to the magazines. Perhaps you will even remember kindly then the old woman
who made you spend a whole afternoon sitting indoors and listening while
she talked about people and events you were fortunate enough to escape yourself when you wanted to be out among young friends of your own age.[3]

This passage is intricately charged with Faulkner's personal sentiments. Although Miss Rosa places law in the highest echelon of respectable vocations, the profession suggests to her effeteness and ineffectuality. Innocuous, utterly domestic in its scope, writing, she further suggests, is a less
active, more demeaning vocation than the law.

Miss Rosa concludes her prefatory remarks to the lengthy tale about
Sutpen and his family by observing that she has "made" Quentin spend the
whole afternoon inside when he might have been out playing with his
young friends. Actually Quentin has no choice. Miss Rosa tells him that he
has been "fortunate enough to escape" the people and events she is poised
to evoke and dramatize for him, but, ironically, her very telling will still
further implicate Quentin in events and lives for which he already feels a
compulsive responsibility. During the course of the novel Quentin will
learn that his greatest misfortune may be that he has to remain a passive
rather than active participant in the events; no matter that he has entered
the events through his imagination's will, he will experience a growing
awareness of ambivalent guilt and hatred and shame.

Of course Quentin Compson is not William Faulkner. Somewhere in
that no-man's-land between protagonist and author flourished the dynamic mediating forces that permitted Faulkner, the artist, to fuse Quentin's angst with his own and to transcend himself through the imagination.
Nonetheless, although the published novel stood ineluctably as a testa-
ment to the power of his imagination as an artist, Faulkner, the citizen of
Oxford, Mississippi, had to go on living with the old, unchangeable daily
frustrations, ambivalences, and trivial responsibilities after the eruptive
creative juices had cooled and hardened into *Absalom, Absalom!*.

Almost as though a dozen years had not intervened and as if, like Quentin Compson, he were again listening to Miss Rosa expound her low estimation of the legal and writing professions, Faulkner described Gavin
Stevens in *Knight's Gambit* as "a split personality: the one, the lawyer, the
county attorney who walked and breathed and displaced air; the other, the
garrulous facile voice so garrulous and facile that it seemed to have no con-

nection with reality at all and presently hearing it was like listening not even to fiction but to literature."[4]

In fact, Faulkner had relentlessly pressed this kind of negative expression into service in novels that followed *Absalom, Absalom!*. In *The Unvanquished,* appearing in 1938, Bayard Sartoris remarks of his infatuation with Drusilla: "I thought then of the woman of thirty, the symbol of the ancient and eternal Snake and of the men who have written of her, and I realized then the immitigable chasm between all life and all print—that those who can, do, those who cannot and suffer enough because they can't, write about it."[5] Two years later, in *The Hamlet,* the collective community of Frenchman's Bend concludes of its new teacher, Labove, ironically a former football star at the state university, that, "although his designation of professor was a distinction, it was still a woman's distinction, functioning actually in a woman's world like the title of reverend."[6] Providing autobiographical information to Malcolm Cowley, the highly esteemed American literary critic who was concluding his introduction to the forthcoming Viking compilation, *The Portable Faulkner,* Faulkner summarized "literature in the South" from the time of the Civil War in this way: "Oratory was the first art; Confederate generals would hold up attacks while they made speeches to their troops. Apart from that, 'art' was really no manly business. It was a polite painting of china by gentlewomen. When they entered its domain through the doors of their libraries, it was to read somebody else's speeches, or politics, or the classics of the faintly school, and even these were men who, if they had been writing men, would have written still more orations."[7]

For Faulkner, regarding writing or teaching literature, a profound and seemingly unavoidable domesticity or womanish quality would persist in plaguing both callings and practitioners, plague him personally with self-doubts about his own "distinction."

On February 7, 1949, just slightly more than four months after the late-September publication of *Intruder in the Dust,* Faulkner wrote a two-page letter he intended to mail to Robert Haas, one of Random House's three principals, imploring him to interpolate into the very next printing of the book a new passage, the conclusion of which reads: ". . . so that in five hundred years or perhaps even less than that, all America can paraphrase the tag line of a book a novel of about twenty years ago by another Mississippian, a mild retiring little man over yonder at Oxford, in which a fictitious Canadian said to a fictitious self-lacerated Southerner in a dormitory room in a not too authentic Harvard: 'I who regard you will have also sprung from the loins of African kings.'"[8]

Two countervailing dynamics are in tension within this passage: on the one hand, Faulkner regarded his accomplishment in *Absalom, Absalom!*

proudly enough to presume that "all America can paraphrase the tag line" to remind itself of a former truth; on the other hand, Faulkner still viewed himself with considerable self-deprecation, alluding to the novel's author as a "mild retiring little man over yonder at Oxford." In addition, by juxtaposed inference, Faulkner equated himself with Quentin, the "fictitious self-lacerated Southerner." Contemplating what he had written, Faulkner evidently decided he had been too harsh on himself; before actually posting the letter, he discarded both ribbon and carbon copies of page 2 and retyped it with one quite major recasting of a phrase: for "a mild retiring little man" he substituted "the successfully mild little bloke."[9] Thus, he asserted an identity with the valiant English, as he had been doing sporadically in dress, speech patterns, and physical mannerisms since his days in the RAF in 1918.

In a different kind of letter, postmarked Oxford, October 25, 1952, Faulkner confided to Saxe Commins, his Random House editor and beloved friend, his urgent need to get away from his home and family. But, he told Commins, he would be unsuccessful in convincing Estelle that his reason for wanting to leave home was to save his talent from total disintegration "since she (E.) has never had any regard or respect for my work, has always looked on it as a hobby, like collecting stamps."[10] To what degree Faulkner was projecting onto his wife his own uncertainties and disillusionments is not clear. But he seems to have felt that what he took to be her attitude toward his vocation represented the general attitude toward it: his life's work was seen by others to represent little more than a "hobby."

Paradoxically, Faulkner's preoccupation with the apparent uselessness of the writer in society increased with his growing reputation. Three years later, in two sardonic public statements, he elaborated the image of a career he had first described privately to Saxe Commins. In his speech on receiving the National Book Award for Fiction on January 25, 1955, he claimed that "the pursuit of art is a peaceful hobby like breeding Dalmatians."[11] Five days later, in an interview he gave to Harvey Breit, his friend and associate-to-be on the People-To-People Program initiated by President Eisenhower, Faulkner added to the notion of the writer's uselessness the idea of his inherent dislocation in society: "The writer in America isn't part of the culture of this country. He's like a fine dog. People like him around, but he's of no use."[12]

These foregoing citations, culled from myriad references to the ineffectuality of the writer that Faulkner made in print or in public statements over his forty-year career, indicate an abiding preoccupation with failure— not with the failure to become a productive artist, but a failure to fulfill his own conception of himself as an active human being. He never succeeded at squaring his self-image as a writer with his image of those he admired as contributing individuals in society. The fact that writing required isolation, contemplation, and introspection minimized its value in a world that revered "doers" and "things." He was not a "doer"; at best, he was someone to be indulged or merely tolerated.

Faulkner's ideal of the active, heroic person was the soldier, an ideal he conceived to have been embodied in the career of his great-grandfather, the "Old Colonel," William Clark Falkner. In this leader of soldiers, railroad builder, hard drinker, and duelist, Faulkner discovered the romantic apotheosis of the man of action and great deeds. That the Old Colonel also found time to be a lawyer, politician, and writer added to his luster, but Faulkner saw his great-grandfather first as a soldier. He portrayed him as such in fiction, although he suggests doubts about the Old Colonel's ethical and moral behavior in *The Unvanquished*.

Rejected by the American armed forces for service in the First World War because of his small stature, Faulkner was accepted in 1918 as a flight training cadet by the RAF in Toronto. His stint lasted only from July to December 1918, when he returned home to Oxford. He received an "Honorary Rank of Second Lieutenant" in 1920.[13] His disappointment in having failed to go abroad and participate in battle is a commonly accepted biographical fact. We know, too, that he concocted tales about dogfights over Europe, crack-ups, and near-misses. The twenty-one-year-old Billy Falkner imagined himself, or at least one of his selves, as a heroic flier returned from the Great War, sporting a steel plate beneath his skull and, with the aid of a cane, managing to master a limp.[14]

Faulkner himself is embodied in one, if not in all three, of the wounded pilots he dramatizes sitting out the war in an English hospital in "The Lilacs," a poem possibly composed while he was stationed in Toronto. An early, subsequently revised draft of this poem mentions by name and distinction the three fliers: "John, the poet," "James, the motor car salesman," and "myself," the latter being the narrator who had been shot down over Mannheim in his "little pointed eared machine."[15] In his first novel, *Soldiers' Pay*, published in 1926, a Faulknerian avatar surfaces in the persona of Donald Mahon; another appears as the central protagonist of "Turn About," a short story published in the *Saturday Evening Post* on March 5, 1932. As late as the mid-forties, Faulkner was still alluding to himself as a pilot who had seen action over Germany. In fact, it was over Germany, he claimed, that he had lost his dog tag, an event about which he reminisced to his nephew, Jimmy Faulkner, in a patriotic confidence-boosting letter mailed from Hollywood.[16]

As sensitive as Faulkner was to the fact that he had "missed the war," he was equally aware of those writers who had not missed it: the English poets Siegfried Sassoon and Wilfred Owens, whose verse he admired greatly; the American novelists John Dos Passos and Ernest Hemingway, who had seen action on the front lines and whose fiction not only palpably re-created scenes of war but also reflected postwar disillusionment in a more poignant and authentic manner than anything Faulkner had approximated in *Soldiers' Pay* or in his "war" poetry and short stories. No matter how flexible it was becoming, his embryonic imagination was no match for their actual experience. Faulkner was highly conscious of his lack of experience. His first novel, *Soldiers' Pay,* and Hemingway's first, *The Sun Also Rises,* both appeared in 1926. Faulkner could have had no doubt about the superior sophistication of Hemingway's novel.

By 1929, however, Faulkner had reached a literary maturity equal to or even exceeding that of Hemingway. The year that saw the publication of *A Farewell to Arms* also marked the appearance of *The Sound and the Fury.* One of the twentieth century's greatest novels, *The Sound and the Fury* demonstrated that Faulkner had taught himself to set aside all his romantic notions of heroic figures poised on the tips of their shining sword points. In this novel, Faulkner focused on Yoknapatawpha, a minute integer of the county anyway, and in subsequent novels and short fictions he was to select shifting aspects of this region, a physical locale as well as his own heart's geography. Here he isolated Compson and Bundren children, Snopeses and Tulls, and Peabodys, Bookwrights, Armstids, Ratliffs, and McCaslins, lawyers, politicians, senators, judges, deputies, tenant farmers, ministers and reverends, soldiers, hunters, poor whites, blacks, Indians, and a few northern abolitionists, town merchants, traveling salesmen, fascists, and convicts: hypocritical, bigoted, pretentious, disillusioned, or well intentioned but ill-fated, misbegotten, all!

The Yoknapatawphans who Faulkner most admired were the ones who exemplified courage and fortitude in maintaining the struggle of living: the "doers," not those who were constantly on the lookout to take advantage of others, to survive at another's expense by dint of superior education, inside information, or chicanery, those whom Faulkner equated with the idle poor as well as the idle rich. The latter category, like the De Spains and Compsons and Sartorises, should have been stewards as their forebears had been to their respective clans and communities but instead, through complacency, laziness, alcoholism, and greed, had allowed themselves to deteriorate into ineffectual Southern gentlemen. Some of them lacked moral principles; others had scruples but lacked moral energy.

After soldiering, the occupations or avocations that commanded Faulkner's greatest respect were flying, hunting, farming, athletics, horseback riding, and sailing. Each of these activities provided opportunities for displaying courage, fearlessness, physical prowess, and a touch of foolhardiness—all the attributes Faulkner equated with men of action and with manhood. During the last fifteen years of his life, Faulkner owned a sail-boat, the *Ring Dove*. He kept horses at Rowan Oak for riding and jumping and engaged to a limited extent in fox hunting. He enjoyed athletics as a spectator of football, basketball, and baseball games on the Ole Miss campus, which was within walking distance of his home. Similarly, while living part of each year in Charlottesville, from 1956 until his death in 1962, he was often seen spectating at the University of Virginia's track and baseball field. As for flying, hunting, and farming, it seems fair to say that as serious vocations these had more reality in Faulkner's thoughts and dreams than in actuality.

Faulkner was in reality a Writer: a fully dedicated, highly skilled, totally committed and engaged man of letters whose trophies, racks and wattles, blue ribbons, and bumper crop harvests were his published short stories and novels. These alone were the tangible manifestations of his victory over odds, the proof of his endurance and fortitude and skill. Yet his literary vocation did not provide Faulkner with what he most wanted to project about himself: an uncompromising sense of manliness. Surely it was not any real doubt that he could hold his own intellectually with academics and critics that made him avoid engaging in literary discussions; rather, his idiosyncratic taciturnity saved him from that nagging sense of inadequacy which his profession never ceased to engender in him. The same feeling may account for his unwillingness to reread his own novels and stories, or even keep many of them on the premises. Reminders of pain they must have been! More so, at times they might have appeared to him as paltry little to show for his life's work. After all, what were a few stacks of books and perhaps three large cardboard cartons filled with manuscripts as the "earthly estate" of forty years? Doubtless, his sense that the writing profession was not really "part of the culture of this country," rather "a peaceful hobby like breeding Dalmatians," motivated him to deflect conversations directed toward his writing into discussions on farming, horses, flying, sailing.

If, in Faulkner's perception, writing as a profession projected a somewhat less than active, manly image, it had also failed to provide him with the outward, tangible rewards for hard work by which he might have been able to consider the pursuit at least economically worthwhile. In *Absalom, Absalom!*, Miss Rosa suggests to Quentin that becoming a self-supporting writer would be one viable alternative to languishing in the South. But his profession had been excluded from the list of occupations approved by the American Gospel of Wealth, the sturdy Puritan Ethic. His novel *Sanctuary* had made money for him only indirectly, not from publisher's royalties but from the proceeds of Hollywood's movie version, *The Story of Temple Drake*. Also, he had made considerably more income from his first association with William and Howard Hawks in scripting *Today We Live* from his short story "Turn About" than he had earned from its original sale to the *Saturday Evening Post*. Paradoxically, it was his scriptwriting assignments for M-G-M in 1932 and 1933, Universal Studios briefly in 1934, mainly for Twentieth Century-Fox in 1935 through 1937, and his sale in 1938 of the movie rights to *The Unvanquished* that had sustained him financially during the decade of his most impressive fiction writing. Although adapted into screenplay form, *The Unvanquished* was never made into a Hollywood extravaganza like *Gone with the Wind;* yet, ironically, its sale had given Faulkner the financial leverage he required to purchase Greenfield Farm and, by extension, become a "farmer."

By the end of 1941, William Faulkner was financially and spiritually bankrupt as a result of his failure to make fiction writing support and satisfy him in a climate of well-being. During late November and into December 1941, he unsuccessfully attempted to gain employment at Warner Bros. by writing and submitting at the studio's request an original story outline of a previously rejected screenplay called "The Damned Don't Cry."[17] Additionally, during the next few months he wrote "5 20–25 page story lines for various studios or individuals, none of which came to anything."[18] In fact, Faulkner spent the first seven months of 1942 working himself up emotionally while his financial condition steadily deteriorated as he progressed toward signing a seven-year contract with Warner Bros. as scriptwriter.

The following five excerpts from letters Faulkner wrote to various associates between January and July 1942 demonstrate the progressive justifications he evolved for not engaging physically in the war, while yet convincing himself he would be participating in it. To Robert Haas, Faulkner wrote: "The world is bitched proper this time, isn't it? I'd like to be dictator now. I'd take all these congressmen who refused to make military appropriations and I'd send them to the Philippines. . . . I have organized observation posts for air raids in this county. . . . But that's not enough. I have a chance to teach navigation (air) in the Navy as a civilian. If I can get my affairs here established, I think I'll take it."[19]

A little more than two months later, Faulkner again wrote to Haas: "I am going before a Navy board and Medical for a commission, N.R. I will go to the Bureau of Aeronautics, Washington, for a job. I am to get full Lieut. and 3200.00 per year, and I hope a pilot's rating to wear the wings. I dont like this desk job particularly, but I think better to get the commission first then try to get a little nearer the gunfire."[20] The tone of the second letter struck a familiar, if distant, chord. It suggested almost a repeat of Faulkner's experience in 1918. Having been rejected by the American armed services, then accepted into the Canadian Royal Air Force, he had been honorably discharged, but without seeing action, and was awarded his Second Lieutenant's wings *post facto*. With this hoped-for desk job would come the regalia and outfit, a costume symbolic of an active-duty flier, superficially indistinguishable from that worn by a "real" pilot. Faulkner's Washington desk job would be his Harvard AT-6, his Corsair, his P-38 Lightning. He could wear the outfit with distinction, just as he had dressed up frequently in his RAF uniform during the late teens and early twenties on the Ole Miss campus and in Oxford, affecting the pose of a wounded pilot returned from his tour of duty "over there."

The following letter to Bennett Cerf, another executive of Random House, written in early June 1942, marks the turning point in Faulkner's jockeying for a moral and pragmatic position: "Good for Don. Do you know how he managed to get into the Air Force? They turned me down on application, didn't say why, may have been age, 44. I have a definite offer from the Navy, but I want an Air Force job if possible. . . . The Navy job is at a desk in the Bureau of Aeronautics in Washington. I want to stay out doors if possible, want to go to California. Incidentally, has Random House any job in California I could do?"[21] To soothe his conscience he continued to express his overt intentions of offering himself up to the service. Of course he would prefer the more romantic branch, the Air Corps. Failing to get this commission, he would settle for a Navy desk job. Yet, on closer, more realistic scrutiny, it seemed that even this alternative would not suffice to relieve him of his financial distress. Later in the same month Faulkner wrote to his New York literary agent, Harold Ober:

> What chance might I have of getting some specific assignment to write a piece that would pay my fare and keep me in Cal. for a month? That is, a drawing acct. of $1,000.00, so I can leave $500.00 here with my family? If I can get to Cal. I believe I can get myself a job at least $100.00–$200.00 a week with a movie co. . . . I've got to get away from here and earn more money. I know no place to do it better than Cal. if I can get hold of $1,000.00 that's what I will do. I would need that much to take up the service commission, buy uniform and transport myself to where I can report for duty and live until I draw pay, even. The comm. (if I pass board) will pay me $3200.00, but I will have to live in Washington, which will leave little over for family, and nothing at all to pay the food bills, etc.[22]

Previously, Faulkner had written Cerf about his "definite offer from the Navy," which ten days prior he had already mentioned to Haas as most likely providing him with an opportunity to obtain "a pilot's rating to wear the wings." Now, in truth, he was admitting to Ober he had doubts about even passing the board examination for the Navy desk job. Furthermore, he realized, passing it would not deliver him from his fundamental dilemma. To Cerf, Faulkner reiterated his monetary and emotional destitution and concluded with what appeared to be a resolute decision: "My best chance to earn money is Cal. Mainly I must get away from here and freshen my mental condition until I can write stuff that will sell. Am I in shape to ask an advance from the firm? if so, how much? I would like to pay the grocer something before I leave, but I have reached the point where I had better go to Cal. with just r.r. fare if I can do no better."[23]

With the unfelicitous assistance of William Herndon, a West Coast agent who had arranged a seven-year contract for him with Warner Bros., Faulkner excitedly prepared to make the first of what would be an off-and-on, four-year sojourn in Hollywood to work as a wartime screenwriter. On July 18, 1942, Faulkner wrote to James J. Geller, then head of Warner Bros. Story Department, of his decision to report for work later that month: "Your letter of July 15 at hand. I also have Mr Buckner's letter describing the job he has in mind. It is a good idea and I will be proud to work with it and I hope and trust I can do it justice."[24]

Officially, Faulkner went on the Warner Bros. payroll on July 27, 1942, at a rate of three hundred dollars per week. Not even a month earlier, desperate to secure work, Faulkner had written Harold Ober, outlining remuneration he had received for Hollywood writing performed between 1932 and 1937: "I believe the agents who have tried since to sell me have talked about $1000 per week. I dont think I am or have been or will ever be worth that to movies. It just took them five years to find it out. I will take anything above $100.00. I must have something somewhere, quick."[25] And even though this sum was considerably more than he himself had suggested as acceptable, he would later complain that the starting salary had been far below his expectations. The "good idea" to which Faulkner referred in the excerpted letter to Geller was "The De Gaulle Story,"[26] a project that had been sanctioned not only by Washington but also by representatives of De Gaulle, then based in England. The motion picture was to be top priority and would provide the most up-to-date information regarding the combined efforts of the Fighting French and British forces allied against Hitler's demoniac fascist regime.

For quite a while Faulkner believed that the work he was doing for the studio had delivered him from the abyss. It allowed him to earn a steady weekly income, albeit one below his level of pay for Hollywood work he had done in the thirties; moreover, it seemed to satisfy his need for pride in vocation. He was, after all, participating actively in the war effort and not as a bystander, or commander of "observation posts for air raids," or even as a uniformed officer sitting at a desk in Washington. Indeed, at first anyway, he even may have felt a tinge of the heroic in his "service" status. And for much of 1942, until the end of November, at least, if we can deduce from the massive output of material he produced for "The De Gaulle Story," Faulkner actually found he could be proud of himself in his role as writer.

But by December 1942, Faulkner was both frustrated with the lack of success in his first major writing assignment for Warner Bros. and homesick. Worse, he had convinced himself that the arrangement into which he had entered with Warner Bros. was a bad one. His pay was paltry rather than generous as he had first perceived it to be; he felt his contractual term of seven renewable yearly options with Warner Bros. was too confining; his "war work" was not as essential as he had thought and hoped it might be.

In an uncharacteristically garrulous letter to his stepson, Malcolm A. Franklin, on December 5, 1942, Faulkner cynically expressed his belief that only soldiers and those working directly on the construction of war materiel were essential. In the group of people who were engaged in work "not essential . . . to winning a war or anything else," he included "real estate agents and lawyers and merchants and all the other parasites who exist only because of motion picture salaries."[27] With eloquent bravado, Faulkner implored his stepson to enlist, asserting his own desire to participate actively in the war. Significantly, Faulkner actually spelled out his fundamental reason for insisting Malcolm not allow himself any outs. Going to fight was a matter of manhood:

> But it is the biggest thing that will happen in your lifetime. All your contemporaries will be in it before it is over, and if you are not one of them, you will always regret it. That's something in the meat and bone and blood from the old cave-time, right enough. But it's there, and it's a strange thing how a man, no matter how intelligent, will cling to the public proof of his masculinity: his courage and endurance, his willingness to sacrifice himself for the land which shaped his ancestors. I dont want to go either. No sane man likes war. But when I can, I am going too, maybe only to prove to myself that I can do (within my physical limitations of age, of course) as much as anyone else can to make secure the manner of living I prefer and that suits my kin and kind.[28]

Faulkner had missed the First World War, and it was apparent to him that he must miss the Second, thus losing a final chance to put his manhood to the test. Furthermore, it was obvious to Faulkner that writing propaganda for the Fighting French was not going to satisfy his need to contribute to winning the war. Perhaps he thought he could participate vicariously through his stepson, Malcolm, and his brother John's eldest son, Jimmy Faulkner, who was training to be a Marine pilot. But Faulkner had another strategy also. Concluding his letter to his stepson, he said:

> The next step opens out here, of course, and this stops being a letter and becomes a sermon. So I'll take this step in one jump, and quit. We must see that the old Laodicean smell doesn't rise again after this one. But we must preserve what liberty and freedom we already have to do that. We will have to make the liberty sure first, in the field. It will take the young men to do that. Then perhaps the time of the older men will come, the ones like me who are articulate in the national voice, who are too old to be soldiers, but are old enough and have been vocal long enough to be listened to.[29]

The rest of Faulkner's life pivoted on this eloquently expressed raison d'être. Availing himself of the rights and privileges accorded older men, he could prove his manhood. His soldiering would be "vocal"; he would become "articulate in the national voice" and be "listened to." Being "listened to," in fact, became one of Faulkner's highest priorities. Although his portrait had appeared on the January 23, 1939, cover of *Time* magazine, signaling the epitome of critical acclaim, the public had not given him its ear at any time during the twenty years since he had first published *The Marble Faun* in 1924. Now Faulkner seemed to have realized that if his voice was to be heard, he would have to broadcast on a frequency to which the public was tuned—one that carried neatly packaged moralizing.

After his brief respite home for Christmas in Oxford, Faulkner returned to Hollywood in January 1943 and resumed where he had left off trying to write a war-effort screenplay. This one was entitled "The Life and Death of a Bomber." On the previous November 14, Faulkner and Joe Berry of the Warner Bros. Location Department had toured the Consolidated Aircraft factory in San Diego to gather information for a proposed script about the civilians involved in building American bombers. According to Faulkner's notes from the tour,[30] the movie was supposed to provide favorable publicity for Consolidated in the way *Wings for the Eagle* (Warner Bros., 1942) had done for Lockheed. On January 21, 1943, Faulkner submitted a twenty-page "Outline for Original Screenplay,"[31] the theme of which is the need for national unity in support of America's servicemen. In showing how a labor dispute and a love triangle interfere with work at the factory and cause a defective bomber to be sent overseas, Faulkner dramatized the tragic consequences of placing selfish motives ahead of national security interests. However, like "The De Gaulle Story" before it, and far more quickly, "The Life and Death of a Bomber" was canceled.

For the next two months, Faulkner worked on a succession of unfulfilled—and unfulfilling—projects, none related to the war. Possibly as a result of this last fact, Faulkner found himself living "a damned dull life" and vowing again "to soldier, if possible."[32] Then a development suddenly occurred that once more stirred Faulkner's enthusiasm and pride. Howard Hawks wanted him as scriptwriter for his next war movie, "Battle Cry."[33] On April 7, 1943, Faulkner began his second major project. This time he would prove himself useful both to Warner Bros. and to the nation. Incorporating sequences describing American, French, English, Chinese, Dutch, Greek, and Russian forces striving for the causes of liberty and universal peace, "Battle Cry" was remarkable for its experimental form. In its variegated shifting in and out of time sequences and montaging of disparate scenes and locations, it more closely approximated one of his own novels, such as *As I Lay Dying,* than it did movies of the period. A month later Faulkner described the project in a letter to his daughter, Jill: "I am writing a big picture now, for Mr Howard Hawks, an old friend, a director. It is to be a big one. It will last about 3 hours, and the studio has allowed Mr Hawks 3 and 1/2 million dollars to make it, with 3 or 4 directors and about all the big stars."[34]

But abruptly and without any advance warning, almost four months to the day from its inception, the "Battle Cry" project was canceled, and Faulkner was temporarily out of a job. Not a week before, in a letter bordering on the euphoric, he had written to his wife, Estelle:

> I will stick at this picture until Hawks says it is finished, my part of it, I mean. He and I had a talk at the fishing camp. He is going to establish his own unit, as an independent: himself, his writer, etc., to write pictures, then sell them to any studio who makes highest bid. I am to be his writer. He says he and I together as a team will always be worth two million dollars at least. That means, we can count on getting at least two million from any studio with which to make any picture we cook up, we to make the picture with the two million dollars, and divide the profits from it. When I come home, I intend to have Hawks completely satisfied with this job, as well as the studio. If I can do that, I wont have to worry again about going broke temporarily. The main problem I have now is to get myself free from the seven-year contract for a pittance of a salary. . . . I have a promise from the studio that, when I have written a successful picture, they will destroy that contract. This is my chance.[35]

Although no one can document with certainty its extenuating and culminating circumstances and reasons, the shut-down of "Battle Cry," which during its short-lived existence stimulated Faulkner to generate thousands of typescript pages leading to a "Second Temporary Draft" composed or adapted almost exclusively by him, must have come as a bleak and nauseating reality. Indeed, if Faulkner believed he had satisfied his immediate boss, Hawks, he could have had little expectation that his efforts had merited him a more lucrative, less constricting contract with the studio. Doubtless, this seemingly gratuitous denouement to his highly concentrated attempt to prove himself not just competent, but exemplary, as a screenwriter could only have reinforced his cynical judgments about Hollywood. Certainly this would break his spirit! None of the projects on which he would work during 1944 and 1945 would either compel or engross him to this degree or delude him with hopes of becoming a well-paid, respected scriptwriter.

Earlier, in a letter to Jimmy Faulkner dated April 3, 1943,[36] Faulkner had spoken in the moralizing voice of public convention. His message was marked by considerable fantasizing in which, at one point, he even reminted a myth about the World War I flying experience he had originally propagated twenty-five years earlier: "I would have liked for you to have had my dog-tag, R.A.F., but I lost it in Europe, in Germany. I think the Gestapo has it; I am very likely on their records right now as a dead British flying officer-spy." Having established his credentials as a combat pilot, Faulkner moved on in his letter to the virtues of becoming intimate with fear so that true courage could emerge and then concluded with a prediction about his future course: "This is a long letter, and preachified too, but Uncle Jack and your father are too old to do what you can do, and I must stay in civilian clothes to look after things for us when everybody comes back home again." For one thing, Faulkner saw the need to become a "preacher" if he were to reach the public with his writing and make money from the recognition of his efforts; for another thing, he recognized that, to be effective in his role of provider for his family, he must officially assume the primogenitive position as family patriarch. Within the next five years, Faulkner would become both "preacher" and patriarch. He did so, however, at the expense of his art.

The first manifestation of this may have occurred in mid-August 1943 when Faulkner returned to Oxford with a check in hand for one thousand dollars, a loan from producer William Bacher to be applied against future movie royalties for an as-yet-unwritten screenplay. He was to write the script on the basis of some partially developed ideas about "a fable" of the First World War. He wrote Robert Haas: "The argument is (in the fable) in the middle of that war, Christ (some movement in mankind which wished to stop war forever) reappeared and was crucified again. We are repeating, we are in the midst of war again. Suppose Christ gives us one more chance, will we crucify him again, perhaps for the last time. That's crudely put; I am not trying to preach at all. But that is the argument."[37]

Sadly, Faulkner failed consciously to recognize that in fact he was substituting the role of the preacher for that of the dramatist.

Back in Hollywood in February 1944, Faulkner worked on the only two scripts for which he received credits from Warner Bros. during the forties: "The Big Sleep" and "To Have and Have Not." The following year he tried unsuccessfully to adapt Stephen Longstreet's *Stallion Road* for film. By mid-September 1945, Faulkner had left the Warner Bros. studio for good, although his Warner Bros. "Off Payroll Notice," dated September 19, 1945, simply stated: "Suspended for not to exceed 6 months."[38] On October 15, 1945, Faulkner wrote a restrained and deferential apologia to Colonel J. L. Warner almost begging for a formal studio release from his contract: "So I have spent three years doing work (trying to do it) which was not my forte and which I was not equipped to do, and therefore I have mis-spent time which as a 47 year old novelist I could not afford to spend. And I dont dare mis-spend any more of it."[39]

Faulkner's exodus from Egypt/Hollywood had not been motivated by a salutary financial alternative, nor was he returning to marital stability and domestic comforts in Canaan/Oxford. In fact, the situation that greeted Faulkner in September 1945 was not much different from that which he had left in July 1942. In a sense, it was even worse since Rowan Oak had further deteriorated, as had his marriage to Estelle. The effect of his recent lengthy separations from her had been compounded by his relationship with Meta Carpenter Rebner. In truth, had he not had Meta's companionship for the duration of his stay in Hollywood and the hospitality of A. I. Bezzerides, a screenwriter and at one time a close friend of Faulkner, during his 1944 and 1945 stays, Faulkner's proneness to alcohol might have destroyed him. Surely he would have been fired from his job.

Ironically, in a letter Faulkner wrote to Malcolm Cowley nearly a year before his September 1945 departure from Warner Bros., he expressed his belief that he could keep Hollywood and Yoknapatawpha separate, mutually exclusive: "I can work at Hollywood 6 months, stay home 6, am used to it now and have movie work locked off into another room."[40] And almost a year later, referring to the prose set piece that Cowley had requested Faulkner write to be included originally in *The Portable Faulkner* that Cowley was feverishly preparing for Viking Press' spring 1946 publication schedule, Faulkner remarked similarly, "I think this is all right, it took me about a week to get Hollywood out of my lungs, but I am still writing all right, I believe."[41] Even though this recently completed fictional tour de force would come to be regarded as one of the finest postwar prose pieces Faulkner would compose, still it looked backward, not ahead, treating material he had conceived almost two decades earlier. Yet, little could he realize when he wrote the preceding cover letter to Cowley, which accompanied the "Appendix" to *The Sound and the Fury,* that never again would he be able to lock Hollywood away in another room or get it out of his lungs.

And, in point of fact, the "Appendix" itself would be explanatory or "preachified." It would bring to the surface through overt, objective clarification that which had remained so beautifully evocative and enchantingly mesmeric in the "longer version" of *The Sound and the Fury* published seventeen years before. In the new piece, among other revelations, Faulkner would tell an audience not altogether certain whether Quentin had or had not actually committed incest with his sister Caddy the "truth" of the matter. Of Quentin III, Faulkner would record that he "loved not the idea of the incest which he would not commit, but some presbyterian concept of its eternal punishment."[42] Although at the time Faulkner's shift in literary aesthetic would go unnoticed even by his most ardent and fastidious admirers, it would appear that Faulkner was no longer content to leave his readers guessing or to allow them to formulate their own determinations. Actually, the "Appendix" he had written was the product of his newly developed compulsion to explain his messages, make sure he was being heard, understood, assimilated, and, above all, respected.

In retrospect, one almost might view the composition of the new "Appendix," occurring at the tail end of Faulkner's Warner Bros. years, as having arisen out of the same compulsive urgency that in the early months of 1942 had driven him to write "5 20–25 page story lines for various studios or individuals," that financial imperative to sustain his vocation as fictionist. This time, also, hoping to enhance prospects for sales of Cowley's forthcoming anthology of his own work in *The Portable Faulkner,* Faulkner had supplied the grateful editor with what equally might be considered a kind of story outline, albeit ostensibly prose fiction. And in this respect, Faulkner's "Appendix" might even be seen as a valedictory to his Hollywood career, incorporating, as it does, not only one of Hollywood's compositional formats, that of the story outline whose technique he had mastered, but even the infusion into its plot of certain traces of that ambience indigenous to his recently abandoned residence. In updating Caddy's biography from the point at which he had suspended her in 1910, the year she had just married "an extremely eligible young Indianian she and her mother had met while vacationing at French Lick the summer before," Faulkner writes: "Divorced by him 1911. Married 1920 to a minor moving-picture magnate, Hollywood California. Divorced by mutual agreement, Mexico 1925. Vanished in Paris with the German occupation, 1940."[43] Furthermore, by 1945, the time frame in which Faulkner as well as his "suspended" characters are concurrently operating, it appears that Caddy is yet very much alive. She has been recognized by the city's public librarian posing beside a German staff general—the actual year is 1943—somewhere on the French Riviera. The arrested scene has been spotted in a photograph from a "slick magazine." Undoubtedly, this allusion was not accidental. It thrust Faulkner directly back into his original working out of "The De Gaulle Story." And as he wrote the "Appendix," if Faulkner had conjured Caddy as heartbreakingly exiled, anomalous, and tragically doomed, there is little doubt he must have considered his own isolated dislocation back home at Rowan Oak and his impecunious condition resulting from his books being out of print equally lamentable and humiliating.

From September 1945 through mid-1947, Faulkner languished in Oxford. His publications during that time could hardly have seemed of much consequence to him since all three represented virtual recyclings of material previously published and previously publicly ignored. His friend Saxe Commins compiled and issued a diminutive paperback printed on cheap pulp paper entitled *A Rose for Emily and Other Stories,* which was distributed in April 1945 through the Editions for the Armed Forces. A year later, the Viking Press brought out *The Portable Faulkner.* This book contained a chronological ordering of much of Faulkner's best fiction and was accompanied by what was to become a seminal introduction consisting of an illuminating overview of Faulkner's all-encompassing thematic design. The third book, *The Sound and the Fury & As I Lay Dying,* issued in 1946 by the Modern Library, brought together in one volume two of Faulkner's favorite novels, both of which had been published more than fifteen years earlier and now were out of print, seemingly unavailable even in secondhand bookstores.

But with these publications, something outsized began to occur. Four years after the publication of the Modern Library edition in December 1946, Faulkner would travel to Stockholm to receive the 1949 Nobel Prize for Literature. If Cowley's *Portable Faulkner* had served to reintroduce Faulkner's fiction to America, Saxe Commins' little collection of Faulkner's finest short stories may have helped to introduce Faulkner to European scholars and students as well as to returning American soldiers. In any event, the Modern Library edition put before the American public two of Faulkner's very best novels together with the newly conceived, highly significant "Appendix" for *The Sound and the Fury,* a slightly different version of which originally appeared in *The Portable Faulkner.* For its author this edition was both a novelistic and an autobiographical exercise, a way in middle age for him to reconnect with the great fiction of his mature youth.

In another interesting exchange between Faulkner and Cowley during the period in which the latter was completing his *Portable* introduction, both men realized the importance of making the piece not only insightful but also accurate, and Faulkner trusted Cowley perhaps more than he had or ever would again trust any critic. But at one point he expressed hesitancy. Mistrusting not Cowley, however, but himself, he thrice insisted on the deletion of certain facts he realized might shadow his credibility. Having read the first draft of Cowley's introduction, Faulkner wrote: "If you mention military experience at all (which is not necessary, as I could have invented a few failed RAF airmen as easily as I did Confeds) say 'belonged to RAF in 1918.' Then continue: Has lived in same section of Miss. since, worked at various odd jobs until he got a job writing movies and was able to make a living at writing."[44]

Two important attitudes toward his career surface in this letter: Faulkner openly expresses his indebtedness to Hollywood for having allowed him to earn money as a writer, no matter (in this letter, at least) the cost to his art and his spirit; second, he no longer seems willing to perpetuate the myth of his flying career in the First World War. On the same subject, in a follow-up letter to Cowley's response, Faulkner sounds almost desperate: "Yours at hand. You're going to bugger up a fine dignified distinguished book with that war business. The only point a war reference or anecdote could serve would be to reveal me a hero. . . . I'll pay for any resetting of type, plates, alteration, etc."[45] In a third and final reference to this matter, Faulkner reaffirms the fact that he did not want to be made to appear heroic, especially when "compared with men I knew, friends I had and lost."[46] In this letter he does not completely repudiate the self-created myth of having been wounded, but rather evasively suggests he may have been in some kind of foolish mishap on a "practice flight." Does he not even intimate that he had been the victim of his own imagination's desperate seeking for recognition and sympathy? It is clear that in middle age he did not want to perpetuate the apocryphal tales about his combat service fabricated in youth. After all, he was almost fifty years old. It was time to begin creating a new image, and Faulkner's disavowal, especially when compared to the obvious fabrication in his April 3, 1943, letter to his nephew Jimmy Faulkner three years earlier, suggests that he was at last looking at himself realistically.

But Faulkner's image as a public spokesman tended to be as false as his warrior image. *Intruder in the Dust* (1948) is a highly calculated, blatantly contrived tract on the growing national problem, civil rights. Only secondarily is it about individuals with personal problems. With its civil rhetoric, flamboyant bombast intermingled with propagandistic sentimentality, it qualified as prime Hollywood fodder. Its sale to M-G-M for fifty thousand dollars outright ironically gave Faulkner relief from penury for the first time. The receipt of the 1949 Nobel Prize in 1950, with its stipend of slightly more than $30,000, betokened ultimate public acceptance and success—success Faulkner could equate with a measure of fulfillment of his manhood because it embodied two fundamental prerequisites: making money and being heard. What he had mentioned to his stepson, Malcolm, in his December 5, 1942, letter about men like himself "who are too old to be soldiers, but are old enough and have been vocal long enough to be *listened to*" (emphasis added),[47] he reiterated in his Nobel Prize address: "So this award is only mine in trust. It will not be difficult to find a dedication for the money part of it commensurate with the purpose and significance of its origin. But I would like to do the same with the acclaim too, by using this moment as a pinnacle from which I might be *listened to*" (emphasis added).[48]

The lofty, eloquent rhetoric embodied in Faulkner's undeniably moving speech did not seem new or startling to those who had been familiar with his fiction, but his avowed affirmation of man's ability to endure and his will to prevail stunned them. Little might they have intuited that this apparently complete reversal of attitudes was the residual product of Faulkner's mature years in Hollywood. After all, neither "The De Gaulle Story" nor "Battle Cry," his two major war screenplays from the forties, had been produced, thus depriving readers of insight requisite to being prepared for and understanding such an "about-face." And even those movies that had earned him screen credits that they might have viewed, *The Big Sleep* and *To Have and Have Not,* were so inextricably collaborative as to muffle and distort whatever voice he originally lent to them.

Nonetheless, the hallmark, or stigma, was in place, even if the public would remain at a loss for adequate explanations for his emotional sea change. Less than six months later, on May 28, 1951, Faulkner again would take to the podium. And again he would preach his newly-arrived-at stance on mankind—this time to an audience gathered in the University High School auditorium in Oxford, Mississippi, for the commencement of the Class of '51, the valedictorian of which was his daughter, Jill. The address, which has come to be known as Faulkner's "Never Be Afraid" speech, was laced with two very remarkable echoes. One implicit theme was that of being "listened to." Faulkner devoted the initial two of only five paragraphs comprising this brief speech to the distinction between youth and age, highlighting with an aphorism the obvious paradoxes in these diametrical conditions. Presuming to have established a position of credibility and moral authority by aligning himself with the older generation, he proposed to offer relevant observations, not absolutes, as a result of his maturity and experience as a man who had traveled beyond Oxford. However, his prevailing insistence was on being listened to; he hoped what he was about to tell them would be heard, at least by those in attendance young enough to yet effect changes:

> So you young men and women in this room tonight, and in thousands of other rooms like this one about the earth today, have the power to change the world, rid it forever of war and injustice and suffering, provided you know how, know what to do. And so according to the old Frenchman, since you can't know what to do because you are young, then anyone standing here with a head full of white hair, should be able to tell you.
>
> But maybe this one is not as old and wise as his white hairs pretend or claim. Because he can't give you a glib answer or pattern either. But he can tell you this, because he believes this.[49]

Most striking in this passage is a second echoing theme, which in retrospect appears to have its direct corollary in lines Faulkner wrote into the "First Extended Treatment" and retained verbatim in his "Second Temporary Draft" of "Battle Cry." In his commencement speech, the thrust of Faulkner's argument and the crux of what he had to tell his audience with such urgency was: "What threatens us today is fear. Not the atom bomb, nor even fear of it, because if the bomb fell on Oxford tonight, all it could do would be to kill us; which is nothing, since in doing that, it will have robbed itself of its only power over us, which is fear of it, the being afraid of it."[50] In both complete drafts of "Battle Cry," Faulkner has an Italian prisoner relate a tale about a fat German officer humiliated by his captives despite his tyrannical domination over them. When he has finished, Battson, his American guard, says, "Well? Is that all?" The Italian replies, "It will never be all, as long as they can laugh. How can you conquer people who can still laugh at you?" "You can starve them," a soldier interjects, and the Italian responds, "You can only kill them by doing that. You can kill them much simpler. But when you do that, you have failed. The man whom you must destroy, as the only alternative to his obeying you, that man has beat you."[51]

Soon public statement became a way of life. Viewing Faulkner's behavior in the fifties from the sidelines, but with a surprisingly perspicacious eye, Phil Stone remarked in the following excerpted letters to Carvel Collins:

> For some time now Bill has not been getting publicity. My prediction is that between now and October 1 he will do or say something startling that will again attract public attention. Watch for it. I have no idea what it is because I have not talked with Bill since he got back from Virginia.[52]

Please refer to the second paragraph of my letter to you under date of July 19 and read the enclosed clipping. My guess came true with sixteen days to spare.[53]

In Stone's follow-up letter to Collins, he enclosed a clipping that was a copy of Faulkner's letter to the editor published in the Memphis *Commercial Appeal,* September 15, 1957. The letter reflected Faulkner's highly controversial pro-integration stand.

The last twelve years of Faulkner's life were marked by public appearances and addresses, letters to editors, interviews, readings, question-and-answer sessions for teachers, students, and critics, press conferences, semiautobiographical essays, moralistic tracts, acceptance speeches, and keynote addresses. With some exception, moreover, the considerable body of fiction he wrote in his last years virtually all tended to moralize and preach.

And even Faulkner's most-well-sustained later prose from the fifties, indeed that which sporadically would rise to the qualitative levels achieved between 1929 and 1942, was marked by more than a striking similarity to filmic story outlines, treatments, and screenplays. For instance, the three masterful prose "prologues" Faulkner composed to buffer his "experimental play-novel," *Requiem for a Nun* (1951), might qualify as background treatment to the play itself, which in format appeared almost identical to "The De Gaulle Story," "Battle Cry," and the other fully developed screenplays he had written in the forties. So, too, did two semiautobiographical essays published in 1954, "Mississippi" and "Sepulture South," read like story outlines. And when one considers that the basic purpose of a treatment is to expand surface narrative elements posited in a story outline with additional plot tributaries, some dialogue, as well as to include initial scene blocking and stage directions or camera angles, the two essays, and especially *Requiem for a Nun,* become easier to locate derivatively in relation to their prototypic models, if not adapted incarnations.

Also in 1954, Faulkner brought to the public ear *A Fable,* whose early drafts he had written substantially in the California home of A. I. Bezzerides ten years earlier and which, if nothing else, seemed to represent the political, religious, and philosophical tenets that had polarized during his Warner Bros. tenure when he had hit financial and spiritual bottom. In 1957, *The Town* was published; in 1959, *The Mansion.* Both appeared almost as elaborate apologiae for earlier work forestalled because of financial difficulties reaching crisis levels after the 1940 publication of *The Hamlet.*

The Reivers, Faulkner's final novel, published not two months before his death in 1962, reprised the semiautobiographical genre he had resorted to in "Mississippi" and "Sepulture South" and in the "Foreword" to *The Faulkner Reader.* It projected a pervasive surface rendering of narrative content and, despite its opening flashback, maintained a serial structure parallel in its linear chronology and resolution of plot, albeit predominantly through the use of farce, itself among the most accessible of comic techniques. *The Reivers* provided Faulkner's loyal reading audience with a novel not only easy to read and follow because of its uncomplicated syntax and diction and superficial plot but also diverting because of its informing gentle sentimentality, nostalgia, and tall-tale humor. Cinematic in its surface presentation, it would manifest an easy adaptability to the film medium: without stretching, *The Reivers* might even be considered Faulkner's most self-consciously constructed and successfully articulated "screenplay."

The Nobel Prize, however, was the catalyst that afforded the public recognition of Faulkner's work that had eluded him for so many dispiriting years. At least evanescently, that pinnacled moment in Stockholm reversed a lifetime of consistent disappointment and losing: he was pronounced Winner. Yet there seems little doubt that Faulkner felt increasingly that he had alloyed and compromised his talent, at first for the money Hollywood had paid him for diluted "Faulkner," then in exchange for continuing public adulation—a sweet emollient to his vanity, despite his vociferous protestations to the contrary. For Faulkner, the fifties would be marred by despondency and complicated by acute alcoholism.

The fiction of Faulkner's final period, 1948–1962, is virtually all residual, if not derivative. One need merely study certain letters written mainly during the thirties and early forties when Faulkner's imagination was aflame, to document the foreshadowing of *Intruder in the Dust, Requiem for a Nun,* and *The Reivers.*[54] *The Town* and *The Mansion,* of course, had been planned as early as the late twenties; there had never been any doubt that these novels would be written. Sadly, their postponement, most likely precipitated by Faulkner's sojourn at Warner Bros. during the early-to-mid-forties, allowed the new, publicly articulate Faulkner to work over that wonderfully fresh "old" material he and Phil Stone had shared in concocting during their youth. Both *The Town* and *The Mansion* seem warmed over. They contain a good deal of moralizing and rhetorical posturing. They may even be said to be sentimental.

Faulkner never forgot the legacy of the Artist he had inherited from his own youthful ego: to complete what he had initiated. Indeed, he had an obligation not only to himself and to his material but also to the "living" fictional characters into whom he had breathed life. He had to permit them to conclude their own literary destinies. But the Faulkner of the fifties was different from the Faulkner of the twenties and thirties. Lawrance Thompson described the bulk of Faulkner's creative effort in the fifties in a prepublication critique of *A Fable* for Saxe Commins:

Perhaps stylistic weaknesses should be listed, here, as the underlying and all-important weaknesses, because they may be seen as causing and determining those other weaknesses of characterization, action, structure. For example, in characterization, Faulkner permits character after character to talk like Faulkner, to rant like Faulkner, and to mouth Faulknerian clichés. So the separate characters frequently blur into each other, and into Faulkner. Take another example, which involves both action and structure, as controlled by style: Faulkner has always seemed only one remove from a dramatist, because he has so frequently presented his narratives through episodes which give us characters pushed out on the stage, so to speak, or into actions where they characterize themselves. This is, essentially, a dramatic principle of characterization. But in *A Fable,* the principle of narration tends toward mere description, and as a result the reader gets the sense that he is watching the action through the wrong end of a telescope.[55]

In essence Thompson said that the creative artist had been transformed into a world-class rhetorician and polemicist. As a world traveler, lecturer, and keynote speaker; as a speculator on the future of race relations, atomic holocaust, and the state of literature; as a cultural ambassador for the American State Department and chairman of President Eisenhower's People-To-People Program committee, Faulkner had donned the fabled coat of many colors he had dreamed in youth of possessing. He appeared to wear it with dignity and distinction. He projected a certain austerity, suggesting always that he was the moody and idiosyncratic genius of grass-roots Jefferson, Yoknapatawpha County, Mississippi, The South, U.S.A.

Faulkner's actual state of mind and health, however, were not reflected in the outward manifestations of having "made it." Faulkner's onetime dearest friend, poetry mentor, and resident collaborator in many of the early Snopes tales, Phil Stone, discerned Faulkner's radical artistic and social deterioration. Writing to Ward Miner on September 29, 1952, Stone, in alluding to and thanking the former for his book, *The World of William Faulkner,* stated as an aside: "Another thing is that such critiques make me a little sad because they seem to be in the nature of literary obituaries. After all, the Nobel Prize was for work he did between 1928 and 1940 and he has done very little since then of the same stature as the work of that period. I think now that he never will and I think that his great success and the adulation that has followed it has really been a misfortune."[56]

On the following day, Stone wrote to Robert Coughlan in attempting to correct misinformation the latter was planning to use in a *Life* magazine article on Faulkner: "There are two things in general in which I think you give an incorrect impression. The first thing is that you emphasize too much the fact that Bill occasionally, very occasionally, throws a drunk. I think you should re-work this part and avoid so much reference to his drinking. On the whole he drinks very little." [57]

If Stone, isolated from Faulkner by a chilling of their friendship in the fifties, failed to gauge the intensity of Faulkner's alcoholism, his editor Saxe Commins did not. Publicly, the image of Faulkner as a drinker carried with it an almost manly distinction; it was discounted, condoned as being proverbially the writer's occupational hazard. Coughlan, misperceiving Faulkner's condition, credited him with being a manly drinker, one whose overindulgence, although risky business, had neither gotten the better of his talent nor led to his physical debilitation. Saxe Commins, on the basis of firsthand knowledge, knew better. On October 8, 1952, he wrote a report to Robert Haas and Bennett Cerf covering the details of his abruptly made trip to Oxford at Estelle Faulkner's behest for the purpose of ministering to a very ill Faulkner: "The fact is that Bill has deteriorated shockingly both in body and mind. He can neither take care of himself in the most elementary way or think with any coherence at all. This may be only evidence of his condition in a state of acute alcoholism. But I believe it goes much deeper and is real disintegration." [58]

Not a month later, Faulkner himself would sound a refrain that became a chant during the remainder of the decade. His keening would take on many variations, but essentially it would revolve around his despair in losing his artistic integrity. On "Saturday," probably November 1, 1952, Faulkner wrote to Saxe Commins regarding *A Fable:* "I must have peace again; I have almost got to teach myself again to believe in it. I seem to have reached a point I never believed I ever would: where I need to have someone read it and tell me, Yes, it's all right. You must go ahead with it." [59]

The last time Faulkner had experienced such uncertainty was during his apprenticeship thirty years before when, as a matter of habit, he asked Phil Stone to read and correctly parse his new poems or to listen to him read aloud his first novels and advise him on matters of structure and stylistics. But more than technical help Faulkner needed "peace again." The constant magazine and newspaper play he was getting, which would increase as the civil rights issue intensified, deprived him of the solitude necessary for his work. Without fully realizing it, Faulkner was caving in under the pressures arising from his celebrity.

Shortly he was to become an eminent cultural emissary. In 1950, he traveled to Stockholm. In 1951, Faulkner went to France and England for three weeks. In 1952, he returned to both countries before traveling on to Norway. Ostensibly, he made these trips to refresh himself and to imbibe the atmosphere in which he was setting what he thought would be his magnum opus, *A Fable*. In truth, the trips allowed him to see a young lady, Else Jonsson, whom he had met while in Stockholm to receive the Nobel award.

Ironically, just weeks before leaving for Europe in 1951, Faulkner had visited Los Angeles, where, while helping script the Howard Hawks production of *The Left Hand of God*, he had spent time with his paramour of the thirties and forties, Meta Carpenter Rebner, and had lovingly given her an inscribed copy of *Notes on a Horsethief* as a token of what appeared not only to be a memento of their past relationship but also a sign of its future.[60] Even more ironic, in July 1951, just three months after returning from his tryst with Else Jonsson, Faulkner flew to New York to work with Ruth Ford on a stage adaptation of his recently completed play, *Requiem for a Nun*. Ruth, like Meta Rebner, was an attractive reminder of his otherwise distasteful sojourn in Hollywood during the mid-forties. "Ruth and Bill" had been under contract to Warner Bros., and on parting, Faulkner kept alive what obviously had been more than just a casual friendship through a series of amorous letters dating from 1947 through 1952. In October 1951, Faulkner returned East, this time traveling to Cambridge to work with Ruth, Lemuel Ayers, and Albert Marre on further revisions of the stage version of *Requiem*. Faulkner's professed commitment was to make good on an earlier "promise" to deliver to Ruth a vehicle in which she could star.

Although more elaborate, this literary gift resembled those Faulkner had handmade and presented to ladies of his affection in the twenties: *The Marionettes, Vision in Spring, Helen: A Courtship, Mayday*. Indeed, in 1927, he had given a hand-bound, typed copy of *The Wishing Tree* to his eight-year-old stepdaughter-to-be, Victoria Franklin.[61] Similarly, in 1948, he typed out and presented an inscribed copy of *The Wishing-Tree* to Ruth Ford's daughter, Shelley, as a Christmas gift. Actually, both gestures and both copies had been intended by Faulkner as tender persuasions to love calculated less to appeal to the children than to their divorced mothers.

Unfortunately, like so many other relationships, this one with Ruth Ford would be interrupted by a formal occasion: marriage. Faulkner's typed response to Ruth's personal announcement and invitation to her wedding to Zachary Scott in 1952 would be a mixture of congratulation and mild remorse. But Ruth was not the only woman who might assuage his needs. In 1949, almost on his own home turf, Faulkner also had allowed himself to be smitten by and fall in love with a twenty-one-year-old Memphis girl named Joan Williams and was at this same time frequently plotting clandestine, intensely passionate trysts with her, having convinced himself that the relationship was justified by his responsibility to be her writing mentor.

In approximately 1952, Faulkner typed out the following fragment to help Joan Williams develop the central character in a novel entitled *The Wintering* (not to be published until 1971). Describing a celebrated older writer, this story fragment exposes William Faulkner himself in a telling moment:

> The writer had received all awards there were, a fact he gave little thought to being still too busy being an artist. But now thinking of himself as this person, he could not help but smile at the incident of himself having lied to drive forty miles on a hot morning to meet a bus bringing a twenty-two year old girl forty miles to meet him secretly too. Perhaps, he admitted, it was not even so much the incident as it was his own satisfaction at finding himself a white-haired bloke and still capable not only of love, but of a fool-young fearfulness at the thought that his love might not keep a rendezvous.
>
> Or perhaps it was just the happiness who [*sic*] brought to a white-haired bloke to find he was still capable not only of love, but of a fool.[62]

Doubtless, the integuments of the incident described had a basis in fact, and the situation had sparked memories of repeated female rejection in Faulkner's youth. Just the memory of this seemed sufficient to reconnect Faulkner with his past, somehow make him feel young again, no matter that his youth had been painful in this regard. Faulkner had again referred to himself as a "bloke," twice, in fact, just as he had done in his letter to Robert Haas requesting an insertion of material for *Intruder in the Dust* in 1949, the implication being that after all he was just an ordinary guy with ordinary feelings and responses: manly, libidinal urges and compulsions.

In truth, Faulkner was meeting with sexual success in his later years where in youth he had failed. He had failed to win his childhood sweetheart, Estelle Oldham, who had married Cornell Franklin, a man with more social position, wealth, and savoir faire; subsequently, he had also lacked success in his courtship of Helen Baird. He experienced even-more-short-lived relationships with Shirley Kirkwood, Gertrude Stegbauer, Elise Huntington, and Mary Victoria Mills, young ladies he more than desired, yet likely failed to entice with his somewhat less than masculine physiognomy, high-pitched voice, and decidedly ascetic mannerisms.

When he finally did win Estelle's heart, his passion had diminished. Quite probably the humiliation of having to accept his formerly pedestaled lady, a divorcée now with two children, tainted whatever passion and exuberance he might have had for a presumably virginal Estelle Oldham. In a perverse, though doubtless unconscious, way, marrying Estelle may have been a way of publicly displaying himself as a cuckold. Now, to the contrary, thanks to his celebrity, Faulkner seemed to be filling and maintaining a role that he had not since youth imagined himself capable of playing: that of "ladies' man." In 1951, four women were on his string: Meta, Ruth, Else, and Joan. In 1953, Faulkner would meet another young lady, Jean Stein, with whom he would take up where he had left off when Joan Williams became Mrs. Ezra Bowen.

Like his drinking, Faulkner's extramarital affairs were symptoms of extreme distress. Faulkner was not a "womanizer." His affairs simply provided him with a definite assurance of his manhood. To be past fifty years of age and still capable of not only attracting but also nurturing and maintaining lusty relationships with at least four young women was reassuring, at least superficially. And even if Faulkner might not have consciously rehearsed this awareness, his wife, Estelle, certainly did in the following excerpts from two letters she wrote to Saxe Commins in 1954:

> As for me—I'm hurt, but not despairing—*Nothing* can alter my love and devotion—nor upset my faith in Bill's actual love for me—although right now, he swears he doesn't care . . . All I want is Billy's good—and to prove it, I'll do *anything* that is best. . . .[63]

> I am much too old and poised (I hope) to give vent to personal animosity— In fact, am not sure that I feel any—Certainly I do not blame Joan—In all probability, had *I* been an aspiring young writer and an elderly celebrity had fallen in love with me—I would have accepted him as avidly as Joan did Bill—
> Who am I, to judge her anyway? I don't—
> And in a way, I feel sorry for Bill—He *is* in a mess, and I daresay is going to have a bad time of it. . . .
> Bill's article, "Mississippi," in next month's Holiday explains the two Bills— He is so definitely dual I think—Perhaps artists must needs be—[64]

Faulkner was not as adept at verbalizing the psychological dynamics of the problem as was his wife. She recognized her husband's affairs for what they were: "I know, as you must, that Bill feels some sort of compulsion to be attached to some young woman at all times—it's Bill—At long last I am sensible enough to concede him the right to do as he pleases, and without recrimination—It is not that I don't care—(I wish it were not so)— but all of a sudden [I] feel sorry for him—wish he could know without words between us, that it's not very important after all—"[65]

Estelle knew that it was the physical presence of these women, rather than their ultimate personal attachment to her husband, that was most significant to him. In fact, when Commins wrote to Faulkner on location in Cairo where he was scriptwriting Howard Hawks' movie *Land of the Pharaohs* to inform him of Joan Williams' recent marriage, Faulkner responded

with shocking callousness: "Thank you for your letter. I knew about it. . . .
Incidentally, a queer thing has happened to me, almost a repetition; this
one is even named Jean. . . . She is charming, delightful, completely transparent, completely trustful. I will not hurt her for any price. She doesn't
want anything of me—only to love me, be in love. You will probably meet
her next fall when we are home again. The other affair would have hurt of
course, except for this." [66]

Although it made almost nothing out of what vague rumors it may have
received regarding his love affairs, the press got great mileage out of Faulkner's drinking reputation, at times indicating that he was less than sober
during his trips abroad in the fifties. These were frequent. In 1954, he went
to Lima and São Paulo for the International Writers' Conference. In 1955,
he was sent by the American State Department to Japan and Manila; he
returned via Italy, France, and Iceland. In 1957, he was in Athens for two
weeks, and in 1961 in Caracas, Venezuela, for two weeks. [67] In the final decade
of his life, Faulkner seemed something like the traveler he had dreamed of
being when in his twenties he had worshiped a romantic image of himself
as a tramp.

Before finally making his youth's grand gesture, his 1925 walking tour
through Europe, he had nurtured his wanderlust and restlessness by vaga-
bonding between Oxford, Greenville, Pascagoula, and Charleston, Mississippi; Helena and Clarksdale, Arkansas; Memphis, Tennessee; and New
Orleans, Louisiana, and back. In the thirties he frequently traveled to Los
Angeles and New York. By the fifties, he was able to travel on the grandest
scale of all—continent-hopping—and he indulged in this with relative
abandon and considerable bravado. He continued to consider flying a
highly masculine endeavor. At this time, oceanic crossings by plane were
still in their pioneering stage as a means of public transportation, and although others were piloting him, flight remained almost as exotic and dar-
ing as it had seemed to him during his teens and twenties.

One result of Faulkner's increased financial stability was freedom to
pursue his interest in sailing; he became an avid, if maladroit, sailor. He
not only maintained his own sailboat, the *Ring Dove*, but also was co-
builder and for a brief time self-proclaimed captain of the houseboat *Min-
magary*. He was Master of the Sardis Reservoir. During this period when
he seemed to fancy he was articulating in the national voice, Faulkner also
showed an enthusiasm for other sports as well as sailing. In January 1955,
Sports Illustrated carried "An Innocent at Rinkside," Faulkner's description
of a hockey match at Madison Square Garden between the New York
Rangers and the Montreal Canadiens. In May 1955, the same publication
presented "Kentucky: May: Saturday: Three Days to the Afternoon," a
more poetic than factual account of the running of the Kentucky Derby.

These pieces, it would appear, informed the public that Mr. Faulkner was not only a fictionist of the highest order, not only a crusader for civil rights and freedom of speech (if not "freedom" of the press), but also a well-rounded man who actively enjoyed active sports.

Actually he did indulge in one sport at which he was more active than ever, that of riding and jumping horses. In a sense this activity represented a refinement of his interest in hunting. In the past he had accompanied rough-hewn, hard-drinking, tobacco-chewing good old boys on deer and bear hunts into the Delta and had written extensively about them by extrapolating metaphorically from his own limited personal experience. In the fifties Faulkner's idea of the hunt would assume more sophisticated proportions. Riding to the hounds either in Albermarle County, Virginia, or just outside Germantown, a community near Memphis, Tennessee, he associated with a socially elite class of people. This reinforced his sense of "having arrived." In the past, Faulkner had cast himself as a farmer, a man of the soil. Although he may not have struck an exact likeness of Cincinnatus at the plow, at least he could boast of trying to earn a livelihood from his livestock and crops. But by the mid-fifties Faulkner had decided to let his nephew, Jimmy Faulkner, acquire Greenfield Farm. He could still stable his horses at Rowan Oak, jump them in the paddock and field, and occasionally ride in Bailey's Woods.

Martin Dain and Ed Meek photographed Faulkner handling his ungroomed horses during the late fifties and early sixties. They also captured a very shabbily dressed Faulkner, a virtual tatterdemalion, completely at ease among his unkempt horses in the shadow of ramshackle outbuildings.[68] A portrait that Faulkner commissioned "Colonel" Cofield, an Oxford photographer, to make of him in December 1960 captures and highlights the disparity between the public image Faulkner meant to project and the private one of a physically deteriorated man. The formal portrait depicts Faulkner stiffly seated on a bench, "dressed to kill" in his full fox-hunting regalia: jodhpurs, high-top black boots with spurs, crop, whip, formal black top hat, white silk scarf with stickpin, and riding jacket. Faulkner had requested that Cofield hand-tint many, possibly all, of the nineteen copies of this portrait he ordered so that the coat might appear in its vibrant scarlet hue with Belgium blue lapels and gold accented brass buttons, with additional touches of black on the stickpin and a stroke of gold to offset the vest peeking out from the scarlet jacket. To complete the impressive rendering of this man of leisure, Cofield carefully retouched the white mustache with light black flecks of oil paint, though he left Faulkner's imposingly white hair untouched.[69] The overall effect must have seemed utterly sensational to Faulkner, who, with enormous pride in early 1961, gave a copy of this portrait to virtually every member of the Faulkner family and to various close associates. To Bennett Cerf, Faulkner sent a different pose from the same sitting, one that captures him standing nearly full length, hands resting on his thighs, clasping the coiled whip. The inscription on its mat read: "To Random House. Love and Kisses. Tally-ho. / William Faulkner."[70] This pose, together with the inscription, epitomized the Anglophile in Faulkner: to be "British," whether bloke or squire, was to attain the ultimate sophistication.

If we find it difficult to square the contrast between Cofield's portraits of Faulkner the Virginia huntsman with those taken by Dain and Meek in the same period, we have no difficulty making a comparison between 1961 depictions of Faulkner in riding habit with a picture made right after the First World War that shows Faulkner, standing stiffly against his cane, in an RAF uniform which he had brought back with him from flight school in Toronto and had embellished with store-bought metal regalia.[71] These portraits forty years apart represent costumed incarnations of the same man attempting to project an image at once ideal and real. As a "wounded," "decorated" flier and as a fully garbed aristocrat accustomed to riding to the hounds with the most elite Virginians, Faulkner could accept himself as a success: a man's man who had succeeded in pursuits requiring courage and skill; a man of action, arrested in perpetuity by the camera's all-discerning eye.

During the fifties, at least two bemusing ironies must have dawned on Faulkner. The first centered on Hollywood; the second on his literary co-eval, Ernest Hemingway. Faulkner had left Hollywood in frustrated disgust in 1945 as penniless as he had been when he first journeyed to Warner Bros. in 1942. Yet in 1948, M-G-M's purchase of rights to *Intruder in the Dust* set him free from financial worry. No doubt because of his increasing celebrity, Universal Pictures, then Twentieth Century-Fox, purchased the rights to and adapted movies from five of his novels: *Pylon* (*The Tarnished Angels*), *The Hamlet* (*The Long, Hot Summer*), *The Sound and the Fury*, and *Sanctuary* and *Requiem for a Nun* (*Sanctuary*). Faulkner had no hand in scripting these fictions for the movies, and with the exception of *Intruder in the Dust*, which he viewed and found vaguely satisfying, he consciously avoided seeing them in the theater.

Prior to the 1948 publication of *Intruder in the Dust, The Wild Palms,* published in 1939, had been Faulkner's last novel conceived wholly as a novel rather than as a literary collage mainly of previously published short stories, as had been the case with *The Hamlet* in 1940 and *Go Down, Moses and Other Stories* in 1942. Faulkner had experienced a virtual nine-year lapse in the writing of new fiction between *The Wild Palms* and *Intruder in the Dust*. Ernest Hemingway had suffered a similar silence in the output of his fiction. Ten years after *For Whom the Bell Tolls* appeared in 1940, *Across the River and into the Trees* was published, followed in 1952 by *The Old Man and the Sea,* which received a Pulitzer Prize. Faulkner's *A Fable* would garner a similar award two years later. While both books made considerable noise at the outset, giving the illusion of matching the greatness of their respective author's earlier fiction, neither was to prove to be as significant as earlier books by Hemingway and Faulkner. Nevertheless, in 1954, Hemingway received the Nobel Prize, as Faulkner had four years before.

Faulkner had many times before and would many times after 1952 decline to pass judgment publicly on Hemingway and on his work. As an exception, Faulkner did contribute a review of *The Old Man and the Sea* for the Autumn 1952 issue of *Shenandoah.* In its qualified praise, it read almost like an epitaph not just for Hemingway but in many respects for Faulkner himself. With a kind of prescience, Faulkner seemed aware that not only Hemingway's work from 1940 on but also all his own work—from the assumption of his duties at Warner Bros. in 1942 to the present moment—had smacked of too much tampering, conscious artifice, and self-imposed moralizing. Faulkner concluded his seemingly complimentary review with an equivocal understatement. "It's all right. Praise God that whatever made and loves and pities Hemingway and me kept him from touching it any further."[72]

Although Hemingway got considerable press from his Pulitzer Prize–winning book and from his elevation to Nobel Prize status, it was Faulkner's decade. As a social presence, Faulkner was in the fifties what Fitzgerald had been in the twenties and Hemingway in the thirties and forties. His much-photographed likeness—that solemn, grave, mustachioed visage with its deeply set eyes and aquiline nose, a ubiquitous pipe forever poised—became imprinted on the public mind. His sarcastic, sardonic, controversial comments frequently flashed across newspapers worldwide. He was quoted and discussed on the cocktail circuits and in academia's austere colloquia and seminars. He had outgrown even his own conception of what his youthful dreams had fantasied and wildly, though not wildly enough, might have envisioned for himself.

The only problem was that the acclaim had taken so long to catch up with his dreams that, by the time it did, he no longer felt a burning urgency to preserve the privacy needed for writing. The momentum of his activities literally pulled him up by his roots. He was homogenized and processed for public consumption in high schools and colleges and lecture halls and reading sodalities across the country and in every nation devoted to studying American society and its literary heritage. As the decade wore on, Faulkner must have come increasingly to realize that the image he projected no longer had any relevancy. Whether or not he appeared to the public as a manly, well-rounded, successful writer, a personage who had overtaken and assimilated the American Dream, made very little difference to him. And he had become numb to receiving myriad awards lavished upon him. Somehow, they seemed trivial and empty.[73]

A. I. Bezzerides has said:

> To me, Bill seemed to have become a victim of his own legend and was living a part that seemed totally false: the esteemed writer, the Nobel winner. The man who had written these great things bore no relationship to the young man who had written these wonderful things he had written when he was a struggling writer trying to make a scratch, trying to earn a living, writing things he was impelled to write, not written deliberately, but impelled to write because they came out of his subconscious. Now, here he was very conscious of the greatness he had achieved without the memory of the consciousness that had actually done the achieving. He was living a role that seemed fraudulent to me. It seemed sad to me.[74]

For all his success, there seems little reason to believe William Faulkner ever completely succeeded in squaring with his role as writer his own personal dissatisfaction over sensing himself to be a physically inactive individual, a "vegetable." His perceived inadequacies would remain ambivalent, if chronic, irritants to be temporarily, repeatedly assuaged. However, at least once, he would actually document explicitly what amounted to a justification for and resolution of all his activities, literary and physical. In his confessional "Foreword" to *The Faulkner Reader,* dated November 1953, Faulkner isolated the underlying "anguish" that had "driven" him to write: his urgency to "uplift man's heart." And although he would like to "hope" his efforts might lead to change, improvement in the human condition, admittedly, he stated, his prime motivation was "completely selfish, completely personal." Referring to himself in the collective voice of all serious writers, Faulkner focused on the "selfish" results his writing could effect:

> He would lift up man's heart for his own benefit because in that way he can say No to death. He is saying No to death for himself by means of the hearts which he has hoped to uplift, or even by means of the mere base glands which he has disturbed to that extent where they can say No to death on their own account by knowing, realizing, having been told and believing it: *At least we are not vegetables because the hearts and glands capable of partaking in this excitement are not those of vegetables, and will, must, endure.*
>
> So he who, from the isolation of cold impersonal print, can engender this excitement, himself partakes of the immortality which he has engendered.[75]

Ultimately, we may conclude, the handcrafted life masks William Faulkner designed to give the illusion that he was one of life's active, productive, virile men were assimilated to his death mask. We can only conjecture about the ambivalent dynamics of this process. It is, in any event, inconsequential. What is significant is how we regard the living corpus of Faulkner's writing: this *exists* to remind us that living productively may be the human spirit's most profound justification for not staying dead in the first place, likely, its only way of saying No to death.

TWO

POET-AT-LARGE

"I was not interested in verse for verse's sake then. I read and employed verse, firstly, for the purpose of furthering various philanderings in which I was engaged, secondly, to complete a youthful gesture I was then making, of being 'different' in a small town. Later, my interest in fornication waning, I turned inevitably to verse, finding therein an emotional counterpart far more satisfactory for two reasons: (1) No partner was required (2) It was so much simpler just to close a book, and take a walk."
—William Faulkner, "Verse, Old and Nascent: A Pilgrimage," October 1924 [1]

"Being a poet, of course I give no fart for glory."
—William Faulkner, letter to Malcolm Cowley, May 7, 1944 [2]

Billy Falkner [3] was already writing verse when Phil Stone first met him in Oxford, Mississippi, in 1914. For the next decade, Stone would encourage, browbeat, and cajole *his* student not only to practice writing by emulating such then-considered masters as Swinburne, Keats, Shelley, and Housman but also to stay current by voraciously reading the contemporary voices of Amy Lowell, T. S. Eliot, H. D., Richard Aldington, E. E. Cummings, the Imagists, and the Symbolists. Stone supplied the books, the personal criticism, and the contacts to whom he and Faulkner, as editor and author (in that order in Stone's proprietary hierarchy), might submit the youthful poet's increasing repertoire of poetry. From their mutual efforts, two poems actually achieved national publication: "L'Apres-Midi d'un Faune," in the August 6, 1919, issue of the *New Republic,* and "Portrait," in the June 1922 issue of the *Double Dealer.* But no further offers to publish the "young Southern poet of unusual promise," as the "Notes on

Contributors" section of the New Orleans literary magazine referred to Faulkner, seemed to be forthcoming.

Notwithstanding, on June 20, 1923, William Faulkner took the initiative to write the Four Seas Company of Boston, offering for possible publication a collection of poems, some of which may have been revised from earlier versions in *Vision in Spring,* a typed, eighty-eight-page booklet Faulkner hand-bound in 1921. He had entitled this manuscript *Orpheus, and Other Poems*. It was rejected more by Faulkner than by the publishing firm that had offered to publish it if money were advanced for its printing costs. Instead, Faulkner assembled a different manuscript consisting of poems written during the months of April, May, and June 1919 entitled *The Marble Faun*.[4] Phil Stone took up the beat, and together both young men were soon conspiring to get Faulkner published in book form by the Four Seas Company, a firm that had published at least two books of poetry Stone had purchased over the years and no doubt had shared with his protégé: *Sour Grapes,* 1922, by William Carlos Williams, and *Images Old and New,* 1916, by Richard Aldington.[5]

Apparently satisfied that the Faulkner/Stone consortium would subvent the four hundred dollars required for publication of the projected volume of poetry Faulkner had sent, the Four Seas Company proceeded with typesetting and had page proofs to Faulkner by late September 1924. By October 16, these proofs were back in Boston, fully corrected. On October 19, Stone sent a thick packet containing not only the form letter they were to print and send out to prospective buyers of *The Marble Faun* but also an undetermined group of *new* poems from which the publisher might wish to choose a few for promotional purposes. One of these poems was entitled "Mississippi Hills: My Epitaph."[6] Stone's offerings were accompanied by a simple, yet suggestive, proviso: Four Seas would be free to make use of any of these new poems, provided that Faulkner would have unencumbered right to them for his next book.

Ultimately, the anticipated publication date of November 1, 1924, was delayed and postponed again, partly because of Stone's tardiness in completing and submitting his preface. December 15 became the official date of publication. The earliest presentation inscriptions suggest that Faulkner and Stone received their first copies of *The Marble Faun* on December 19, 1924.[7]

As well as marking both the apex and almost simultaneous culmination of his aspirations and achievements as a poet,[8] the period prior to publication of *The Marble Faun* was climactic for Faulkner because of his significant inability to maintain a respected job. After an absence of nearly six months in 1918 spent as a civilian worker in New Haven and as a cadet in the Royal

Air Force in Toronto, Faulkner had returned to Oxford to live. With one other major exception in 1921, when he had clerked in Lord & Taylor's Doubleday bookstore in New York, he remained a resident of that small northern Mississippi town until publication of *The Marble Faun*. Although he frequently expressed his restlessness by traveling to Greenville and Clarksdale, Mississippi, and Memphis on social outings, he had failed to make a break with the confining environment of his family and relatives and university friends—that narrow world in which convention would have him pursue and hold a *responsible* position and where for three years, in the guise of university postmaster, he actually tried to work at a routine job.

On October 31, 1924, under severe censure and coercion, William Faulkner officially resigned from the postmaster's job, which Phil Stone had been instrumental in securing in 1922 through his growing influence as a young Mississippi lawyer. Although this resignation seemed to cause Faulkner no great recrimination, it must have carried with it certain embarrassment in the tightly knit social community of which he was, at least marginally, a patrician member (his father, Murry, was a member of the university administration).

At just about the same time, Faulkner received an unequivocal request to cease his activities as scoutmaster of the local, church-affiliated troop, which he had directed for a number of years. Although he had developed a reputation as a positive force in teaching young people the pleasures and values of outdoor camping and mastering new skills, some individuals condemned him, both privately and publicly, as a negative influence because of his notorious habit of drinking.

Responding more than two decades later to Malcolm Cowley's last-minute request for biographical information he might incorporate into the dust jacket copy for *The Portable Faulkner,* Faulkner alluded to this occasion of his *resignation* from the scouts: "When I came back from RAF . . . I didn't want to go to work; it was by my father's request that I entered the University, which I didn't want to do either. That was in 1920. Since then I have: Painted houses. Served as a 4th class postmaster . . . Oh yes, was a scout master for two years, was fired for moral reasons."[9]

During the last week of November 1924, Faulkner, accompanied by a friend, Mr. Kelly, attended a party at the home of Mrs. Homer K. Jones in Memphis.[10] He recorded some of the circumstances of this gathering and the incidents proceeding from it in the following handwritten letter, which he sent to his host once he returned to Oxford, Mississippi:

My dear Mrs. Jones—
   I seem to recall, when Mr Kelly and I were with you one evening last week, giving you a copy of one of my poems. Mr Kelly and I were having such a

grand time then that I dont know what I wrote; whatever it was, I am sure it is undecipherable, so I am taking the liberty of sending you a correct copy of the verse, as you are interested in literature. Also, this was [the] poem which I tried so unsuccessfully to recite.

I am sorry to have needlessly annoyed you about the pipe and scarf. The pipe I later found, having left it somewhere else. The muffler I had after we left you, I am reliably informed. What I am asking pardon for, is failing to call you again as I should. Almost immediately after calling you that morning I was arrested on a moral charge, and by the time I was a free agent again, I had forgotten it. Please forgive me, and thank you for the whisky-and-soda. I dont know whether I drank it or not, but it was a beautiful tipple.

Please give my regards to Mr Jones.
Sincerely yours,
William Faulkner[11]

The contents of this letter suggest more than a few simple biographical facts about William Faulkner: they disclose an ambience, a sense of the youthful Faulkner in all his recklessness, his brash and dashing bravura and pretentiousness, the poet pursuing his own image of the Bohemian artist, the absent-minded genius whose main concerns are for his Art. Withal, there is still the lingering hint that its author is a sensitive Mississippi gentleman aware of his social responsibilities, propriety, and good breeding.

More important, this letter underscores a magical time in Faulkner's life. Possibly, this period between Faulkner's first officially published book and his recent dismissals from his job as well as from his scouting duties may have been the beginning of the one, short-lived time in his entire career when he would be a "free agent," beholden to no one other than himself. He was, as this letter implies, very much aware of himself as a single male, free (forgetting for the moment his brief arrest for public drinking) to pursue his destiny as a writer, a poet, indeed, soon a published poet. Faulkner would evermore regret the passing of this period in his career; frequently, he would refer to it when responsibilities grew too weighty for him to fathom.[12]

Also, this letter indicates habits that would recur throughout Faulkner's life. For instance, in future correspondence he would often allude to misplaced pages of manuscript, pipes, or articles of clothing. And on at least one other occasion while inebriated, Faulkner would be inspired to recite and inscribe for companions poetry that moved him.[13]

Finally, implied in this letter are Faulkner's arrogance and his own enormous sense of self-worth. Indeed, he must have recognized in Mrs. Homer K. Jones a genuinely sophisticated taste for serious literature; otherwise, he surely would never have deigned to recite to her from his most recently completed work, let alone inscribe for her a copy of "Pregnacy" [*sic*], a new poem that obviously moved him out of his usual reticence to perform for her. Nor would he have submitted for her further approbation a "correct copy"[14] of the poem had he not considered her a discriminating and worthy critic. If anything, he had very little patience with sycophants. He disdained those he judged frauds in the literary world.

However, to those whom he admired, or was drawn to romantically, or owed his loyalty, he would consistently make gifts of his books and manuscripts, those things he regarded as most precious. This habit, like the others mentioned, would persist throughout his career. And as with so many of Faulkner's *gifts*, the handwritten copy of "Pregnacy" that he gave to Mrs. Jones that evening in the week of November 23, 1924, at the Joneses' house survived. Like many other recipients of his gifts, Mrs. Jones must have intuited Faulkner's potential and future greatness from his own self-confidence, his exaggerated presence. Why else would this woman have saved the scribbled poem Faulkner himself, on sober reflection, considered to be so "undecipherable" that he felt obliged to send along a typed carbon copy in his letter apologizing for his recent behavior?

The version of "Pregnacy" that is transcribed below had been hastily written out by Faulkner in brown ink on the verso of what must have been a handy piece of letterhead stationery printed with the logo: "Dr. Willis C. Campbell / Clinic / 869 Madison Ave. / Memphis, Tenn." Apparently, Faulkner's pen ran out of ink before he could complete his rendition of the poem; the last line and a half, as well as one correction and his signature, "William Faulkner," at the bottom of the leaflet, are in pencil:

Pregnacy

As to an ancient music's hidden fall
Her seed in the huddled dark was warm and wet,
And three cold stars were riven in the wall:
Rain and dark and death above her door were set.

Her hands moaned on her breast in blind and supple fire,
Made light within her cave: she saw her harried
Body wrung to a strange and tortured lyre,
Whose music ~~was once~~ once was pure strings simply married

One to another in simple diffidence
Her strange and happy sorrows once were wed:
But what tomorrow's ~~song~~ chords be recompense,
For yesterday's simple song unravishèd?

Three stars in her heart, when she awakes
As winter's ~~sleep~~ sleep breaks greening in the rain,
And in the caverned ~~earth~~ earth spring's rumor shakes,
As in her loins, the tilled and quickened grain.

Inebriated or not, or to what degree, remains a matter of speculation and ultimately of little consequence. What is significant is the sense of artistic decorum that Faulkner felt necessary to maintain at this stage of his career. There are few substantive changes that the "correct copy" makes manifest; rather, the carbon copy supersedes the original re-creation as much for neatness as for correctness. Faulkner was, whatever his inability in holding a steady job, an artist, specifically, a poet whose first book, *The Marble Faun,* was at the time this letter was written less than two weeks away from removing him from obscurity. Furthermore, he was a very proud poet, and for someone of Mrs. Jones' caliber, it would not do for him to leave her with a slovenly impression of his newest work. At age twenty-seven, as poet-at-large, William Faulkner of Oxford, Mississippi, already had a self-styled image to maintain as well as a vision to project to the literary world of Memphis, Tennessee, and beyond.

But Faulkner's poetic meteor would soon burn out. He would travel to New Orleans, settle for a time in the Vieux Carré and discover that his true calling was not composing poetry at all but writing prose, some of the most poetic prose the English language would ever know.

THREE

"ELDER WATSON IN HEAVEN"

"I think that the trouble with Christianity is that we've never tried it yet."
—William Faulkner [1]

"No offense," I says. "I give every man his due, regardless of religion or anything else. I have nothing against jews as an individual," I says. "It's just the race."
—Jason Compson in *The Sound and the Fury* [2]

In the early months of 1942, Robert W. Daniel, a graduate student in English at Yale University, wrote to various friends, family members, and acquaintances of William Faulkner, soliciting materials he might borrow and display in what that summer at Yale in the Sterling Memorial Library would be the first major American exhibition of Faulkner's books, letters, and manuscripts.

Although Faulkner's portrait had appeared on the January 23, 1939, cover of *Time* magazine to coincide with publication of his new novel, *The Wild Palms,* transforming him into an overnight celebrity, it would have been a hedged bet that few of *Time's* subscribers had read many, if any, of Faulkner's labyrinthine novels. Yet, in the minds of contemporary critics as admired as Malcolm Cowley, Cleanth Brooks, and George Marion O'Donnell or in the estimation of such recognized artists as Robert Penn Warren and Conrad Aiken, Faulkner was unequivocally the most profoundly original, provocative, universal, and seemingly enduring writer their country had produced in the twentieth century.

But there existed a vast paradoxical disparity between Faulkner's reputation as a literary genius and the income resulting from his superior talent when translated into and measured against royalties accruing from sales of his books. Thanks to the *Time* exposure and the fact that the two stories comprising *The Wild Palms* had relatively accessible, linear, less complex plots and simple diction, this new book did enjoy strong initial sales. However, the following year, *The Hamlet* did not perform as well, and many sets of printed sheets were placed in storage, unbound.[3] Along with a modest trade print run, Random House would offer on May 11, 1942, a deluxe edition of *Go Down, Moses and Other Stories,* specially bound in an issue of 100 autographed copies. Whereas *The Wild Palms* and *The Hamlet* had appeared in signed, limited editions of 250 copies each, this new edition would prove to be Faulkner's most severely limited collector's item to date. The limited publication owed less to wartime conservation measures than to economic exigencies. Careful not to project the status of their foremost author in a pale, Random House could not afford to dispense altogether with issuing a limited edition; after all, his publishers had used this promotional tactic with each newly published book since *A Green Bough* had appeared in 1933. Neither were they eager to produce an expensive book that would diminish profits from the overall sales potential of the new novel. Rightly, they were dubious that by this time many readers, or even collectors, would be willing to pay double the $2.50 retail price of the trade edition just for the opportunity of purchasing a Faulkner autograph.

Not only did Random House trim its production run to correspond with its reevaluated estimation of expected sales, as it related to both signed, limited copies and dust-jacketed trade copies, but it also at the last minute upped the retail price from its projected $2.00 to $2.50. Since the printer had already finished its run of dust jackets showing the $2.00 price on the upper corner of its front flap, workers at the plant had to clip those prices by hand. As a result, very few copies exist with the original retail price; buyers had to rely on clerks or printed stickers to determine the book's cost.

Fearing the worst, Random House's principals went one step further: without informing Faulkner, the reigning triumvirate of Bennett Cerf, Donald Klopfer, and Robert Haas decided to append to the intended title of Faulkner's novel, *Go Down, Moses,* a tell-tale trailer, "and Other Stories."[4] Their rationale at the time was that the short story was by far the more respected of the genres. The public had been conditioned to respond to this form as it most popularly appeared in the pages of *Saturday Evening Post, Scribners, American Mercury, Harper's,* and a myriad of lesser quality magazines. Faulkner was shocked; he had labored over the inclusion of each juxtaposed "chapter" of what he came to believe was an integrated, cohesive novel, not a compilation of short stories. He had consciously recrafted the original magazine stories comprising these chapters in *Go Down, Moses* with this overall intention and novelistic design in mind. Yet, he would have no recourse other than to wait for the "Third Printing" to appear in 1948 with his originally conceived title.

Doubtless, Robert W. Daniel would have had little awareness at this time of the precarious sales status of Faulkner's books, his tenuous financial straits, or his failure to make a livelihood from his vocation, nor could Daniel have imagined that within a matter of months, almost concurrent with the opening of his exhibition at Yale, Faulkner would have assumed the role of a $300-a-week scenarist at the Warner Bros. studio in Burbank, California. Yet, Daniel was certain of one thing—he had been fully imbued with a belief shared not only by a consensus of the critical element at Yale University but also by the American academic community at large, which had placed upon William Faulkner's fiction its highest imprimatur and upon Faulkner himself its ultimate accolade: that of writers' Writer!

Thus, Daniel focused all his energies on the task of mounting an exhibition that would present to the public a sampling of Faulkner's literary career. The exhibit opened in mid-July and ran through the better part of August 1942, and although it was not seen by many summer-vacationing Yale students, nor by many who had contributed artifacts (mostly Mississippians for whom the cost and logistics of wartime travel were prohibitive as well as difficult), it did generate a legacy in the form of a relatively authoritative bibliography Daniel arranged and titled *A Catalogue of the Writings of William Faulkner.* [5]

There is no evidence that Daniel ever engaged Faulkner's assistance on this project. Many family members, however, including Faulkner's mother, Maud, and his great-aunt, Alabama McLean of Memphis (the Old Colonel's daughter), and old and current friends, the most instrumentally helpful among whom was Faulkner's mentor/lawyer Phil Stone, saw or contributed to the show. Among them was Mrs. Ben F. Wasson, Sr., mother of Ben, Jr., Faulkner's Greenville, Mississippi, friend, early agent, and editor of at least one novel, *Sartoris.* In Mr. Wasson's brief reply on his wife's behalf, written on March 16, 1942, he mentions he is forwarding "the only paper Mrs. Wasson has been able to find from the pen of William Faulkner." In addition, he continues, "I fear this paper will not be of much value to you, but you are welcome to it for whatever it may be worth." [6]

Although Mr. Wasson failed to detail the contents he was contributing, some of the materials he may have sent Daniel can be deduced. Assuming that Daniel acted on Mr. Wasson's generous offer, it can be surmised that at least two poems were sent by Mr. Wasson, almost certainly made part of the exhibition, and retained by Daniel after the exhibit's close sometime in late August 1942. These poems were entitled "Elder Watson in Heaven" and "Pierrot, Sitting Beside The Body of Colombine, suddenly Sees Himself in a Mirror."

There seems little doubt that both these poems were part of, if not the entirety of, the "paper" that Mr. Wasson sent to Robert W. Daniel in mid-

March 1942. Furthermore, due to the similarity of format and the fact that these two poems were the only original Faulkner materials in the Yale-Faulkner Exhibition manila folder Daniel still retained in his files thirty-five years after that time, a concurrence of composition dates, as well as provenance indicated by the penciled notation on the "Pierrot" poem, might also reasonably be assumed, thus assigning to "Elder Watson in Heaven" 1921 as the likely year of its composition.[7]

The following rendition of "Elder Watson in Heaven" has been transcribed from the Wasson typescript, which to date remains the only extant original copy of this unique Faulkner poem, written when its author was twenty-four years old and absolutely positive that his literary calling was poetry and that fame, at least, was imminent.

Elder Watson in Heaven

Elder Watson, lying still,
Protrudes a red haired meagre shank;
Treasure above has he, as well
Ten thousand dollars in the bank.

Elder Watson, when erect
And circumscribed with moral good,
Presents the world an iron curve
Of dogma and of platitude

In which his soul, that sober flame,
And presbyterian, and dight
With subtleties equivocal,
Need fear no sudden change of light

When through the shining gates he moves
While music mounts the golden air;
And his reward, as promised him,
Is spread before him everywhere.

Here there is no five percent,
Nor driven bargains, we are told:
Nor bankers' checques: this is a life
Insurance premium, paid in gold.

This, too, will be a recompense
For that ten thousand left behind;

And, feeling Fate's incurious hand,
He drew the shroud across his mind

And to his waiting children, said:
"Walk upright in the sight of God"
Nor did he look back on his clay
As through the opening gates he trod

With confidence, and gravely smiled,
Pausing on the shining stairs
As passionately to him rose
The hurried mourning of his heirs.

Perhaps he smiled, and then, like God,
Saw Elder Watson in the wrack
Of worn theology, sleeping there
Profound, defenseless, on his back.[8]

Structurally and narratively, "Elder Watson in Heaven" might be likened to a lighthouse situated on the treacherous shoals of William Faulkner's skeptical sensibility, a lighthouse whose beacon, no matter how dimly, would sweep the expanse of his entire literary career, illuminating a specific obsession: telling stories. In microcosm, this poem might easily serve to highlight that particular penchant as raconteur Faulkner demonstrated almost from the beginning of his writing career and that eventually would contribute to his consciously orchestrated shift from poetry as his dominant mode of expression to the broader freedoms of prose: that compulsive drive of his to conceive, elaborate, and narrate complete fictions from single threads or images.

Indeed, this poem is structured to yield a sense of narrative progression. Constituted of three distinct sections, though not so demarcated, told by at least two separate persons and arguably by a third-person voice controlling the concluding quatrain, it succeeds in more than just making an opinionated statement about a particular condition inherent in a specific person's character. Actually, it creates and defines its own environment and context in which its protagonist moves from point A through point B to destination C and is self-contained by means of an organic sense of circularity. Remarkably, the poem's climax effects a condition that increasingly would come to characterize virtually all of Faulkner's best fiction: a suspension of authorial judgment capable of requiring readers not only to participate in the narrative but also presumably to render individual interpretations rather than be satisfied with traditional absolutes as to motivation and outcome of human behavior.

Specifically, the initial five quatrains and first two lines of the sixth stanza are told in the present and, with one exception, future tenses by an internal, first-person narrator who in the fifth stanza, not unlike the narrator of "A Rose for Emily" (1930), identifies himself as the collective, communal "we." The narration itself operates on parallel levels with the objective description of Elder Watson (his physical appearance, position in the community, financial status) alternating with and consistently being undercut by subjective double-entendres: words and phrases ironically weighted toward the sarcastic, cynical, biting, snide, vindictive, and sardonic. Thus, to isolate just one example, it matters little that the protagonist has "treasure above" because, we are mockingly told, he has already enjoyed having "ten thousand dollars in the bank." Words qualified or standing alone, such as "moral good," "iron curve of dogma," "platitude," "sober flame," "presbyterian," and "subtleties equivocal," evoke responses quite opposed to those superficially intended to generate sympathetic approval by the narrator.

Obviously delighting in his wordplay, Faulkner also allows three derivative echoes to infiltrate his poetry: one, possibly an allusion to Eliot's apelike character at the heart of "Sweeney Among the Nightingales," describes Elder Watson's "red haired meagre shank" and his "erect" stature; a second, borrowing from the seventeenth-century tradition of the hyperbolic metaphysical conceit, suggests that for Elder Watson heaven will be "a life / Insurance premium, paid in gold," one calculated to "recompense" him when he dies for having had to relinquish his "ten thousand dollars." Decidedly, a third set of echoes in "Elder Watson in Heaven" seems to hark back to the poetry of E. A. Robinson. If dissimilar in rhythm and measure, tone, even particularized focus on religious personages, Robinson's secular "portraits" yet appear thematically compatible and may well be sources or models for Faulkner's "Elder Watson."[9]

If the first section of the poem begins with Elder Watson "lying still" and uses this static occasion to describe his immediate as well as "promised" state (the reader is led to believe Elder Watson is merely stirring in restive sleep), the second section is announced by a sharp shifting of tense and voice. Commencing with the second half of the sixth stanza and running through the seventh and eighth stanzas and told in the third-person, imperfect tense by an omniscient narrator, this section elaborates considerable physical action initiated by Elder Watson himself. Having drawn the shroud across his sleeping mind, accepting death's invitation, he first admonishes his gathered "children," presumably at bedside, then without looking back passes through heaven's opening gates, pausing on the "shining stairs" just long enough to remark the "hurried mourning" of his "heirs."

As abruptly as the second section begins and ends, the third section opens and climaxes in the ninth and final stanza. But this shift is not without its own idiosyncratic and unexpected reversal. Up to this point, the voices describing the scene and the situational story they showcase have been very assertive, if deliberately ambiguous, to effect the appropriate attitude and tone espoused by their particular narrators (not to be confused or necessarily fused with Faulkner's attitude and tone). Although the third-person, past tense, omniscient voice is retained in the climactic quatrain, the deliberate pose of the unidentified narrator is blurred. Referring to the newly arrived spirit of Elder Watson in heaven, the voice conjectures conditionally that "*perhaps* he smiled" (emphasis added). The suggestion is strange indeed: that the Elder might be suffering painful insights from his new vantage, seeing his former self for the hypocrite he had been. The poem returns to its opening scene, in which Elder Watson, although now apparently dead, is "sleeping there / Profound, defenseless, on his back." Curiously, however, now the body is being punished in "the wrack of worn theology." Finally, most poignant of all is the more likely possibility that even though in heaven, Elder Watson "perhaps" has failed to see the very implications of his former sanctimoniousness. Either way, the reader is not told whether Elder Watson's soul shall be redeemed, his salvation made manifest through ultimate awareness of his sins and absolution resulting from his asking and receiving penance from God. Regardless, the closure carries the reader back to the poem's opening lines and creates an atmosphere of endless circularity, which forces him continuously to attempt to reassess his own interpretation in light of the dramatically suspended final authority the poet consciously withholds.

Thematically, even a cursory gloss of this poem reveals its author's unveiled, blatantly cynical distrust of fundamental, formal religion and his sardonic and skeptical attitude toward those charged with the responsibility of formally upholding their faith. With severe ironic intent, Faulkner levels his indictment at a respected Presbyterian Elder whose moral and ethical positions in the community, though seemingly unblemished, are undermined by his hypocrisy and sanctimoniousness. Indeed, Elder Watson may be more contemptible for his base greed than for his arrogance, inflexibility, or triteness.

Between 1929 and 1932, Faulkner would achieve his most mature fictional expression of these themes and attitudes. In composing the following set piece, which Jason Compson delivers in the third section of *The Sound and the Fury* (1929), and venting all his cynicism and sardonic humor toward the Church and its ministers, Faulkner might almost have had in mind his own character, Elder Watson, evoked seven years earlier. With minimal substitutions, "five thousand dollars" for "ten thousand dollars," first-person, present tense narrative for third-person, past tense, and prose for poetic technique and format, it is not difficult to make the leap with the author from groping to mastery of style and theme:

> After all, like I say money has no value; it's just the way you spend it. It dont belong to anybody, so why try to hoard it. It just belongs to the man that can get it and keep it. There's a man right here in Jefferson made a lot of money selling rotten goods to niggers, lived in a room over the store about the size of a pigpen, and did his own cooking. About four or five years ago he was taken sick. Scared the hell out of him so that when he was up again he joined the church and bought himself a Chinese missionary, five thousand dollars a year. I often think how mad he'll be if he was to die and find out there's not any heaven, when he thinks about that five thousand a year. Like I say, he'd better go on and die now and save money.[10]

In his next novel, *As I Lay Dying,* published the following year (1930), Faulkner would focus almost entirely on the theme of hypocrisy as it manifested itself in word and deed, in civil as well as in religious contexts. In addition to Reverend Whitfield, who, as an extended embodiment of Elder Watson, has committed a real, mortal sin, adultery, as opposed merely to hoarding wealth, and who seems to suffer for his unassuagable spiritual depravity, Faulkner would present Elder Watson's secular, female counterpart, Cora Tull, a self-righteous, rigid, and highly dogmatical arbiter of community values and religious standards. Like Elder Watson, she proves to a fault, literally, to be dependent on material wealth and ultimately distracted by it. In the first of her three monologues, or "chapters," Cora convincingly makes clear her capacity for justifying and squaring the earthly omnipotence of finances with the heavenly austerity of election and salvation:

> "She ought to taken those cakes anyway," Kate says.
> "Well," I say, "I reckon she never had no use for them now."
> "She ought to taken them," Kate says. "But those rich town ladies can change their minds. Poor folks can't."
> Riches is nothing in the face of the Lord, for He can see into the heart.
> "Maybe I can sell them at the bazaar Saturday," I say. They turned out real well.
> "You can't get two dollars a piece for them," Kate says.
> "Well, it isn't like they cost me anything," I say. I saved them out and swapped a dozen of them for the sugar and flour. It isn't like the cakes cost

me anything, as Mr Tull himself realizes that the eggs I saved were over and beyond what we had engaged to sell, so it was like we had found the eggs or they had been given to us.

"She ought to taken those cakes when she same as gave you her word," Kate says. The Lord can see into the heart. If it is His will that some folks has different ideas of honesty from other folks, it is not my place to question His decree.

"I reckon she never had any use for them," I say. They turned out real well, too.[11]

With her hypocritical pretense of piety, Cora is as accountable for earthly and spiritual fallibility as is the Reverend Whitfield who, for all his apparent suffering, ultimately acquits himself of his impiety in the name of God's mercy, presumptuously suggesting, "He will accept the will for the deed." That conditional "perhaps" on which the climax of "Elder Watson in Heaven" hinges has been replaced by a much more subtle, if essentially similar, sense of the ironic. As a participatory condition imposed by his conception of the novel itself, Faulkner heightens the effect of exasperation the reader experiences by coercing him to accept being spoken to by the character, not by an outside narrator.

With the publication of *Sanctuary* (1931), Faulkner would reintroduce Horace Benbow, a male counterpart of Cora Tull, and in *Light in August* (1932), Faulkner would flesh out, through the characterization of Reverend Gail Hightower, his earlier portrayal of Reverend Whitfield. He would offer as dominant modes of expression stark, realistic detail combined with riveting, self-indicting interior monologues that would engender a palpable protagonist capable of commanding empathic responses from the reader, not just a nod to the satirical projected by a stereotypical Elder Watson or even the two-dimensional abstraction Faulkner named Reverend Whitfield.

In *Go Down, Moses* (1942), Faulkner would actually fuse the clerical with the temporal in the person of Ike McCaslin, exploring a life ranging over at least seven decades dedicated to squaring moral and ethical issues with religious requirements of spiritual right living. For all his apparently proper responses, Ike appears finally to fail at reconciling ambiguities of the human heart in conflict with itself and with its Maker. Faulkner further seems to suggest that neither society nor its most cherished, sacred rituals and myths raised to religious significance can ultimately accommodate Ike's own incapacity to act on his best intentions and most deep-seated convictions. If "The Bear" postulates hope and the possibility for Ike to come to terms with his heritage and make appropriate reparations and changes, "Delta Autumn" would seem to seal his disappointing failure to succeed at these tasks.

Even as late as September 1950, disguising his pervasive contempt for
hypocrisy, especially that of wearing churchly robes, Faulkner would reas-
sume the more direct satirical pose he had adopted in treating Elder Watson. This time his spleen would vent itself in a humorous, retaliatory condemnation of three Protestant ministers whom he believed had egregiously
overstepped their ordained bounds by decrying from their pulpits an up-
coming petition and vote to legalize the public sale and consumption of
beer in Lafayette County, Mississippi. Indeed, they had even resorted
to having printed and disseminated in church copies of the following
broadside:

TO THE VOTERS OF OXFORD:

Your vote on Tuesday, September 5, may decide whether or not BEER will
be sold in Oxford.

We believe that the sale of beer in this city would be detrimental to the best
interests of this community for the following reasons:

1. We had it from 1934 to 1944. It was so obnoxious that it was voted out.

2. Beer is an alcoholic beverage. A bottle of 4 percent beer contains twice as
much alcohol as a "jigger" of whiskey.

3. Money will be spent for beer that should be used to purchase food, clothing and other essential consumer goods.

4. Since the recent act of the Legislature authorizing towns of 2,500 and
above population to vote on beer, Starkville and Water Valley have voted.
Both have voted against the sale of beer. There must be some good reason.

It is our opinion that the majority of the people are against the sale of beer
in Oxford, but you must GO TO THE POLLS ON TUESDAY, SEPTEMBER 5, in
order to express your opinion.

> Yours for a better Oxford,
> H. E. FINGER, JR.
> JOHN K. JOHNSON
> FRANK MOODY PURSER [12]

To maximize his audience, Faulkner would eschew the relatively private
domain of poetry in favor of the more immediately direct and accessible

medium of the prose broadside; he would have the Oxford *Eagle* print single-sheet copies of his own response similarly entitled "To the Voters of Oxford" and, accompanied by members of his immediate family, would personally assist in distributing it door-to-door in Oxford. Employing in his "Beer Broadside" a pseudoscientific pose to reinforce his rebuttal of the ministers' arguments, "William Faulkner / Private Citizen" would contend that clergymen, without exception, should not interpose themselves through the influence of their office in public elections and other matters of temporal preference. To do so was to arrogate judgments best left to the democratic process.

The following transcription of the now-infamous "Beer Broadside" of William Faulkner is rendered from the copy formerly belonging to Faulkner's stepdaughter, Victoria Franklin Fielden:

TO THE VOTERS OF OXFORD

Correction to paid printing statement of Private Citizens H. E. Finger, Jr., John K. Johnson, and Frank Moody Purser.

1. *'Beer was voted out in 1944 because of its obnoxiousness.'*

Beer was voted out in 1944 because too many voters who drank beer or didn't object to other people drinking it, were absent in Europe and Asia defending Oxford where voters who preferred home to war could vote on beer in 1944.

2. *'A bottle of 4 percent beer contains twice as much alcohol as a jigger of whiskey.'*

A 12 ounce bottle of four percent beer contains forty-eight one hundredths of one ounce of alcohol. A jigger holds one and one-half ounces (see Dictionary). Whiskey ranges from 30 to 45 percent alcohol. A jigger of 30 percent whiskey contains forty-five one hundredths of one ounce of alcohol. A bottle of 4 percent beer doesn't contain twice as much alcohol as a jigger of whiskey. Unless the whiskey is less than 32 percent alcohol, the bottle of beer doesn't even contain as much.

3. *'Money spent for beer should be spent for food, clothing and other essential consumer goods.'*

By this precedent, we will have to hold another election to vote on whether or not the florists, the picture shows, the radio shops and the pleasure car dealers will be permitted in Oxford.

4. *'Starkville and Water Valley voted beer out; why not Oxford?'*

Since Starkville is the home of Mississippi State, and Mississippi State beat the University of Mississippi at football, maybe Oxford, which is the home of the University of Mississippi, is right in taking Starkville for a model. But why must we imitate Water Valley? Our high school team beat theirs, didn't it?

Yours for a freer Oxford, where publicans can be law abiding publicans six days a week, and Ministers of God can be Ministers of God all seven days in the week, as the Founder of their Ministry commanded them to when He ordered them to keep out of temporal politics in His own words: 'Render unto Caesar the things that are Caesar's and to God the things that are God's.'

WILLIAM FAULKNER
Private Citizen[13]

Once again, the bottom line, though couched along broadly humorous and satirical lines and not a little Swiftian in attitude, intent, and tone, was unmistakably one of outrage against hypocrisy, specifically, religious cant.

Perhaps the final incarnation of Elder Watson is Flem Snopes, whose funeral in *The Mansion* (1959) is the occasion for this description:

He (the deceased) had no auspices either: fraternal, civic, nor military: only finance; not an economy—cotton or cattle or anything else which Yokna-patawpha County and Mississippi were established on and kept running by, but belonging simply to Money. He had been a member of a Jefferson church true enough, as the outward and augmented physical aspect of the edifice showed, but even that had been not a subservience nor even an aspiration nor even really a confederation nor even an amnesty, but simply an armistice tem-porary between two irreconcilable tongues.[14]

This evocation functions on two levels: first, as an affirmation of Faulkner's overall thematic continuity, with the "irreconcilable tongues" of money and salvation sounding in a funeral scene, and, more important, as a full circling back to Faulkner's literary origins, that melting pot filled with poems and inchoate Snopeses that Faulkner and Phil Stone doubtless stirred together, certainly by the early twenties.

This survey of literary treatments of a fundamental thesis that com-pelled William Faulkner during a career spanning more than forty years by no means exhausts poignant examples one might select to reinforce it. It should, however, serve to order and stabilize a preoccupation of Faulkner's that is often easier to isolate through individual citations and confirm as a pervasive pattern of perception and response than to trace to its sources. The publication of "Elder Watson in Heaven" pushes back the time frame in which William Faulkner seriously undertook what would become a salient theme in his most highly developed fiction and fixes it with some degree of certainty in the year 1921.

FOUR

BILL AND BUZZ:
FELLOW SCENARISTS

"I too like my town, my land, my people, my life, am unhappy away from it even though I must quit it to earn money to keep it going to come back to."
—William Faulkner, letter to William F. Fielden, April 1943 [1]

"I'm so impatient to get home, I am about to bust. Thank the Lord, I have work to do, something I believe in. If I were just sitting here, waiting for a contract to expire, I reckon I would blow up."
—William Faulkner, letter to Estelle Faulkner, August 1943 [2]

The following interview occurred during a five-day visit I had with Albert I. Bezzerides and his wife, Silvia Richards, in their home at Woodland Hills, California, September 3–7, 1983. A screenwriter for more than fifty years, Mr. Bezzerides, as he explains, had a close association with Faulkner in the forties. Undoubtedly, the interview is the result of luck and timing, with some persistence mixed in. I trust it captures the special candor and articulateness, the strong, reliable sense of intuition and insight that for me best characterize "Buzz" Bezzerides. In editing the longer version of the interview yielded by the tapes, I have taken the liberty of placing in quotation marks snippets of conversations that, in the recounting, Mr. Bezzerides may have reconstructed from memory's contexts. I have rearranged a few portions of our conversation from this time in the interest of continuity and clarity.

LDB: Can you recall your first encounter with William Faulkner, the writer, and with Bill Faulkner, the friend?

AIB: In 1931, when I was at Berkeley going to college, I was given a book on my birthday by my girlfriend who always said to me, "Al, you can write, you have to write," and when I lost confidence in myself, her urgings to make me write were very helpful because they made me believe in what I was doing. She gave me Faulkner's *As I Lay Dying,* and I remember that as I read it I had a totally new experience: the frustration of trying to read what he had written, trying to understand what he was saying; the anger of not being able to comprehend it; flinging the book across the room, then running to pick it up and going back to the beginning and trying to read it over again, desperate to understand it, and finding it difficult, cursing Faulkner for writing the way he did, but yet incapable of putting it down. The phenomenon of this man writing that book with its strange complexity, the inner feelings that it has, unstated statements that it makes, your having to read into it the things that he is saying—all of this was a remarkable experience for me, so I never forgot Faulkner. I read everything he wrote as the books came out. I tried, anyway, always with the same fury.

One day, perhaps around 1936 or 1937, my wife and I and a friend of mine, Jim Holmsey, and his wife, Gwen, were at the Pig-'n-Whistle in Hollywood, and who was sitting in a booth toward the back? William Faulkner! He was a smaller man than I had imagined him to be, with his mustache, with his pipe; he was seated with a young woman who turned out to be Meta Carpenter.[3] There wasn't anything that could have prevented me from getting up and walking along the row of booths to his booth and saying, "Sir, you haven't the slightest idea who I am, but I know who you are; you're William Faulkner, and I have read everything you have written. I think you are a great writer." He got up immediately and said, "Thank you, sir," in his accent, and we shook hands. Then I turned around, went back, and sat with my people, embarrassed as hell.

At Warner Bros. they had a writers' building, and on the ground floor, there was a long hallway with offices on both sides; at the end of the hallway, it opened up in what they called the "bullpen" where a lot of secretaries worked. I had an office at the very end of the hall on the right-hand side; the office across from mine was empty. I usually left my door open because I didn't like being alone in the office. One day I looked up and saw this diminished figure of the man with the pipe and the mustache leaning— he had a way of leaning backward when he walked—slowly into the bullpen. He went into the empty office, sat down, crossed his legs, and started puffing a pipe. This was some five or six years after I had "met" him at the Pig-'n-Whistle. I remember sitting there looking at him, and he looked across at me. I got up, went over, stood beside his chair, and I said, "I don't know if you remember me," and he said, "Yes, sir, I do," and I said, "My name is Bezzerides, and since I saw you last, I'm under contract with Warners. What are you doing here?" He said, "I'm under contract here at

Warner Bros., too." I asked him, "How are you going home tonight?" because it was during the war by then. He said, "Well, I take a bus and go to the Highland Hotel." I said, "I've got a car. I usually take a carpool and take turns; you can ride with me." That began my friendship with William Faulkner.

LDB: During the war years of 1942 and 1943, who were some of the other writers with whom you and Faulkner associated at Warner Bros.?

AIB: There was Arthur Sheekman; he was a comedy writer and a very nice guy. John Fante was another. I also remember W. R. Burnett, who wrote *High Sierra* and other pictures, a very successful screenwriter and novelist. There was a wonderful Western writer named Frederick Faust who wrote under the name of Max Brand. Later he volunteered his services as a reporter for the war and was killed in Italy. Faulkner and I were friendly with Frank Gruber, Tom Job, and Jo Pagano as well.

LDB: You mentioned seeing Faulkner at the studio and being very surprised. Had there been any advance notice of his arrival? Was there excitement? Was he being brought there because of his name?

AIB: Well, that Faulkner was at the studio under contract startled me, but when I heard the conditions under which he had been put to work, I was appalled. I was getting about $1,000.00 per week at that point. I was stunned to discover he was getting $300.00 per week, which was what I had started at. The way I learned this—he didn't talk much about himself—came about one day while he was cleaning out his pipe. He pulled out a rather wicked-looking knife, and I said, "Jesus Christ, where did you get that thing?" and he said, "I bought it to cut Herndon." I said, "Why would—?" and he interrupted, "To cut the agent who got me the contract." I asked him why he would want to do that, and he told me that William Herndon had signed him to a seven-year contract with Jack Warner—by then I had heard about Jack Warner boasting how he had the best writer in the country under hire for peanuts. Faulkner told me how Herndon had written to him and said if Warner agreed to hire him, Herndon wanted to be able to tie Warner down right away, not give him a chance to renege by examining his client's drunkenness. Apparently Faulkner had given Herndon the right to sign him to the binding contract with only nominal raises. So when he discovered what had actually evolved, he bought this knife. I said, "If you would have cut him, you would have ended up in jail," and he said, "Yes, I know," and so that's what had prevented him from doing it. That's how I discovered how Faulkner got there at Warner Bros.

As for the little circle of writers at Warner Bros., they all knew who he was; they were all awed by the fact that he was there. He didn't mix with any of them, was older by perhaps ten years or so than most of us. He took the ride from me. I'd drop him off at the Highland Hotel, and as our friendship developed, we would have meals together, at Musso's, Schwab's, etc., and we were together often.

LDB: Did the fact that you were almost eleven years Faulkner's junior inhibit your friendship? Did it remain one of awe, or did it become a closer relationship?

AIB: We grew to be very good friends, and one of the reasons I think we were was I never asked him about writing or talked to him about his writing. I recall once a writer named Elik Moll wanted to meet Faulkner. It was an honor to meet Faulkner. You couldn't walk up to him and say I'm so and so and meet him because his manner was one that discouraged that kind of behavior. So, Elik asked if I would introduce him. I promised I would that night but warned him not to ask Bill about his writing because this would offend him, and he said, "I won't; I give you my word." That afternoon as we were leaving the writers' building, Moll came up to the group, and I told Bill, "This is a friend of mine, Elik Moll. Moll, this is William Faulkner." "Yes, sir." Bill didn't offer his hand to shake; he didn't even take his hand off his pipe, and he kept walking, leaning backward like he usually did—I don't know how he kept his balance. As we walked along, I was stunned to hear Moll begin talking about *Go Down, Moses* and the story about the bear, the confrontation in that story and the emotional feelings he had gotten from it. Then, to climax it all, if you can call it a climax, Moll asked him, "How did you do that?" I just took one look at Faulkner, and I knew there was never going to be an answer to that question. Faulkner didn't say a word; he pretended he didn't hear. Moll looked at me, and I shrugged and dropped back because I was appalled that he had asked this question after he had promised me he wouldn't. Then he repeated his question to Faulkner. Again Faulkner made not a sound, not a word, and then Moll dropped back. I got with Bill, and as we were crossing the empty lot to my battered, old Willys, I said, "Bill," and he said, "Bud," and I said, "You know, Elik Moll," and he said, "Who?" I said: "The fellow I introduced to you; he asked you a question, and you didn't answer. Why didn't you answer?" He informed me in a very terse way that anybody who would ask such a question didn't deserve to be answered. And that is the sort of relationship Bill had with people at the studio. So long as they didn't violate his privacy, didn't ask ridiculous questions, he was there.

LDB: In the writers' building, did Faulkner ever ask you for any kind of assistance, or did he ever run story lines by you?

AIB: Never! He never ever discussed his stories or screenplays.

LDB: Then you were probably not aware that summer of '42 when you two first met that Faulkner was at work on "The De Gaulle Story" for Robert Buckner.

AIB: I was not!

LDB: In that vein, can you give me some image or impression of the atmosphere that existed during those years. Was there an air of austerity, high seriousness, a somberness, or, despite the war, was there cheerfulness among the people working at the studio?

AIB: We were making pictures, essentially. It seemed to me that we were all isolated from it. We all knew the war was raging, knew what was going on, knew the atrocities that were taking place; but we certainly weren't deterred by it at the studio.

LDB: Well, wasn't Hollywood experiencing blackouts, food and gas rationing? Weren't all kinds of precautions being made for a potential invasion of the West Coast?

AIB: Oddly enough, that didn't seem to reach into the studio, because we were making pictures to entertain people. Sure, many of the movies were patriotic, sentimental war pictures. And I do recall that because I worked at the studio, my draft status was deferred. Even when I went to work at Paramount in '44, my draft status didn't change, and I felt safe about that. The movie industry was considered a wartime effort. What it was doing, in a sense, was serving to entertain people in a tense situation who needed to be diverted from the realities that were going on. In a peculiar way, it all served as a massive propaganda resource.

LDB: You mentioned earlier taking Faulkner back and forth in your carpool from the Highland Hotel to Burbank. At what point did Faulkner accept your invitation to stay in your home on 621 North Saltair just north of Santa Monica?

AIB: Well, we got acquainted in this first session in 1942 which lasted, oh, five months, something like that, and then he went home, back to Mississippi, because he missed not being home. He returned to Hollywood for nearly seven months in 1943. In February of 1944, I got a telegram. All it said was he was arriving at the depot on a certain day, and I just went there and picked him up. At that point he didn't have a place to stay, and I said, "Why don't you stay with us?" So he moved in with me and my family in western Los Angeles. There was a bedroom that wasn't being used; he took over that bedroom and started to write *A Fable* there, or at least he was working on it, because I would hear typing at three o'clock in the morning. One day I asked him what he was doing, and he told me he was working on his "new fable."

LDB: Did Faulkner stay with you for a long period?

AIB: Oh, yeah! He stayed for nearly six months in 1944 and almost four months in 1945.

LDB: And, of course, you charged him no rent.

AIB: Not a thing! And he never volunteered to pay. But, then, I understood that the money he was earning was peanuts, and he was always broke. He had this meticulous little book in which he kept all his expenditures. If you looked at it out of the edge of your eye, you could see that the balance was always near zero; you could hardly ask him to pay anything.

LDB: Did you have children at that time?

AIB: We had a daughter, Zoe, and a son, Peter. To give you a slant on the kind of person Faulkner was, he was sitting some twenty or thirty feet away from the dining-room table, clear across the room from my son in his highchair, when Peter pushed his foot against the edge of the table and the highchair started to fall back. Faulkner, with an explosion of movement, darted across that space, grabbed the chair before it toppled to the floor, and rescued my son. To watch Bill move was something to see because this man, who ordinarily seemed to be moving backward when he walked, and who usually seemed so passive, could explode into action.

LDB: Did this suggest to you a violence or passion?

AIB: Absolutely! This man was so intense behind that seemingly quiet surface, almost seething.

LDB: During these stays did Faulkner eat many meals with your family?

AIB: We almost always ate dinner together. He didn't have a car, so he came home with me and became a part of the family. Yet, there was always a kind of distance between us. He always managed to keep himself separate. If he sat with people in the living room, you always had a feeling he was not really there; he was in his head somewhere. He was off thinking about what he was doing. I think we probably bored him to death because he participated very little in conversation or anything. And we just took that; we weren't upset by it. He tried occasionally to be helpful—he was friendly with Yvonne, my wife, and he was friendly with the kids—but he really wasn't there. In the summer of '44, Estelle and Jill came to visit Bill. He had moved out for a few months, rented a bedroom in a private house. Jill and Zoe became good friends; they swam, rode horses together.

LDB: Jill was maybe eleven years old at the time?

AIB: Something like that.

LDB: Tell me about the horseback riding.

AIB: We used to go to Jack House's stable in Glendale quite often that summer. It was located very near Warner Bros.

LDB: Who rode?

AIB: I didn't ride. My wife rode, and Zoe rode.

LDB: Did Faulkner ride at all?

AIB: Faulkner rode; Jill rode. They loved riding.

LDB: Was Jill close with your daughter?

AIB: They were very friendly.

LDB: In a different vein, were you aware of Faulkner's social affairs? His intimate friends?

AIB: No. I never knew many of the people he went out with or knew socially, other than for Meta Carpenter, of course. Except for her, I don't believe he knew many people intimately. A lot of people have taken credit for intimacies with Faulkner, but they never happened.

LDB: How about places he might visit or frequent?

AIB: He really didn't do much. He would go to the Players' Club or to Musso's to eat with friends if he were living alone or when he was staying at the Highland Hotel. Then they would get out of there, walk around a little bit, then he would go to his room and retire. Occasionally he would visit with Jo Pagano or Tom Job, their families. Once at Pagano's house he was drunk, sitting on the floor next to their child, and he was given a shot of whiskey, which he held up to the child proclaiming, "God's gift to man," as he sipped it. I recall Pagano telling me this and how shocked he was that Faulkner thought whiskey was God's gift to man.

I remember one incident that occurred between Faulkner and John Fante, who was also working at Warners with us. John wanted to socialize with Faulkner. One night Bill, Fante, and I went out. I think we went to Musso's to eat but started drinking there in the back room, then left without eating, carrying a bottle of wine out with us, going from bar to bar. After we got drunk, we began to tell dirty jokes and sing dirty songs. Finally, old Faulkner began to sing a song about "Fucking in the cowshed / Fucking on the bricks, / You couldn't hear the music / For the swishing of the pricks." And he sang it with a strong Scotch accent. It was three or four in the morning when we got home. Afterward, when we got sober, I remembered the song and tried to get Faulkner to sing it again, so I could learn all the other stanzas to the song. He just chuckled, but he wouldn't sing it again. He had to be drunk to sing that one, and I found that kind of amusing.

LDB: You mentioned that on returning to California in 1944 Faulkner had sent you a telegram asking if you would pick him up. Was this customary for him to rely on other people?

AIB: Oh, yeah! He had a way of using people. After I got acquainted with him and understood the relationship he had with Meta, I also knew that he had just used me to go to the railroad depot to pick him up or to do various other chores. He used Meta in a different way, though; he used her in the sense of diminishing his loneliness. Although, when he was out here in California, it's true he was away from the commotions of his family, he was alone, totally alone, and his way of going home was to have a relationship with the young Southern woman, Meta Carpenter. I always felt sorry for her because I could see she was being used; I don't think she was even aware of it. But I realized there was no chance that their relationship would go beyond what it was here in Hollywood, because that would have required him to make a commitment and take her back to Oxford. That simply wouldn't have happened.

LDB: Was there anything specifically he said or just your closeness to the situation that led you to this conclusion?

AIB: After being with Bill and knowing him the way I did, I realized that he just simply couldn't make any permanent relationships.

LDB: Was he really that selfish of a person?

AIB: Absolutely! He was a very selfish fellow and didn't seem to be aware of the demands he was making, the burdens he was putting on people.

LDB: He put demands on you and others around him. In what respect?

AIB: It was done rather quietly—you found yourself inviting him to do something because he needed it. You were very aware of his needs.

LDB: Even his alcoholic bouts required other people.

AIB: True. If he got dead drunk and fell on the floor, somebody discovered that he was dead drunk lying on the floor, called the hospital, and took him to the hospital where he was put together again.

LDB: The irresponsibility of the drunkenness! Do you feel he knew someone would always help him, be there at his side, or do you think he really didn't care?

AIB: There were times when I felt this kind of drinking bordered on suicidal, because if someone hadn't walked in and done something about it, he might very well have died. A doctor once told me, "You better tell your friend that he's going to get a heart attack and die if he doesn't watch his drinking." So I told Bill. The next thing I knew, he had gotten terribly drunk, and he had vanished. Then I noticed that his bags in the Highland Hotel where he was staying at that time had vanished. Two bags had vanished, along with the books that he had—he was always surrounded by books. I couldn't understand what the hell had happened. His clothes were there; he hadn't packed and left. So I began looking for him, yelling, "Bill, Bill," all over the place. There were two entrances to the Highland Hotel. You got out at the front, where it ran along Highland Avenue, and went up three or four floors where he was staying, or you got off at the lobby on the top floor to the street level—it was built on the side of a steep hill. So, I finally went out into the street at the back end of the upper floor and yelled, "Bill," and got no answer. But I saw him climbing the hill with the two bags in his hands. So I ran up to him and I said, "What the hell do you think you're doing?" And he said, "If I got a bad heart, I want to find out." I said, "If you find out, it will kill you." He said, "I want to know," at which point I knocked the bags out of his hand, picked him up in my arms, and started carrying him down the hill. As I was carrying him over my shoulder, I saw him make a tremendous grimace while he tugged with pinched fingers against his collar, and I said, "What are you trying to do?" "I'm trying to get down." I remember bursting into laughter because I thought his trying to get loose from me by tugging on his own collar while still in my arms was so ridiculous. He was chuckling drunkenly as I put him down, and I said, "Well, come on." Then I let him walk, because the indignity of being carried by me like a child back to his room was too much for either of us.

LDB: Can you recall other incidents, surely less comical, in which Faulkner required your assistance?

AIB: Whenever Faulkner got drunk and passed out I would take him to some sanitarium that specialized in such things. There was a special nurse that he knew whom I would call. He'd come, and they would put him on juices and sober him up. The first time he got drunk I took him to a sanitarium in Los Angeles. It was a rugged place downtown, filled with old men and drunks to whom they fed orange juice, juices, and things and kept on a diet and gradually got them back on their feet. They put Faulkner on a cot, and he was lying there. I remember being startled by this sight. Faulkner was very stubborn and refused at first to drink the orange juice; he refused unless they would give him a drink first. The nurse said, "All right, Bill," and filled Faulkner's whole glass from the whiskey bottle. Faulkner drank it and said, "Ah, that's good"; then he accepted the glass of orange juice and drank it down to the last drop. I was appalled, and that's when I blew up. "Look, he's drunk," I shouted. "We're paying you all this money, and you're giving him whiskey out of a bottle. What the hell gives?" With that the male nurse interrupted, "I'll give you some, too," and we touched glasses. I drank it. It was tea, and I was stunned because I could see Faulkner was so very drunk he couldn't even tell the difference between tea and whiskey.

On another occasion, I took Bill to a sanitarium on Van Nuys Boulevard in Van Nuys. After I left him there, I got a phone call from him.

"Bud, they stole my watch; somebody stole my watch," and I said, "Jesus Christ." He said, "You got to get me out of here," and I said, "No, Bill; you have to stay there; if they stole your watch, they can't steal anything else, because you didn't have anything else; you left your wallet in the front office. If your watch is gone, it's gone, but you have to stay." I was kind of firm about it, not so much because I wanted to be firm with Bill but because I didn't want to run around finding another place. But I came back, and when I got to the place I asked about the watch being stolen. The nurse said it wasn't possible; she didn't understand how the watch could have been stolen. Then I discovered that Bill had stuffed the watch in his shoe in order to be able to tell me that it had been stolen, so that I would come and get him out of there.

Always after he came out of the sanitariums—I took him to four or five—I'd give him a ride in the car. We would go running around to different parts of Los Angeles just to get him back into the air again. I remember one day driving along Vine Street, and as we stopped at Sunset, two girls in their pretty dresses started to cross the street in the pedestrian lane. They looked at us lingeringly as they went by. Then the light changed, and we drove on. An hour and a half, perhaps two hours later, Faulkner said something I couldn't quite hear because he always mumbled, and I said, "What did you say, Bill?" He said it louder so I could hear it: "I could sure do with a strange woman!" I thought that was very funny!

Another time after he was released, I drove Bill all the way to Ventura along the coast and then came inland up to Ventura highway, which wasn't a freeway in those days, past the orange groves, back into town. He would just tilt his head, nod at something, and I would look off. Maybe it was something remarkable that he was looking at or just a vague thought he was having. Once we stopped at an orange grove to smell its fragrance. You could see the ocean in the distance. During these trips, I always talked because he never said a thing; he never said one word. I found the silence a little difficult to stand, so to fill the silence, I would talk about hunting or trucking trips I had made out of Fresno in my youth. Once, during one of my transitions or pauses, Bill said, "Bud," and I said, "Yeah, what is it, Bill?" He said, "Bud, you're an animal, but I'm just a vegetable!"

LDB: Surely, Faulkner was appreciative of you, not only for allowing him to stay in your home but for your friendship and occasional ministrations.

AIB: Yes, he was! I'm sure of it. Shortly after Bill left Hollywood for good in September of 1945, perhaps a year or two later I was assigned to do a picture for Paramount about sponge divers off the coral reefs. It required doing research. I took my wife and family to Tarpon Springs, Florida, and to parts of Cuba. On our way home, I called Faulkner. I didn't say we're here, and we would like to come visit. I called to say that we were in Florida and were about to go back to California; I thought I'd call to say hello. And he said, as I knew he would, "If you don't come to visit us, I'll never see you again." And he really meant it. We went on a train to Memphis, and he came and picked us up at the depot in a car that had no floorboards in the driving compartment. I sat with my foot on the sloping part of the dash, and we drove for hours, it seemed, through the darkness to get to Oxford. On arriving, I remember spying that fabulous house in the woods on the edge of town. Estelle was up and she greeted us. We talked for quite a while, then went to bed. We were given a room adjacent to another large room upstairs where Faulkner and his wife slept while we were there. There were sliding doors between our two rooms. My daughter slept with Jill.

LDB: Was the visit all that you had expected?

AIB: Yes, for the most part it was quite pleasant, though I remember wanting to leave after a few days, yet feeling that it was too soon. You can't leave that soon. A decent amount of time had to pass. I realized that Faulkner was trying to pay me back for the hospitality he had received in California. He couldn't pay in any other way, so the only way he could do it was by giving us his hospitality, and he did. He was just great. Mrs. Faulkner, the fragile woman that she was—she was so thin I wondered how she could be in good health—was wonderful. We had marvelous meals. He would go into the back smokehouse and pick out a ham, and we would eat ham that had been smoked by them.[4] We met some of the blacks who used to be servants but who now had jobs in town. Although their status had changed, there was enough of the past there that you could see where the slaves had lived out in the back. Faulkner tried to give the image of a house that had proper servants and stuff. He had trained a young black to serve the table, but he did it very badly. I remember Faulkner being very tolerant with that, trying to explain to him how to do things and so on.

LDB: How long did you actually stay at Rowan Oak?

AIB: We were there quite a while. Perhaps a week. I remember one day walking with Faulkner over to the drugstore where he was going to exchange a stack of mystery stories for a new stack. I asked him, "Why do you read all of these damn mysteries?" and he said, "Bud, no matter what you write, it's a mystery of one kind or another." As we walked into town,

he with his armload of books, I just following along, I noticed that as acquaintances greeted him, there was an air of contempt in their "Good
morning, Bill." The way they looked at each other and then looked at him,
it was as if they didn't know who he really was, or if so, begrudged him his
celebrity.

One day we went out to Bill's farm. He had planted some kind of corn,
and it hadn't come up. He discovered that they had given him corn in-
fested with worms. So he went over to the place where they sold seed, and
there was a bunch of men sitting in a circle: "Good morning, Bill." The
look they had for him was contemptuous as he pointed out politely that
the corn hadn't seeded, the seed hadn't germinated. He wanted to get
more seed. They said, "Well, try again, Bill," and it was kind of a joke. I
can recall my feeling of amazement that these people didn't know who he
was. They had no understanding—none of them read anything—and if
they did know he was a writer, they held that in contempt!

Back at the farm, we were walking along a road, and Bill touched my
arm. I looked down at a poisonous snake. I had almost stepped on it and
could have been bitten. A sense of danger seemed imminent when I was in
the South. There was a sense of hazard, always a sense of hazard. Especially
when Jill and my daughter might not come back, because something terrible could happen. The Southerners didn't seem to be aware of this presence, but I was!

LDB: During your visit, did Faulkner introduce you to any of his family or
old friends?

AIB: I met Phil Stone. We went to his brick law office just off the Square,
but it was just a quick introduction, and all the time we were in Oxford
nobody came to the house. I never met his mother or his brother, John, or
his nephews. I didn't get to meet his stepdaughter, though I did meet Malcolm Franklin, his stepson.

LDB: Did you spend most of your time at the house?

AIB: At the house. I went around some with Bill, but my wife stayed at the
house with his wife, Estelle.

LDB: Was Faulkner doing any writing at the time?

AIB: Not that I recall. I didn't hear the typewriter.

LDB: What made up your day?

AIB: We drove around the countryside quite a bit. I recall one afternoon when Bill took me out to a place where he liked to go fishing. We drove and drove in wooded hills. As we got to the place he wanted to show me, he stopped the car, seemingly surprised, and looking around with mounting anger. He began to swear, "God dammit! God dammit! They never leave anything alone; they always destroy things, and pretty soon this country won't be anything like it was." It seemed the stream had been dammed up, and instead of a stream, it was a lake the authorities were busy stocking with fish for the tourist trade. Faulkner fulminated about how they had destroyed a natural stream that was a beauty in the area. The lake would eventually fill with mud, would be polluted after a while, wouldn't even tolerate fish. He was furious. So, on the way back down, with him fuming away, we stopped suddenly and waited a while and pretty soon an arm was thrust into the car through the open window and in it was a bottle of what he called liquor, brewed at some still in the woods nearby. He paid the fellow, and as we sat there, he uncorked it, and we drank the clear liquor. It was like drinking fire! He drank lots of it; I didn't drink much. I could see that it didn't affect him. When he didn't want to get drunk, he could drink any amount, and it didn't matter, but when he wanted to get drunk, the liquor would begin to take hold, and he couldn't stop drinking. He didn't drink just to drink; always it was to escape something.

On another excursion, Bill and I were driving through town, around the Square. Somebody said, "Bill, Bill." It was a woman, a car full of women, and one said, "Did your guests from California arrive?" He said, "Yes," and introduced me. And the woman said, "How is Estelle?" and again this was said with that strange air of contempt. "How is Estelle?" meant, I later realized, "Was she sober or drunk?" They handed Bill a bouquet of gardenias for Estelle and asked to be remembered to her, but there was a strange ridicule in their airs.

LDB: Who were these women?

AIB: They were neighbors, friends, friends of Estelle. But friends who had this attitude startled me. Later that day, after dinner, we all sat outside talking, getting tipsy. Soon we went to our various bedrooms. I was always very aware of that sliding door that separated Faulkner and his wife lying in their bed from us lying in our bed, but there was no sign of embarrassment by anybody. But on this night I awoke about two or three o'clock in the morning, and I heard the fierce, vicious whisper of Estelle's voice: "Don't touch me, Bill. I don't want you to touch me. Don't you touch me." I woke up my wife, and she heard Estelle's protest, and in the middle of all this, there was a sound that I'll never forget, that sharp, intense strik-ing of a hand against flesh. He had apparently slapped her in the face. Just to hear that slap inflicted pain, and then silence. Shortly after that, we be-came aware of a sexual encounter on the other side of the door. My wife and I had been parties to the sadness of the relationship between Estelle and Bill. I remember lying there awake for a long time, conscious of how appalled my wife was. Next morning, Estelle was cheerful as she could possibly be when we sat down to eat with her and Bill. Breakfast was served as if nothing had happened. Later that morning we prepared to leave. We went back home to California, and that was the last I saw of Faulkner.

LDB: That stark bedroom incident between the Faulkners that you and your wife overheard on your visit to Rowan Oak in July 1947, in what way, at least inadvertently, might it have symbolized for you the loneliness you believed Faulkner suffered?

AIB: Bill and his wife did not have a good relationship; for a long time they were on the verge of breaking up, if they only realized it. Faulkner's efforts to touch Estelle were probably a need for sex but also a need for loving and being loved. And I could understand her feelings, too, her angry response. She didn't want to be taken advantage of; they probably slept separately. In fact, things that I have read long after suggest they didn't sleep together. But because we were there, they were forced to sleep together. And in that situation he was apparently unable to control his appetites.

LDB: Did Faulkner experience countervailing pulls on his emotions? When he was out in California during the time you knew him, did he desperately long to be in Mississippi? When in Mississippi, was all he could think about getting away from there and going back out?

AIB: He never wanted to come to California, and when he came out here, he hated it. If Warners could have given him an assignment and he could have written it back there in Mississippi, he would have, because, unhappy though they might have been, Estelle and he were together; they were bound to each other. There was no way to divorce Estelle, separate from Estelle, any more than he could divorce himself from his brothers, his mother, his various nieces and nephews, his stepkids. I don't think he under-stood this, but he was bound to them by an unbreakable bond.

LDB: A sense of responsibility?

AIB: His sense of responsibility, the claims they all made on him because he was the oldest: You're the oldest, you have to be the best. That was never ever forgotten by him. Whether he tried to forget it or not, there was no way to forget that.

LDB: So there was an enormous sense of torment!

AIB: Torment? Absolutely! And he didn't want to be away from them. Couldn't! When he came here, he felt at loose ends, and in his desperation, he tried to make a connection; and what other type could he make than one with a girl from the South, Meta Carpenter. He could have had other women, had relationships with them, but his way of returning to Oxford was to be with Meta, so when he came out here, he was with Meta. When Bill was out here between 1942 and 1945, Meta was between marriages to Wolfgang Rebner. She divorced him in 1939, I believe, and remarried him, but not until after Bill left for the last time in 1945. So they saw each other openly during all those years Bill spent here in Hollywood. And as his mistress, Meta provided Bill with a way of going home. Bill was a very lonely man when he was here, very lonely!

LDB: When Faulkner arrived at Warner Bros. in late June 1942, his first major project was "The De Gaulle Story." In hindsight, what do you feel about Faulkner's effectiveness on this assignment?

AIB: It didn't come off—with Faulkner. That was a project he was going to do that actually excited him in the beginning, but, you know, it didn't come off. Very few of the things that he tried to pull off at Warners came off! This had to lead to a kind of writer's disenchantment. Staying at Warner Bros. became a bore, because he wasn't doing the things that he wanted to do or succeeding at the things he did care about, and he had a point there. I was at Warners, and I was doing things I didn't want to do, too. There was an apparent repetition of failure, which has led many critics to assume that Faulkner didn't like writing scripts, felt it was a total waste of time. In fact, Bill seemed to do them assiduously and actually took considerable care in what he was doing.

LDB: When Faulkner would do one screenplay after another and find they were either not getting produced or, if so, that his work had been rejected and replaced with pages from another writer who would subsequently garner the screen credit, how did he respond?

AIB: He gave up because nothing he did was coming off.

LDB: It wasn't that he didn't like doing the writing?

AIB: Quite the contrary. He actually enjoyed inventing the story lines, filling them in with his dialogue, and he could turn out pages prodigiously. You see, Hollywood is a challenging place. Writers of Faulkner's caliber—Huxley, West, Fitzgerald—all thought that writing for the movies was an easy thing to do. They all, more or less, tried their hand at it, because it was challenging to sit down, do a script, then make a motion picture out of it, and suddenly it comes to life in front of you on the screen. If it's done well, it's really very exciting. If it's done badly, there's nothing worse than a lousy picture where the characters don't ring true. So, Faulkner really thought he could write scripts, thought that he could do stories that were meaningful, and he landed on heavy subjects to do, but they never came off. He had to be bitterly disappointed.

LDB: Why did Faulkner fail to bridge the gap between novelist and screenwriter?

AIB: Well, screenwriting requires a totally different choreography. If you're writing a novel, you can talk about people's feelings, you can write about the things that they think about, you can delve into the characters psychologically, you can write descriptions and develop a progressional story that gradually moves toward and arrives at a conclusion. *The Sound and the Fury* tells the same story four different ways; it's got a totally different hold on you. The magic of that is something that is beyond the capacity of the screenplay. The story in a screenplay is pretty well laid out. The dialogue has to be economical because people won't listen to pages of dialogue. It has to be terse and meaningful and pointed to progress the story, just as the narrative has to be more on the surface, more pictorial.

LDB: You've also suggested a second, more major, dilemma. Was Faulkner attuned to the characters he was being asked to create?

AIB: Take "The De Gaulle Story"—I've now read the script again after forty years. Faulkner's characters talk about things instead of progressing things so that they happen. Things are discussed rather than made to happen. The script is long, and it simply doesn't progress the way a good screenplay should develop.

LDB: Was it possible that Faulkner may not have felt at ease with or at one with the characters themselves?

AIB: Well, the things he wrote about had to do with his own past in a crazy way.

LDB: You're talking now about his fiction?

AIB: Fiction. The minute he got into writing about the war and De Gaulle and Churchill in "The De Gaulle Story," this was not his personal experience. He talked about having been in a war, but he had never gone to a war. He was writing about things that he knew very little about. He knew little about the people. He knew little about De Gaulle, less about Churchill, so when he tried to write about them, they didn't ring true; they were two-dimensional, rather than three-dimensional. I'm sure that when De Gaulle and Churchill sat down and talked, there were some pretty personal things that went on between those two. They weren't superficial things that dealt with heroics and the fate of countries and so forth. It had to do with a man talking to a man. You never get this feeling when you read the script. You really had to get under the skins of those characters, really know them to do that, and I don't think Faulkner was capable of doing that. That required a kind of research that he didn't do.

LDB: In one of the scripts that Faulkner left with you after his last stay in Hollywood, there were a number of fact sheets about De Gaulle and his progress in the early stages of the occupation and about the Free French movement that the story and research departments of Warner Bros. had prepared for him.

AIB: Research done by Warner Bros. and research done by a person out of a driving need to know are vitally different. Reading about whores is one thing, but going to a whorehouse and seeing them living their actual lives is something else.

LDB: Was it that Faulkner was not interested in the material, or was it that he just couldn't connect with most of this material that he was being assigned to write about? Was it too contemporary?

AIB: Bill read newspapers, like all of us did. He was plenty aware of world events. But it was a little exotic to be sitting here in Hollywood in an office on the Warner Bros. lot trying to do a meaningful story about a complex man like De Gaulle and another very complex man like Churchill and a situation of which he had no knowledge. How would Faulkner know what a village in France goes through when it's being occupied by the Nazis unless he were there?

LDB: One of the problems with this script may have been that his imagination wasn't the crucial factor at all; rather, what was required was mere accuracy of detail as opposed to an imaginative rendering. Facts, per se, just may not have been Faulkner's long suit, not Faulkner the novelist, anyway.

AIB: "The De Gaulle Story" probably should have been written by either a French or English writer who knew firsthand about the lives of these people under siege in ways Faulkner had no way of knowing. Faulkner couldn't admit his incapacity for doing it, and that got him into trouble.

LDB: What do you mean by "trouble"?

AIB: I'll tell you what I think was wrong here, where he failed. I remember walking with Bill across the Warner Bros. lot late one afternoon back to the car. He did a kind of dance of rage in which he punched fist into palm, fist into hand, and said, "God dammit! Why do I do it? Why do I do it?" and I said, "Why do you do what?" and he said, "Get drunk the way I do." "Bill," I said, "if you really want to know why you do it, you'd go to a good psychologist and sit down and talk to him, because if you want to know, you can find out." He quickly composed himself and retired into a vast silence. I knew I had touched a touchy subject. He had no intention of really exploring why he did it, and this was the flaw in Faulkner's attempts to try to write about things that he didn't know. How can a man who not only doesn't know what motivates him but doesn't know who he is begin to write about people he doesn't know? How can he delve into them and find out who they are, what they are, when he fights and resists finding out who he is and what he is? Faulkner couldn't take the first step to explore into himself, and it made him incapable of exploring characters not even intimate with his imagination, let alone his daily self.

LDB: And yet, he is very successful in exploring some of the characters, those best within his fictive realm.

AIB: Ah, but those characters are innate to him; they arise out of his past; they arise from his life experience. He is very knowledgeable there, but it's a subconscious knowledge that's very deep within him, and he doesn't— he lacks insight as to why these things actually happen and what they are. He just writes about them.

LDB: He was good at liberating them and letting them do their own act.

AIB: That's right! But he knew them very intimately in a subconscious way, and subconsciously, artistically, anyway, he could control them, put reins on their actions at will. The liberating was a therapeutic thing whether he knew it or not. *The Sound and the Fury,* if it's about anything, it's about his life in a way. He showed me the fence where the idiot prowled.

LDB: He took you there to see the Chandler house?

AIB: Yeah, and he told me about the idiot who lived there, about how he had incorporated him into the story. That really was a story about himself, his cousin, Sally, his brothers, his mother and father and grandparents. It's all there.

LDB: But the characters in "The De Gaulle Story," they weren't real?

AIB: They weren't real *to him*. They didn't relate to his subconscious, to his past.

LDB: And yet, you've said that he did make a very conscientious effort to do the best work he could.

AIB: Oh, well, of course. He was earning a paycheck every week. I'm sure Faulkner tried to be as honest as he could be. He tried very hard to make a good script out of "The De Gaulle Story." He worked like a demon on that. That wasn't for lack of wanting to that he failed. It was—he was incapable of doing it because it was beyond his reach. He was reaching for something that he couldn't grasp.

LDB: This seems to bring us back to the vital notion of responsibility.

AIB: Faulkner was plagued by his sense of responsibility. At an early age he was told by his mother: You're the oldest; you have to be the best. Also, he had it pointed out over and over again that, since he was the oldest son, he would ultimately take on the responsibilities of the family. In his life he knew from watching his father and watching his grandfather that the last thing he wanted was to take on the responsibility of his family. How to avoid taking on the responsibilities that were going to be dumped on him, because he would be smothered by them—that was the dilemma! This was a kid who, having watched his father's failures, his resorting to drunkenness to escape from the irresponsibility of owning up to his failures, knew that he didn't want any part of that as a child, and the only way he could protect himself against it was to avoid doing the things that they wanted him to do: to get an education, to become a lawyer, a banker, engineer like one of his brothers became. He didn't want any part of that, so at an early age he dropped out of school. He went back only because he wanted to play baseball or some ridiculous thing like that, and then dropped out again. He quit his education because he wanted no part of the responsibilities for which this would prepare him.

Now, together with that, he also saw something else. It had to do with the Old Colonel, with the books he had written and with his deeds. The great-grandfather was a womanizer, a politician. He built a railroad, fought in the war; he got involved in duels, and he killed people. I'm saying it roughly, but he was a man who misbehaved, and all of his misbehavior was forgiven because he had written books, done deeds, achieved not only notoriety, but celebrity. What they remembered of him finally wasn't his misbehavior of the past but the books, which constantly made him seem to people who came after him that he was a man of some substance, or he wouldn't have written those books. Faulkner apparently came to believe, or romanticized, that he, too, could be forgiven his irresponsibilities for not doing, not becoming a lawyer, or banker, not finishing school, going to college, not becoming formally educated. He educated himself by reading, and he picked being a writer because, if it forgave the Old Colonel's profligacies, just think of the sins it might forgive for him.

But it didn't give Bill the escape he thought he was going to get, because later on, being an obedient son who attended to his mother and listened to what she said, regardless of whether he agreed with her or not, he finally became a victim of the business of being the oldest son, and it landed on him like a ton of bricks.

LDB: What form did this victimization take?

AIB: Faulkner was endlessly pressed by demands on him by his family. When he was in Hollywood, letters would come, and he would be writing checks, sending them out, or there would be problems that he would have to resolve, and he tried to resolve them, but there was a kind of desperation about him, because he didn't want to be doing this. Yet the thing that he was afraid would happen had happened, and there was no way he could get out of it.

LDB: Is there any connection between the notion of Faulkner's "using" people and this idea of responsibility?

AIB: Well, I told you earlier that after my visit to Rowan Oak in 1946, I never saw Bill again. He had abrogated his contract with Warner Bros.; we

weren't near each other. I didn't go out of my way to call him when he was
here because I felt that it was an intrusion. There was always a sense that,
unless there was need on his part, you were intruding. His relationship to
you was always very casual, as if he had other things to do and you were
getting in the way. So, I made a point of not intruding. The same thing
was true with Meta and Bill. Once he went home, he didn't need the solace
of her companionship.

LDB: Meta relates in her book, *A Loving Gentleman,* that when Faulkner
left Hollywood in 1945, with one brief exception in 1951, she never saw him
again.

AIB: Well, he didn't need her.

LDB: Once you parted, were you aware of Faulkner as a growing presence
in world events?

AIB: When he was awarded the Nobel Prize in 1950, I heard about it and
called immediately. I said, "Bill, this is Buzz." He said, "Oh, hi, hello, Bud.
How are you?" and I said, "I heard about the Nobel Prize. I wanted to call
and congratulate you." He said, "Thank you, thank you very much," and
that was the conversation. Then I hung up and that was it. It was very
short. Once I wrote him a letter; there was no answer. I had written letters
before, and there was never any answer; but when he had needed me, I
would get a letter, meet him at the depot, and so forth.

LDB: You're talking about earlier.

AIB: Earlier. Once the Nobel Prize thing happened, he certainly didn't
need Hollywood, and when he came out here, he knew my phone number; he never called.

LDB: He came out early in 1951 to work on *The Left Hand of God* for Howard
Hawks.

AIB: He never called. When he came out, he never called. So, when I say
that he was a user and he needed people, he had a need for certain people
around him, and when he had that need, he made his demands in his subtle
ways, and people gave of themselves to him. I didn't feel used. I was glad
to do what I did, and I don't think Meta felt used. She was glad to do what
she did because she loved him. I was very fond of Faulkner, and I liked him
very much. I was in respect of him. I had contempt for his inability to

recognize that one has responsibility when he accepts this kind of responsibility from others, but he showed no signs of recognizing it. He took it as his privilege as a great writer to make demands on people, get what he wanted, what he needed.

LDB: And after the Nobel Prize, did you follow his celebrity?

AIB: I actually learned more about Faulkner's activities during the last fifteen years of his life by doing research for the documentary script commissioned by the Public Broadcasting System on Bill's life than from anything else.[5] Stories were told to me about how he was always drunk, always had a bottle of wine or whiskey during his stay at the University of Virginia, made a ritual of drinking there. To me, Bill seemed to have become a victim of his own legend and was living a part that seemed totally false: the esteemed writer, the Nobel winner. The man who had written these great things bore no relationship to the young man who had written these wonderful things he had written when he was a struggling writer trying to make a scratch, trying to earn a living, writing things he was impelled to write, not written deliberately, but impelled to write because they came out of his subconscious. Now, here he was very conscious of the greatness he had achieved without the memory of the consciousness that had actually done the achieving. He was living a role that seemed fraudulent to me. It seemed sad to me. He lived next door to his daughter in a house, and he was back with Estelle again. They hadn't separated. Finally, they even went back to Oxford, where he died and was buried. I think in the end it got to him that he was living the kind of life that he was living. I feel strongly he must have been aware of the fraudulency of what he was doing.

LDB: These intuitions came mostly after the fact, from your work on *William Faulkner: A Life on Paper*?

AIB: I did a lot of research on this and talked to a lot of people. I talked to people at the University of Virginia; I talked to people in Oxford. They all told me a lot of things that had happened in these intervening years. I met his stepdaughter who got out of a deathbed to drink with me and talk to me in the—with the pure, pure anger that she had about how Faulkner had been mistreated over the years by the family and by the people around him and so forth, about the demands that were made on him. She told me things I couldn't use—

LDB: This was Victoria Fielden?

AIB: Yes. And I loved her for doing it, telling me, but I also had to use discretion, because you simply couldn't say these things. Yet, I put together a sequence of events from which I finally came to understand and believe that toward the end of his life Faulkner realized that the life he was living wasn't Faulkner. He and Estelle came back to Rowan Oak. Now the two of them had had a bad relationship for years; yet they were bound together from childhood because they were childhood sweethearts. They had traumas in their childhood, she in her family, he from his, that made them seek out each other in strange ways. I'm sure that if a good analysis were made of this, you would see that they were doomed to be together, and they were.

As a conclusion to the PBS script, I wrote that at the end of his life Hemingway discovered the loss of his faculties and that the grief over this made him put a shotgun in his mouth and pull the trigger. Likewise, Faulkner surely committed suicide by getting drunk so incessantly and riding the least manageable horse, the one that had thrown him several times before and he knew would throw him again. I think the last few months of Faulkner's life were dedicated to committing suicide in a way because he had sensed a loss of faculty.

LDB: To what might you attribute this loss of faculty?

AIB: Oh, the drinking for years had certainly dulled off his sharpness. When I read that he had had shock therapy applied to him by a psychologist who hadn't even asked for permission to do it, had done it without getting permission from the family, I asked a lot of questions about what shock therapy does to a person. One of several very bright doctors put it this way: "It deletes memory, the memory of the past, the pain." Faulkner's great fiction had been written out of the memory of pain; this had been deleted. Suddenly I could understand how in *The Town* Flem Snopes had become a loveable character, not the monster he had been depicted as being in *The Hamlet*. Suddenly Bill was a man who had sweet memories of his past. Certainly Bill must have realized in some strange, profound way that he had lost something terribly important, and this loss drove him to his special kind of suicide.

LDB: Why do you imagine Faulkner submitted at all to the shock therapy?

AIB: I have no idea, in fact—perhaps to curb depression, help him cure his drinking problem. I do feel that Bill couldn't benefit from therapy of any kind. He simply couldn't examine why things happened. He couldn't face the realities of his life; it was too painful! There is nothing simple about this; there is nothing wrong about this either. A lot of people can't face what they have done in their life.

LDB: Do you feel perhaps that Faulkner's reluctance to probe into these personal things had to do with an uneasiness that if he did discover the root, the core of many of his personal problems, he might in the process of removing the source of the disturbance eradicate or annihilate or nullify the need to create fictively?

AIB: No way! If Faulkner had been afraid that more insight would somehow keep him from his writing, he was full of shit! He would have written even better. Writers shouldn't be afraid of insight. The more you know, the better you can understand the people you're writing about.

LDB: Then, speculatively at least, to what do you attribute his unwillingness, Faulkner's emphatic unwillingness—

AIB: To probe? Pure terror! Pure terror at knowing the reality that you come from. Pure terror! Can you imagine how it must have been to be a child, an infant, to be in the presence of a dominating, angry mother and an incompetent, drunken father who failed at everything he did. Faulkner heard this even before he was born, when he was rocked in the amniotic stage. Can you imagine how terrifying it must have been to explore into that—terrifying! No wonder he didn't do it. No wonder people don't do it!

LDB: In summing up, you were born in 1908. Your life has encompassed many radically changing cultural movements in our society. Earlier you expressed your excitement in 1931 on having discovered for the first time Faulkner's *As I Lay Dying*. Now, in looking back over the span of fifty years, how do you see Faulkner? How do you see his work? Will it last?

AIB: I see Faulkner as a very sensitive, very bright, very intelligent, high-I.Q. guy. He was great in the intellectual sense. I see Faulkner in the personal sense, in the sense of relating to people with empathy, as not having been terribly effective. If he had appreciated all the things I did for him when he was at Warner Bros.—knowing him, liking him as a writer, respecting him—it seems to me that there was a little more he might have given back than just a few days over at his place in Oxford. If he had been a sensitive man, and he was sleeping with his wife and we were in the next room, it seems to me he would not have allowed himself to become enraged that night. There was an insensitivity and an inability to relate. That's tragic!

Yet, I think, despite all of this, he was somehow driven to express himself, to prove he was a writer, since he had taken the cop-out of being a writer to escape his responsibility as the oldest son. He had begun to write out of desperation, without even realizing it, and he succeeded in writing things that were Faulkner, the things that he knew, the things that he was, things that came out of his own life. So, in many ways, he was a sensitive guy.

LDB: Are you making a distinction between the man and his fiction?

AIB: Well, he was very sensitive to the things that touched him, that meant something to him. He was totally insensitive toward the feelings of other people. He was basically a selfish, self-serving person.

LDB: But in his best fiction, what you get, most often through artistic implication, is a strong sense of moral value, of ethical substance. Are you suggesting that, although Faulkner may not have been an exemplary person in his deeds, his fiction could still express and project strong positive moral values?

AIB: Up to a limit—there is a limit. In his writing, in the intimate details having to do with intimate relationships between men and women, he fails because in his life he failed. He couldn't face that dilemma in his life, so when he wrote about it, there was no way for him to touch it. If Faulkner had had the capacity to recognize what he was doing to Meta Carpenter, if Faulkner had had the capacity to recognize what his mother had done to him, then he could have humanized the characters in his stories; he would have fulfilled those relationships. But he couldn't, because he couldn't fulfill them in his own life.

LDB: Which isn't to say that he couldn't express sorrow and pain and regret and all other abstracts.

AIB: Pain and regret, perhaps, up to a limit, but when he came really down to the man-woman relationship in his stories—

LDB: But how about the Dilseys and the Riders, the Fentrys and Wash Joneses and Nancy Mannigoes of Faulkner's fiction? He seems certainly capable of expressing powerfully a whole emotional range of sentiments and passions, strong moral and ethical values, standards of right and wrong.

AIB: Oh, yeah, in the larger sense, when blacks were abused, he knew they were abused, were being abused, and when society—look what he does in *The Sound and the Fury* with Quentin and the other characters there. When he does it in that context, it is fine.

LDB: You're saying that in male-female contexts he is less convincing?

AIB: That's right! He seemed incapable of doing it in his life, because he did it again and again with the different women in his life, failed to respect them as persons, not just as women, which he couldn't do either. He thought talking about writing fulfilled his relationship with one of the girls that he was with, but that wasn't what she wanted.

LDB: And that was Joan Williams?

AIB: Yeah, that didn't fulfill anything. That was an incomplete relationship.

LDB: Meta Carpenter Wilde suggested in an interview that Faulkner was probably best as a lover in his letters to her. He was apparently unable to vocalize his sentiments, his passions.

AIB: Yes, but relationships have to do with being a person, not writing letters from 2,000 miles away. Just think how safe he was writing letters from Oxford. Live up to what you said. I can't; I'm 2,000 miles away.

LDB: To bring this back around again, will you give me your estimation of Faulkner's literature, divorced from the man you knew? Will the literature last? Is it authentic? Is it valid? Is it valuable and, if so, why?

AIB: In a peculiar way, when I say that Faulkner had limitations, despite the limitations, something comes across. When you read *The Sound and the Fury* and don't quite get what the hell he's talking about, you read it again and again, and you get it. It is very hard to criticize because you don't know where to attack it and where to praise it, except that a world he recreates really does come to life.

LDB: The best of the writing, then, what does it do? How does it affect us? Will it live?

AIB: I certainly think it will live. God! If the Japanese and the French accept it as great writing because they're involved in doing the abusive things to their own people that we have done to people in our own South, then it's great writing, and it's going to live, because people are going to do these stupid things to each other all along, and his writing is going to say this is where it gets back to. His fiction says, "Look what we did," and it tells about the abuses of the black and white relations. Now there it's not personal. There it's a thing that he is viewing, and he writes very honestly about that. The pains of that are wonderful. When the black and the white kids are growing up together so that they don't know whose breast is whose, or care if this black woman is his mother or not, but when they get to a certain age and something terrible happens, and he writes about this, this doesn't have to do with his utterly terrible relationship with his own mother and father. So he writes about this like a house on fire. And an aspect of our society's heritage comes to life in a way that is incredible. Faulkner has done something! He has said a crime was committed, and this is what it was. And in the best of his writing, like *Absalom, Absalom!*, he says to what degree of white and black you must be before you can be forgiven for being black, what percentage of black blood you must have in you in order for you to be persecuted. That's a hell of a book. If you want to know the crime that was committed against the people in the South, read *Absalom, Absalom!*. You don't have to go any further than that! It tells you! No wonder his own family turned against him! I doubt any one of them even read the Goddamn book!

LDB: Well, they certainly read *Intruder in the Dust*, and they turned against him at that time.

AIB: Yeah, and *Intruder in the Dust* couldn't cast a shadow on *Absalom, Absalom!*.

LDB: Except that it was certainly provocative enough to his family and those around him like his old friend, Phil Stone, whom he had long since outdistanced in sentiment.

AIB: My feeling is that the best of Bill's writing wasn't focused on personal dilemma, although that's where the writing began, but on depicting the crime that was being committed, and Bill had the sensitivity to see the crime, to size it up. In personal relationships, he didn't have that sensitivity, but in the relationships in his South that he saw and could view without personalizing them, he succeeded masterfully.

LDB: He didn't like individual persons, but he loved people.

AIB: People, right! Also, it was difficult for him to touch on the personal for himself, having to do with his own life. He had to enlarge it into a marvelous fantasy.

LDB: The fact that Faulkner could have had some of the insights he had, having grown up in that rather provincial, strangling environment embedded in bigotry and racism—the fact that he could somehow seemingly rise above a lot of that and create a universal literature amazes me. Do you feel that his success had to do with his getting out of Oxford from an early age, going to New Orleans, New Haven, New York, California?

AIB: No! This all happened long before. He got out of Oxford, and in a sense the world in which he was living, and could view it objectively because he got out of the demands of being the oldest child and taking on attendant responsibilities by becoming the writer: first, the bohemian poet, then the writer of *Sanctuary,* finally, the Nobel laureate—though by that late time it no longer worked, as I have said. See, if he had looked at his world subjectively—turn-of-the-century Oxford, Oxford of the teens and twenties—he never would have questioned it. He would have done what his father demanded, what his grandfather demanded before him, what his mother demanded of him, which was really nothing but failure, at least in terms of his father's poor record. He even refused to accept his literary mentor's dicta, in the final analysis—Phil Stone's restrictive and rigid ethical, racial, and literary principles—and that's when Faulkner discovered how to make great, innovative fiction! Not wanting any part of that life in Oxford made him objective and removed him just as if he had gone to Hollywood or New York. He left that town long before, and the way he left it was by wandering about and watching people in their lives, their oppressions, watching the mules pulling the plow, watching the stuff over by the River. This all happened in his teens and early twenties. He just didn't want to be a part of it! His revolt was against a sense of responsibility!

LDB: So he got out of Oxford even though for the longest time he never left at all. He did remove himself from it.

AIB: Intellectually.

LDB: Spiritually, too! He removed himself from it, not by going to Hollywood, New York, not even by going to Memphis, Greenville, or Clarksdale, rather by wandering around the town, the courthouse, the Square, the countryside; and in wandering around he saw and kept seeing objectively the world in which he was living. How much did the intensive reading he was doing in his youth tend to reinforce or augment his perceptions?

AIB: I think that what the reading did for him was to say these writers lived in a world and in their way—the Joyces, Hardys, Conrads, Balzacs—they wrote about the world they lived in. Seeing this and reading it made him see the world he lived in, and when Sherwood Anderson said write about the world you know, bang, that clicked.

LDB: Being close to it and having access to other writers as models gave Faulkner the insight into how other people, writers, living within similar closed societies could yet gain distance and be objective.

AIB: Right! That's right! They provided him with endless examples; their examples made it possible for him to do what he did.

LDB: The literature that he had assimilated, his great-grandfather's image as well, plus the dread of having to fulfill the responsibility of becoming the head of a household in that town—these impelled him toward his vocation!

AIB: Absolutely! Once Faulkner said, "I'm going to be a writer like my great-granddaddy," then he had to be a writer. So he read and did all these things because he had to fulfill what he was going to become. We all make choices. He could have chosen to become a drunk and fail in everything, but he chose to be a writer.

LDB: Perhaps he chose to be both writer and drunk because he was flawed, because even choosing is flawed.

AIB: Right! His writing was flawed, and so was his life. But the point is, he did choose them both.

LDB: And in choosing both, he was forced to make and accept his compromises.

AIB: Yeah, but also he would have been the first to admit that not all of his writing was great.

LDB: He wasn't *born* a great writer, but his circumstances made him choose writing as a way of escaping the realities of his life. He *made himself* a great writer and, in the process, created a greater reality of his own.

AIB: You know something? What I get out of all this isn't a sense of pity but a sadness for Bill and, at the same time, the realization that without all that agony the writing wouldn't have happened. If the agony hadn't been there! If the anguish hadn't been there! I tell you, it makes me want to cry, and yet I wouldn't have denied him any of the pain because, without the pain, he wouldn't have written *The Sound and the Fury;* he wouldn't have conjured *Absalom, Absalom!*.

FIVE

FROM FICTIONIST TO POLEMICIST

"The passion in the two poems is not controlled. Therefore, it stops being clean passion and becomes rhetoric, which a reader doubts a little.
Put the passion in it, but sit on the passion. Dont try to say to the reader what you want to say, but make him say it to himself for you."
—William Faulkner, letter to Joe C. Brown, possibly January 29, 1945[1]

"If one begins to write about the injustice of society, then one has stopped being primarily a novelist and has become a polemicist or a propagandist."
—William Faulkner at the University of Virginia, May 20, 1957[2]

When the Joint Ceremonial of the National Institute of Arts and Letters and the American Academy of Arts and Letters was held on May 25, 1950, William Faulkner was not in attendance to formally accept the Howells Medal being awarded to his recently published *Collected Stories* and for the distinguished body of American fiction he had created over the past two decades. In his June 12, 1950, letter to the secretary of the American Academy, acknowledging receipt by post of the medal and the transcription of Archibald MacLeish's presentation speech, he sounded a plaintive, almost elegiac tone by focusing on the nature of evaluating the quality of others' and of his own work:

> None of mine ever quite suited me, each time I wrote the last word I would think, if I could just do it over, I would do it better, maybe even right. But I was too busy; there was always another one. I would tell myself, maybe I'm too young or too busy to decide; when I reach fifty, I will be able to decide how good or not. Then one day I was fifty and I looked back at it, and I decided that it was all pretty good—and then in the same instant I realised that that was the worst of all since that meant only that a little nearer now was

the moment, instant, night: dark: sleep: when I would put it all away forever that I anguished and sweated over, and it would never trouble me anymore.[3]

Viewed with the matchless perspicuity of hindsight, Faulkner's remarks might seem to contain an amazingly prophetic quality: that on reaching fifty, just prior to writing *Intruder in the Dust,* he intuited there would not be "another one," as "always" there had been another novel to occupy his time and diffuse his energy when he was "too young and too busy to decide . . . how good or not" his work had been, at least not another fiction new or experimental in terms of theme, event, character, technique, and moral content. Perhaps on reaching fifty Faulkner did realize that being able to "decide" that his own work "was all pretty good" signified the abatement of his creativity, his genius. This is not to suggest that during the next fifteen years Faulkner would cease writing and publishing or that he would no longer anguish and sweat over the products of his craft. Indeed, he would maintain his prolific pace and output. But with notably few exceptions (clearly *The Reivers,* possibly the three prose prologues from *Requiem for a Nun,* and isolated characters from *The Town* and *The Mansion* who enchanted him personally), it is doubtful that, given the chance to "decide," Faulkner would have judged his fiction from *Intruder in the Dust* through *The Reivers* "all pretty good."

Significantly, however, there is a redeeming element to be considered in this relatively negative evaluation. Given such an opportunity to "decide" on the quality of his work from 1948 to the end of his life, Faulkner just might have awarded another phase of his writing, nonfiction, with high marks. Quite likely he would have expressed satisfaction with the general reception accorded his essays, public letters, and speeches. But to better understand this hypothetical shift, we must first return to that period in Faulkner's life and literary career when the attitude, emphasis, and technical approach he exhibited in creating dramatic, evocative fiction began to change to rhetorical and oratorical elements essentially harnessed to the production of provocative, nonfiction prose and public discourse.

During those prodigiously creative and prolifically productive years when he was "too busy" writing *The Sound and the Fury, As I Lay Dying, Sanctuary, Light in August, Absalom, Absalom!, The Hamlet,* and *Go Down, Moses,* Faulkner took strenuous measures to guard and preserve his privacy. The following excerpt from his February 11, 1949, letter to Malcolm Cowley eloquently underscores the urgency of his obsession: "I will protest to the last: no photographs, no recorded documents. It is my ambition to be, as a private individual, abolished and voided from history, leaving it markless, no refuse save the printed books; I wish I had had enough sense to see ahead thirty years ago and, like some of the Elizabethans, not signed them.

It is my aim, and every effort bent, that the sum and history of my life, which in the same sentence is my obit and epitaph too, shall be them both: He made the books and he died."[4]

With fastidious resolve, Faulkner heeded his Muse's mandate not to jeopardize the integrity of his fiction by pre-empting or diminishing it through written explications, rhetorical bravado, or offhand apologias and observations for public consumption. He expressed equally skeptical disdain for shoptalk among literary peers and with academicians, holding to his belief, as he wrote Malcolm Cowley on December 8, 1945, that "what I have written is of course in the public domain and the public is welcome; what I ate and did and when and where, is my own business."[5] Unswervingly, Faulkner maintained a position of silence, convinced his inner motivations, compulsions, personal ambitions, and private objectives were his sole property; only the artistic implications of his fiction, existing inferentially for anyone willing to commit himself to his complex art, belonged to the world and to succeeding generations.

Faulkner was highly suspect of the human compulsion to talk, engage in what to him seemed the flatulent and egotistical pursuits of discourse, debate, and speculation. Such activities could only distract him from the business at hand, which was writing his novels, and that could only be accomplished in solitude. Correspondingly, in *As I Lay Dying, The Sound and the Fury, Light in August, Go Down, Moses,* and *Intruder in the Dust,* Faulkner depicted, respectively, Cora Tull, Quentin Compson, Reverend Hightower, Horace Benbow, Ike McCaslin, and Gavin Stevens as characters doomed by the "curse of human speech" to suffer unhappy disillusionment and spend their lives resigned to pomposity and unenlightened self-righteousness. In a May 1946 letter to Malcolm Cowley, Faulkner documented with sardonic and biting indignation his aversion to talk and talking: "Goddam it I've spent almost fifty years trying to cure myself of the curse of human speech, all for nothing. Last month two damned swedes, two days ago a confounded Chicago reporter, and now this one that cant even speak english. As if anything he or I either know, or both of us together know, is worth being said once, let alone twice through an interpreter."[6]

Anyone who knew Faulkner personally would have concurred that he practiced implicitly what he advocated: to avoid preaching at all costs in his writing as well as in social intercourse. He could be unnervingly taciturn with most persons, one-on-one or in groups. Quite often he was given to attenuated silences, which forced others to carry the entire burden of the conversation. His lack of participation in a discussion frequently coerced monologue and soliloquy from those present. At times, his contempt for the spoken word almost bordered on paranoia, as though he actually feared anything he might say could or would implicate him in a universal scandal or at least an interpersonal contretemps.

Accepting this trait in Faulkner's personality makes it less difficult to appreciate how he could write to Malcolm Cowley on July 16, 1948, asking the latter to decline for him an invitation extended by a Yale professor to speak to his students, and to do so without self-consciously considering himself rude or arrogant: "I had a letter from a Mr Pearson at New Haven about coming there to make a talk, something. . . . I dont think I know anything worth 200 dollars worth talking about but I hope to be up East this fall though I still dont believe I will know anything to talk about worth 200 dollars so I would probably settle for a bottle of good whiskey."[7]

Similarly, writing to Mark Van Doren on April 1, 1950, though in a different guise, Faulkner could assert his fundamental distrust for the spoken word by declining to accept the Howells Medal in person: "I would like to be present, of course. I am very sorry that right now I cant even say No. I am a farmer this time of year; up until he sells crops, no Mississippi farmer has the time or money either to travel anywhere on. Also, I doubt if I know anything worth talking two minutes about."[8]

In fact, as early as December 6, 1946, in response to an invitation by Professor Cleanth Brooks to speak to his students at Louisiana State University in Baton Rouge, Faulkner sent a polite, terse refusal by telegram; this at a time when, having recently returned from Hollywood and strapped for income, he could have benefited from the honorarium the invitation promised. He wrote to Brooks: "INVITATION DECLINED THANKS AND APOLOGIES WOULD LIKE MONEY AND TRIP BUT HAVE NOTHING TO SAY."[9] Permitting himself few exceptions, Faulkner would cleave to this attitude and to his policy of refusing to disclose anything pertaining to his personal life and to his literary habits, methods, and implications. He would at least maintain this posture until after that day in Stockholm, Sweden, when he delivered to the public more than his auspicious Nobel Prize speech; unwittingly, he delivered up his own body and soul as well.

Curiously, one of those few pre–Nobel Prize exceptions in which Faulkner would allow himself to go public occurred in Oxford, Mississippi, within walking distance of his home, Rowan Oak, less than half a year after he declined Professor Brooks' invitation to speak at L.S.U. On April 10, 1947, encouraged by a casual conversation Dr. A. Wigfall Green reported having had with Faulkner days before, Dr. W. Alton Bryant, head of the English department at the University of Mississippi, wrote to Faulkner: "The Department of English at the University is interested in bringing several prominent American writers to the campus, and in having them talk to our advanced students in English. Since we consider you one of the ablest American writers, we are happy to extend the first invitation

to you. If you are interested in talking with several groups of our advanced
students, we could pay you an honorarium of two hundred and fifty dollars ($250)." [10]

Dr. Bryant's letter also contained a "tentative schedule" of classes (two
sections of American Literature, Creative Writing, Modern Literature, the
Novel, and Shakespeare) that Faulkner might wish to attend between
April 14 and April 17, 1947, and concluded, "We hope very much that you
can see your way clear to be with us next week."

Apparently, Faulkner found the requirements for his appearances unan-
noying. He would speak informally with members of six different classes
on four different days. His stipulation that the sessions include neither faculty nor outside publicists posed no point of contention. Whether or not
he was aware that the dates of his scheduled appearances corresponded
with the Southern Literary Festival being held at Ole Miss that year, or if
knowledge of it might have affected his decision to visit the campus, remains unknown. From the few accounts that do exist, it seems Faulkner
conducted himself with politeness and came away from the experience,
which initially he must have imagined would be painfully uncomfortable,
with a sense of pride in having competently fulfilled his responsibilities.
Also, he had managed to cash in on an unexpected and much needed
windfall of $250. Surely Faulkner could not have been prepared for the en-
suing flap that his informal talks would precipitate or realize that their cost
to the university would be minimal compared with the extravagant price
he would pay in recrimination and self-doubt over the coming months and
years for having allowed his tongue to speak for his pen.

Indeed, the scandal that eventually assumed international proportions
began four days after Faulkner's last appearance at Ole Miss at the instiga-
tion of the overzealous, self-serving Marvin M. Black, the university's recently installed director of public relations. Black had taken the liberty of
creating a press release for Faulkner's campus visits, which on April 21,
1947, he dispatched to the nation's leading news syndications. [11] On that
same day, he also mailed a sample of his release with a cover letter to Harrison Smith, book editor of the *Saturday Review of Literature,* whom Black
had met briefly before the war and now hoped to interest in publishing his
translations of "contemporary Mexican literature" in return for receiving
first crack at publication of an article he was now "exclusively" offering
Smith: a piece, whose writing he would oversee, based on "some most
valuable material taken down verbatim in the classroom from the questions and answers" [12] generated between Faulkner and the students with
whom he had conversed during the April 14–17 sessions at Ole Miss. The
one-page release included certain of Faulkner's responses that, when excerpted out of context, appeared not only controversial but also provoca-

tive and cast a very cynical, ascerbic pale over Faulkner, rather than suggesting the modest, often self-effacing tone that, as deferential respondent, he actually conveyed during his visits. There can be no question that Black calculated the following release to achieve highest visibility and shock value:

UNIVERSITY, Miss., April 21—Publicity-shy William Faulkner, internationally known author and resident of Oxford, Mississippi, adjoining the State University campus, broke a precedent last week when he came out of his shell to take charge of classes in Creative Writing, Modern and American Literature, and the Novel, at the University of Mississippi.

In answer to a question whom he considered his five most important contemporaries, he replied, Thomas Wolfe, John Dos Passos, Ernest Hemingway, Willa Cather, and John Steinbeck, in that order. Then in reply to a questioner who asked where he would place himself among modern novelists, he put himself second on the list following Thomas Wolfe.

Of Thomas Wolfe he said: "He had much courage, wrote as if he didn't have long to live . . ." Of Hemingway: "He has no courage, has never climbed out on a limb. He has never used a word where the reader might check his usage by a dictionary." On Steinbeck: "I had great hopes for him at one time. Now I don't know . . ."

American literature began with Sherwood Anderson, Faulkner told his hearers. "Previous writers have written in the European tradition using their phraseology and diction. They looked East and then looked West," he said. "Anderson had no inhibitions. His style is like a primer. He writes simply as if he had never read anything." Faulkner considers him the forerunner of Hemingway, Dos Passos, and Thomas Wolfe.

Asked if he is working on a new book Faulkner said he had one under way dealing with the birth and life of Christ.

(Marvin M. Black, Director of Public Relations)[13]

Neither Faulkner nor any university official, except Marvin M. Black, was made privy to the existence of this press release, that is, not for slightly more than two months when Faulkner became indirectly aware of it as the result of a highly disturbing secondhand letter he received in Oxford.

On April 23, 1947, Harrison Smith, also, coincidentally, Faulkner's former publisher, acknowledged receiving the communiqué from Black, concluding, "You have certainly found at home an extraordinary teacher of English."[14] Apparently, Smith had not delayed in getting word to his old friend Bill Faulkner, informing him of what was astir. It did not take Faulkner long either to express to Dr. Bryant his consternation and distress at the possibility that any of his remarks had been transcribed and were being circulated and offered up for national publication. He would be willing to cooperate in correcting and refining any notes that may have surfaced from his talks but with the sole intention of making them available for instructional purposes at the university.[15] Nor did Dr. Bryant tarry in writing to Black:

> Dear Mr. Black:
>
> This letter concerns the possibility of giving publicity to Mr. William Faulkner's talks with six of our advanced classes in English during the week beginning April 21. The desire to publicize Mr. Faulkner's remarks is commendable, for Mr. Faulkner is a widely known figure whose opinions carry weight and authority.
>
> It has come to my attention, however, that Mr. Faulkner does not wish his remarks publicized. Under the circumstances, I strongly sympathize with Mr. Faulkner's attitude. He talked with our students quite informally and in an off-the-record atmosphere, a procedure which was perfectly in keeping with the request made of him by the Department of English. He gave our students a first rate performance and they were delighted. I can understand that under such circumstances a man would feel free, and even be led by the very nature of the discussion, to say things which, however true they might be, he would not wish publicized.
>
> I should add, also, that in negotiating with Mr. Faulkner, I gave no indication that his appearance was to receive publicity, nor did I have such publicity in mind.
>
> It is my hope that Mr. Faulkner's wishes in this matter will be observed as far as possible. In view of the fact that neither Mr. Faulkner nor the Department of English understood that publicity might be given to his remarks, the Department of English would suffer some embarrassment should such publicity be given.
>
> Sincerely yours,
W. Alton Bryant, Head
Department of English [16]

Having gone on record with Black in accordance with Faulkner's wishes, Dr. Bryant must have believed when he wrote Faulkner the following day that he had put a quick and final end to any further activity of the nature Faulkner had described to him (doubtless as a result of Smith's written admonitions). Formally thanking Faulkner represented Bryant's last official duty in an otherwise very pleasing exchange between the university and the eminent writer of Oxford, at least for 1947. Diplomatically avoiding the issue of rumors that notes taken surreptitiously in Faulkner's classroom meetings were being prepared for public dissemination, Dr. Bryant wrote:

Dear Mr. Faulkner:

On behalf of the Department of English, I wish to thank you for the valuable contribution which you made to our students during your informal talks with them in April.

We know that your discussions were superior because our students came away from them with enthusiastic praise for what you had to say. In fact, several of our better students have asked me about the possibility of your talking with them again.

Frankly, we faculty members envied the students the privilege of hearing you talk, but we all feel that everything went better with us out of the room. I am quite sure that the students felt freer to ask questions and enter into the discussion than they would have with faculty members present.

It is our hope that in the future you will find it possible to give a "repeat performance." The first was a smash hit!

With kindest regards,

> Sincerely yours,
> W. Alton Bryant, Head
> Department of English [17]

Faulkner's fundamentally appreciative letter of acknowledgment to Dr. Bryant expressed his mutual belief that the incident had been stopped in its tracks and that no damage had been done. So mollified was Faulkner that he all but agreed to make a "repeat" performance at some future date:

Dear Dr Bryant:

Thank you for your letter. I never had any doubt but that our ideas were one regarding the purpose of the plan. Thank you for going on record also, and along with the gratitude, my apologies for having put you on a spot (if I did so) where you felt it necessary to do so.

I went over the material with Miss Parker. It is fairly correct now (I mean by 'fairly' that it is not complete, still informal) and it is yours to do with as you like. I just hate like hell to be jumbled head over heels into the high-pressure ballyhoo which even universities now believe they must employ: the damned eternal American BUY! BUY!! BUY!!! 'Try us first, our campus covers ONE WHOLE SQUARE MILE, you can see our water tank from twelve miles away, our football team almost beat A. & M., we have WM FAULKNER at 6 (count them: 6) English classes.' That sort of thing I will resist with my last breath. But if the English department, not the publicity dept., uses the material, I shall have no qualms and fears. . . .

If you decide on a 'repeat,' let me know.

Thank you for the check.

> Yours sincerely,
> William Faulkner [18]

But even as these pleasantries were being concluded, the pernicious germ of Faulkner's words, issuing from Black's press release of April 21, 1947, had found a carrier in an influential newspaper. What Ernest Hemingway read in and processed from the May 11 edition of the *New York Herald Tribune*'s book review understandably appeared to him to be libelous defamation of his character: the few denigrating phrases excerpted from a news release issued in University, Mississippi, contained what amounted to character assassination. Faulkner had accused him of lacking "courage" and apparently had made his remarks with taunting, devil-may-care arrogance and blatant disregard for the ramifications of his callousness. Two weeks later, on May 25, 1947, Hemingway forwarded the article to his war friend General C. T. Lanham, exhorting him to write Faulkner on his behalf "only what you personally know to be true" in response to Faulkner's accusations, specifically to address the slur against his "courage." [19]

On June 24, 1947, Brigadier General, U.S.A., C. T. Lanham did write a four-page, single-spaced letter to Faulkner, extolling from personal experience Hemingway's feats of valor, his immense courage under fire, his lifelong sense of adventure in the face of death. The tone and tenor of the following excerpts from Lanham's second and closing paragraphs are representative of the body of the letter, whose detailed enumeration of theaters and campaigns and personal testimonials clearly suggests that neither Lanham nor Hemingway had understood the substance of the implications of Faulkner's originally innocuous comments. However, to be fair, neither could they nor any reader have been expected to intuit Faulkner's intended meanings out of context. Lanham writes:

> It is extremely difficult for me to understand how anyone in writing of Ernest could say, "He has no courage; he has never climbed out on a limb." Certainly his whole life belies that statement—his early days in the professional prizering; his combat experience in World War I; his fighting record with the Loyalists in Spain; his anti-submarine work in the Caribbean in the early part of World War II; his large number of hours in the air in an RAF Mosquito working over the Rocket Coast; and his subsequent work with our Army starting with the assault on the Normandy Coast on D-Day. . . .
>
> In a person-to-person conversation, I could tell you many deeds of derring-do performed by Ernest while with my regiment, but these things I cannot put in writing for many reasons. But I can tell you this, Mr. Faulkner: It takes one hell of a good man to win the affection and admiration of an Infantry regiment in battle even if that man be in uniform. And for a correspondent to do it verges on the miraculous. He has to be something of a superman and this, I can assure you, is just what Ernest Hemingway was and is in the eyes of all of us. I have stated this many times before and I expect to state it many

times more before I'm dead—Ernest Hemingway is without exception the most courageous man I have ever known, both in war and in peace. He has physical courage, and he has that far rarer commodity, moral courage. Finally, I might add this: I have never known a more truthful man or a more generous one.

I trust that this note may in some degree change your written opinion that Ernest Hemingway "has no courage." I'm sure that that statement must be based on false information.[20]

On June 28, 1947, Faulkner responded to General Lanham with the following letter:

Dear General Lanham:

Thank you for your letter.

The statement as you requested it is not correct because apparently it was incomplete as you saw it, and in its original shape it had no reference whatever to Hemingway as a man: only to his craftsmanship as a writer. I know of his record in two wars and in Spain, too.

In April, on request from the English department of the University of Mississippi here (my alma mater) I met six English classes, answering questions about literature, writing. In one of them I was asked to rate the greatest American writers. I answered, I wouldn't attempt it since I believed no man could, but (after further insistance [sic]) I would give my own personal rating of my own coevals: the men whose names were most often connected with mine since we began to write. I named Hemingway, Wolfe, Dos Passos, Caldwell. I said:

'I think we all failed (in that none of us had yet the stature of Dickens, Dostoevsky, Balzac, Thackery etc.). That Wolfe made the best failure because he had the most courage: to risk being guilty of bad taste, clumsiness, mawkishness, dullness: to shoot the works win or lose and damn the torpedoes. That Dos Passos was next since he sacrificed some of the courage to style. That Hemingway was next since he did not have the courage to get out on a limb as the others did, to risk bad taste, over-writing, dullness, etc.'

This was elaborated of course. I spoke extemporaneously, without notes, as I believed at the time, informally, not for publication. Your letter was my first intimation that it had been released, and from what you re-quoted, garbled and incomplete.

I'm sorry of it. A copy of this goes to Hemingway, with a covering note. Whatever other chances I have to correct it, I shall certainly take.

Thank you again for your letter.

Yours sincerely,
William Faulkner[21]

On the same day, Faulkner wrote the following cover letter to Ernest Hemingway, which accompanied a copy of his long letter to Lanham:

> Dear Hemingway:
>   I'm sorry of this damn stupid thing. I was just making $250.00, I thought informally, not for publication, or I would have insisted on looking at the stuff before it was released. I have believed for years that the human voice has caused all human ills and I thought I had broken myself of talking. Maybe this will be my valedictory lesson.
>   I hope it wont matter a damn to you. But if or when or whever [*sic*] it does, please accept another squirm from yours truly.
>
>   Faulkner
> re letter from Brigadier Lanham who commanded (then) an infantry regiment you were with. He sounds like they had a good mess.[22]

The tone and the phraseology of this letter strike an amazingly similar chord to that struck in Faulkner's May 1946 letter to Malcolm Cowley ("Goddam it I've spent almost fifty years trying to cure myself of the curse of human speech, all for nothing"),[23] acknowledging the latter's warning that an esteemed Russian writer, invited to America by the State Department, was intending to drive to Oxford to visit him.

Apparently, for Faulkner, saying and doing were irreconcilable contraries. Obviously, he had not "broken [himself] of talking." In truth, the recent incident at Ole Miss had forced him to bear witness to his own self-victimization and that of one of his contemporaries as a direct result of his indirectly misspoken words. In a sense, feeling obliged to write letters of apology to Lanham and Hemingway had reduced Faulkner to making two childlike acts of atonement for misdeeds he had committed. Thus, it would seem that Faulkner's subsequent refusals to accept Professor Pearson's invitation to speak at Yale in July 1948 and to travel in May 1950 to New York to deliver an acceptance speech for the Howells Medal were direct manifestations of an increasingly overcautious attitude toward speaking in public from fear of committing additional inadvertent scandals.

Yet Faulkner had not learned his "valedictory lesson" from the Hemingway flap, and the following spring he accepted Dr. Bryant's offer to make a "repeat performance" at Ole Miss.

Sometime during the spring of 1948, the exact day seems to have escaped recording, Faulkner did make what appears to have been at least one more appearance on the Ole Miss campus to converse with students. This time he insisted on confidentiality. Perhaps Faulkner persuaded Phil Stone, his friend and lawyer, to attend with him this "interview" in order to help enforce the letter of the law: Faulkner's law. Yet this time also,

though most likely with Faulkner's approval, notes were taken whose compilation resulted in a four-page summary provisionally entitled "Confidential group interview at University of Mississippi, Spring 1948. Including
remarks and reflections by his lawyer, Stone."[24]

Why had Faulkner chosen to make a "repeat" after the debacle his
words had created a year before? Perhaps an urgent need for income compelled him to fly in the face of his better judgment. Merely trying to avoid
making a "repeat" of the flap he had caused in 1947 could have accounted
for his insistence on keeping his 1948 interview "confidential." But this
need for confidentiality might also have engendered out of other more importunate motives than anxiety over risking giving offense to another individual as a result of inappropriate remarks he might make.

Possibly there was a far more subtle reason. Intuitively, Faulkner may
have been aware that he could use this opportunity as a dress rehearsal for
a sustained defense of his forthcoming novel, *Intruder in the Dust,* his first
in six years. He knew its publication would ignite a powder keg since it
consisted of a calculatedly controversial manifesto on race relations in Mississippi, the South, and in the United States. Perhaps better than anyone
else, Faulkner may have suspected just how divisive and inflammatory the
following remarks "Re Negroes," excerpted from the four-page "confidential" interview of spring 1948, might appear if the national media got hold
of them, not to mention the local animosity and friction they would create
among family, friends, and townsfolk in Oxford:

> Re Negroes: They are spiritually tougher than white men—better in that
> sense. The negro has all the white man's virtues, some to a greater extent—
> proof; he has more sympathy with children, more affection for the old and
> helpless of his race. The negro's vices: drunkenness, gambling, lying thiev-
> ery—which the white man taught him.
>
> The negro does not want complete social equality; he wants to buy at the
> same prices, have the vote, have same taxes. If Christianity means anything
> there can be no color line in churches. (Earlier he said that a hotel keeper has
> the right to exclude anyone he pleases—all blue-eyed people for example.)
>
> Faulkner thinks that separate schools are more practical. He believes that
> the negro should have the right to a university education. Suggests that
> negroes should register here at the University and receive tuition and a ticket
> to the University he chooses.[25]

As Faulkner may have judged it, the dilemma originated more in the
delivery format of his message, a result of his present urgency to publicly
vocalize previously fictionalized statements, than in its substance, specifically. After all, in "The Bear" (1942) he had already permitted Ike to dis-

course with McCaslin Edmonds in terms that closely resembled statements he himself made to the group at Ole Miss in 1948 and, presumably, allowed to be recorded in the first of three paragraphs in the section subtitled "Re Negroes" of the four-page "confidential" interview:

> 'Because they will endure. They are better than we are. Stronger than we are. Their vices are vices aped from white men or that white men and bondage have taught them: improvidence and intemperance and evasion—not laziness: evasion. . . .'
>   'All right. Go on. And their virtues—' and he
>   'Yes. Their own. Endurance—' and McCaslin
>   'So have mules:' and he
>   '—and pity and tolerance and forbearance and fidelity and love of children—.'[26]

And in *Intruder in the Dust,* Gavin Stevens reiterates a response similar to the one that Faulkner made in the same 1948 interview and that became the substance of the third paragraph of that same subtitled section "Re Negroes": "In time he will vote anywhen and anywhere a white man can and send his children to the same school anywhere the white man's children go and travel anywhere the white man travels as the white man does it. But it wont be next Tuesday."[27]

By imbedding his implications in the context of his evocative prose and by burying even more deeply his authorial tonalities and nuances of meaning, Faulkner could absolve himself of explicitly endorsing any personally attributable viewpoints; he could disclaim all responsibility other than that of authorial supervision and all accountability for what his characters said and did. Malcolm Cowley recorded in his notebook the following observation that Faulkner made to him while visiting in the Cowley home in Sherman, Connecticut, between October 24 and 26, 1948: "We talked about *Intruder in the Dust.* . . . Stevens, he explained, was not speaking for the author, but for the best type of liberal Southerners; that is how they feel about the Negroes."[28]

However, this was decidedly not the case with direct public statements he might make; his personal accountability was immediate and almost impossible to deflect. Had Phil Mullen, editor of the Oxford *Eagle,* or any stringer from a national wire service picked up on these specific remarks from his interview, Faulkner would have had to claim and defend them publicly, and it is highly doubtful that his assertions in lily-white Mississippi of 1948 would have been perceived as anything short of treasonable. For that matter, had the time been 1962 instead, most of the same detractors, in spirit, certainly, if not physically, might well have been among those who would take up brickbats and nightsticks and set crosses aflame on lawns of "moderates" or "gradualists" or "liberals" like himself, sympathizers espousing such "radical" heresies as allowing Negroes to register for enrollment at the University of Mississippi. Malcolm Cowley's journal notes dated October 25, 1948, record incidents and statements that Faulkner expressed at a party given in his honor the previous Tuesday at the New York apartment of Robert Haas. They contain this observation: "He caused a mild scandal at Ole Miss when he said that Negroes should attend the university."[29] Apparently, what he had said to the group gathered for his spring interview was still quite vivid in Faulkner's memory.

One highly ambivalent and subsequently ironic statement paraphrased from Faulkner's remarks in the 1948 "confidential" interview lingers hauntingly. He said to one questioner, "A writer should be objective. You can't be both an artist and a reformer." This comment was qualified in parenthesis by the following aside: "(Stone's note; 'He got this originally from me, and it is true.')" In this instance there is little reason to mistrust or disbelieve that Faulkner's aesthetic and artistic intentions, reinforced by his one-time literary mentor, were authentically embodied in this expression. But whether or not they were still viable or relevant to Faulkner's present emotional and artistic needs is a different issue.

Postulating plausible answers as to why Faulkner felt compelled to go public while attempting to keep his message "confidential" in the spring of 1948 actually raises two even more fundamental questions. First, what were the central, unifying motives that forced Faulkner to exchange one aesthetic, that of full-time novelist of such recent fictions as *The Unvanquished* and *Go Down, Moses,* for another, one that would divide his creative energies between composing novels and writing political diatribes and tracts on social reform? And second, how did Faulkner justify and effect this transformation? Finding persuasive explanations requires taking a closer focus on his experiences as scenarist for Warner Bros. during the years from 1942 through 1945.

William Faulkner arrived at the Warner Bros. movie lot in Burbank, California, on July 27, 1942, and buoyantly assumed his $300-weekly job with a sense of financial security. Paradoxically, his seven-year contract guaranteeing semiannual incremental raises offset scanty royalties accruing from sales of his novels. He saw his immediate task of writing an original script, soon to be titled "The De Gaulle Story," as just the opportunity he needed to justify and satisfy his personal requirements for demonstrating his patriotism and his manhood. He would be contributing to the cause of victory by creating a movie proclaiming the resilience, durability, and ultimate capacity for triumph of traditional values (hope, sacrifice, honor, courage, endurance, and compassion) no matter how overwhelmingly threatened by agents of destruction and inhumanity they might appear to be at any given moment in history.

Faulkner spent nearly four months of uninterrupted concentration writing and meticulously revising "The De Gaulle Story." Yet, growing more dispirited than ever before, he rediscovered in this first extended stint at Warner Bros. how Hollywood operated. To his utter frustration, which by degrees reached beyond disillusionment to desperation, Faulkner learned that scriptwriters were, as a lot, chattel, or, to recall one of Jack Warner's most unfortunately memorable cynicisms, "schmucks with Underwoods."[30] Worse, writing for Hollywood was not a solitary, individualistic labor, but a perfunctory means to a collaborative end product, which in the process prior to packaging for public consumption might be endlessly subjected to alteration and tampering from all jealous quarters. Unlike a novel, which might benefit from the deft insight of an accomplished editor, a screenplay was continuously vulnerable to others' whims and compromises. Furthermore, this kind of writing demanded of its creator surface narrative, not evocative, poetic prose. Movie scripts depended almost entirely on surface plot. Although extremely inventive at plotting, Faulkner felt uncomfortable giving his characters superficial lines that deliberately exploded suggestiveness with direct explanation. His forte was in creating subtly accretional fictive situations, settings, scenes, and actions that worked through inference and suggestion. The filmic medium required him to show and tell, not suggest and evoke, and disclosures had to be made immediately, not withheld and then slowly unfolded. Hollywood war propaganda was accomplished through blunt, uncomplicated messages.

By December 1942, Faulkner's "The De Gaulle Story" had been shelved, more as a result of the effect Charles de Gaulle's fractious and intransigent personality and attitudes had on President Roosevelt, and through him on Jack Warner, than because Faulkner had been unable to come through with a workable script. Yet Faulkner had also balked. Fighting to retain some semblance of the aesthetic sensibility he had always mustered in composing his best fiction, he deviated from the initial premise of mythicizing De Gaulle, focusing instead on the "little people of Brittany" whose travail under threat of extinction he had found more compelling. Predictably, the Free French representatives overseeing the project found this approach reprehensible and irresponsible; they refused to accept Faulkner's scripts without what amounted to endless revision.

Dejected and humiliated, Faulkner returned home to Oxford for two months to rest before having to be back on the Burbank lot. On December 5,

1942, he wrote to his stepson Malcolm Franklin a letter in which he ex-
horted him to enlist rather than wait to be drafted. Faulkner's rationale
was insightful: "It's a strange thing how a man, no matter how intelligent,
will cling to the public proof of his masculinity." Additionally, he reas-
sured Malcolm, "when I can, I am going too, maybe only to prove to myself that I can do (within my physical limitations of age, of course) as much
as anyone else can to make secure the manner of living I prefer and that
suits my kin and kind." [31]

Sensing his own physical inefficacy, if not complete lack of emotional
involvement, in winning World War II, Faulkner prophetically concluded,
in what had already become an emotionally charged letter rife with moralizing and propaganda: "It will take the young men to do that. Then perhaps the time of the older men will come, the ones like me who are articulate
in the national voice, who are too old to be soldiers, but are old enough and
have been vocal long enough to be listened to." [32] In hindsight, there seems
little doubt that forty-five-year-old William Faulkner had clearly defined
and isolated the major priorities he would attempt to accomplish during
the remainder of his life. And he would graduate with honors from Hollywood's "crash course" in public speaking. It must have seemed obvious to
him that changes were in order. After all, to keep reminding himself of
this, he need only contrast the celebrity and fanfare *Gone with the Wind*
and its author, Margaret Mitchell, had received with the paltry showing of
his own *Absalom, Absalom!,* published that same year of 1936.

Although Faulkner may not have realized it at the time, working on
"The De Gaulle Story" did provide him with some positive reinforce-
ments. Decidedly not an addition to his fictional canon, nonetheless this
major writing project had allowed him to restate and extend themes he
had been working into stories written between 1940 and 1942: "The Tall
Men," "Shingles for the Lord," "Two Soldiers," and early portions of "Delta
Autumn." Certainly oppression and violence and injustice were not new
themes to Faulkner, nor were their countervailing motifs: compassion,
equality, patriotism, and personal liberty. But the medium and the requirements of writing for the screen were distinct from his fictive techniques.
Moreso, the objects of his Hollywood focus were different from those on
which he had concentrated as a Mississippi writer telescoping regional
conflicts and conditions into universal ones. Inhumane plantation owners,
slaveholders, illiterate white trash, rednecks, and crackers given to evil,
rapaciousness, and criminal deeds were now supplanted by arch villains,
such as Hitler, Mussolini, and their fascist, Nazi, and Vichy sympathizers.

On returning to Hollywood in January 1943, Faulkner resumed developing war-effort motifs. Most significantly, he placed his signature or

"voice" on two new studio assignments of considerable substance, a story outline titled "Country Lawyer" and the full-length dramatic screenplay for Howard Hawks, "Battle Cry." His voice would take the form of blatantly misplaced autobiographical and authorial intrusions straining to connect the world at large, through Hollywood, back to Mississippi. His focus was the plight of the Negro in America, specifically the southern branch, and the catalyst for his observations was the Second World War.

In *The Sound and the Fury, Light in August, Absalom, Absalom!,* and *Go Down, Moses* and in short stories as compelling as "That Evening Sun," "Pantaloon in Black," "Delta Autumn," and "Dry September," Faulkner had been elaborating Negro conditions in the South. With a painter's eye for detail, nuance, and hue and with an extraordinary understanding of chiaroscuro, he had created a Bosch-like scape depicting the blacks' pervasive position of inferiority within the societal fabric: one of unremitting degradation which, for all its apparent depravity, seemed to produce character after character who exemplified ethical integrity that elevated them to positions of final moral authority.

Between March 27 and April 16, 1943, Faulkner submitted fifty-two pages of a story outline entitled "Country Lawyer." In a story ranging from 1890 to 1942, Faulkner depicts four generations of two white families, one representing the established, patrician gentry, the other, that of Sam Partridge, rising from obscurity to assume an enduring, if nouveau riche, status of stewardship within the community of Jefferson, Mississippi. Simultaneously, the story parallels the lives of three black families, beginning with the grandparents Tobe and Rachel and with their daughter Caroline who, like Sam, will outlive their offspring and serve to bind all four generations. Faulkner paves the way for the convergences of blacks and whites by having the upstart Sam Partridge defy all unwritten sanctions in defending Tobe without pay against a certain jail sentence. As recompense, Tobe moves into Sam's small house to be his servant. Faulkner uses this occasion to describe their mutual interdependence:

> But now he has a servants' cottage in his back yard, in which Tobe and his wife Rachel and their daughter Caroline live. Rachel cooks for him; his clothes are taken care of. For a while he could not pay them wages, though he is doing better now.
>
> For a little while Tobe seemed to have reformed, stayed at home, did a little work about the house. But now he has returned to his former tramp's life, sleeping wherever dark finds him, trifling and worthless. But Rachel is a different sort, and the daughter will also be a good woman. Her mother is training her to be so. We see here a relationship established upon mutual respect between the white man and the two Negro women which will endure.[33]

With precision Faulkner advances his tale from the turn-of-the-century to 1918; the setting fluctuates from peace to war. We learn that Caroline's son Spoot and his best friend Sam, Junior, Sam Partridge's son, are both soldiers in the First World War. Both have left young, pregnant wives back home. In October Old Sam receives a letter from his son, which reads in part:

> I was assigned to this company because I was a Southerner, and therefore I knew Negroes. I told the Colonel: 'Yes, sir, I know Negroes, a few of them, that I was raised among and who knew me and my fathers just as my fathers knew their fathers. I suppose, what you mean is, understand Negroes.' I told him I didn't know what there was he wanted understood about them; that maybe any human being was his own enigma which he would take with him to the grave, but I didn't know how the color of his skin was going to make that any clearer or more obscure.[34]

Dissolving from Sam's library in his mansion in Jefferson to the front lines in France, Faulkner describes the circumstances which bring Sam, Junior, and Spoot together again:

> A runner enters, followed by a group of Negro soldiers temporarily commanded by Spoot, now a sergeant. Spoot and Sam, Junior, recognize each other; Spoot has been hunting for Sam, Junior, for a year now. But the matter is official yet. Sergeant Moxey turns his party over to the Captain. Sam dismisses them, asks Sergeant Moxey to return.
>
> Spoot returns. Now he and Sam are alone. They are once more the two boys who fed from the same breast, who hunted the bird nest and stole the pig and were whipped for it, who slept in the same bed until after they were both so big that they would have to sleep together by stealth to keep old Rachel from catching them, who hunted together and had never been separated until Sam went to Yale. This is simply a reunion. We will play into it whatever is necessary. It shows mainly the relationship between these two men of different races, how little the difference in race means to them when they are alone.[35]

Not long afterward, both boys are caught under fire in a German advance. As Spoot "tries to cover Sam's body with his own . . . machine gun bullets seek them out and kill them both."[36] Telegrams arrive announcing their deaths. Old Sam and Caroline convey the tragic news to Rachel who, in a coma, regains lucidity long enough before dying to comprehend the tragedy. What follows is "toe-tapped" by Faulkner in this manner:

Sam's parlor, the big house. Rachel's funeral, Rachel in her coffin in state while the Negro choir sings. The family are gathered, a few white friends, old people who have known Rachel and Sam a long time. The dining-room door is open. It is filled with Negroes, standing.

When the spiritual ends, Sam stands at the head of the coffin. On a table behind him are photographs of Spoot and Sam, Junior, in uniform. Sam delivers the oration. (Will use one I delivered in like circumstances over an old Negro servant of my family.)

When Sam ceases, the choir leader gives signal. The choir sings another spiritual into—FADE OUT.[37]

Once again, Faulkner advances the story by a generation. Pearl Harbor has just been bombed. Spoot, Junior, and Carter Hoyt, the intended husband of Sam, Junior's, daughter Lally, are placed in parallel juxtaposition. In this instance, Lally helps Spoot, Junior, study to pass the admittance examination to qualify him for flight training at Tuskegee Institute where a squadron of Negroes is being readied to enter combat. The fate of both young soldiers is left hanging as Faulkner suspends his story.

"Country Lawyer" was submitted but apparently rejected by top management at Warner Bros., then reassigned to other scriptwriters. It was finally brought to the screen in 1947, though the film version bore no similarity to Faulkner's story line. It is tantalizing to speculate on the impact Faulkner's story might have had if it had been produced. Indeed, he had been writing this generational *Bildungsroman* in various manifestations ever since *Sartoris*. Certainly *The Unvanquished*, with its black and white counterparts, Ringo and Bayard, and *Intruder in the Dust*, with Aleck Sander and Chick Mallison, bore remarkably striking affinities, at least in terms of their pairings of members of disparate races. However, if Hollywood had produced the movie as Faulkner envisioned it, there is little doubt that the sympathetic, compassionate, and deferential respect of white toward black, black toward white, would have been sacrificed. In 1943, American audiences would have been disquieted, some outraged; all would have found the premise unrealistic, not "true to life."

Not more than three months later, while working on an original script for "Battle Cry," Faulkner again seized the chance to state his position on the issue of racial relations in America. In this instance, however, he selected a highly unlikely protagonist as his mouthpiece and set the stage for this diatribe in a wholly implausible ambience. Faulkner depicts a small, doomed, rag-tag American battalion guarding, almost by accident, a strategic well against an inexorably advancing German tank force in the African desert. The men have taken time out to vote collectively on whether to abandon their position or stay and fight what doubtless will be their last battle. An Italian prisoner upstages the tense drama with a story about a Greek patriot who helps steal a town bell to keep the occupying Germans from melting it down for bullets. Borrowing from Budd Schulberg's short story "A Bell for Tarchova,"[38] Faulkner stretches his story's climax to create an analogous situation. In fact, it serves as a very transparent excuse to allow himself to preach about voting and universal democracy. But Faulkner fine tunes his poetics by having the Italian specifically direct his statements toward America, a paralyzed black soldier, and his constant defender and companion Akers, a young white Southerner from Alabama. As contrived and forced as this linkage appears, the following eloquent dialogue between the Italian and Battson, the screenplay's Gavin Stevens–type devil's advocate, seems even more disembodied from the immediate action and subsequently was deleted from Faulkner's revised "Second Temporary Draft" of "Battle Cry":

ITALIAN:

So they voted perhaps, what to do, as you are about to vote, because this Greek who was in love, this Demetrios, had lived in America, where all men have a vote in what all are or are not to do—

BATTSON:

All of them except America's folks. There are parts of it where America's folks don't have any say. Ask Akers.

ITALIAN:

That's true. But that condition will change.

BATTSON:

When? They will give America's father and mother and brothers and sisters a vote in exchange for that bullet in his back?

ITALIAN:

I think it will be changed just as soon as the people outside that part of the country, whose concern it is not, stop trying to force them to give America's people a vote. When the people outside that part of the country have cleaned their own house a little, as they had promised to do on the first day of January, 1863—

BATTSON:

So your name is Demetrios. You don't look to me as big or as handsome either as you make yourself out.

ITALIAN:

No. I am not Demetrios. But I have lived in America too, for many years.

(*he continues*)

—clean their own house a little, who have herded America's people into tenements in Harlem and Chicago and Detroit—

BATTSON:

They are free to leave, whenever they don't like it. They can go anywhere they want. They won't have to ride in Jim Crow cars to do it either.

ITALIAN:

So can they leave the Jim Crow part of the country, whenever they like. If the rest of the United States' house were as clean as it should be, as it had given its promise to be on that first day of January, 1863, making them as welcome into it as that old promise implied, I think the Jim Crow people would need much more than just a vote to bribe America's people to remain in the Jim Crow land at all. But perhaps not. Perhaps it is not that simple, not that easy to turn your back on the land, the earth, where you were born and where the only work you know is and where your mother and father and sisters and brothers and children, too, are buried—even if it is only a tenement in Harlem or Chicago or Detroit or a farm in Jim Crow land—

BATTSON:

All right, all right. Get on with your Greek.

ITALIAN:

(*continuing*)

Yes. This Greek. This Demetrios. So perhaps they voted on whether to bring the bell back or not. Or perhaps—[39]

Like "The De Gaulle Story," but for various other reasons, "Battle Cry" was stillborn. Faulkner's lack of success on projects he lavished with his creative energies must have been frustrating, particularly because the evolutionary process he had been working through in his recent fiction and to a large degree in his scriptwriting needed responsive audiences for its expression. For years, Faulkner's perception of the Negro's intolerable plight, especially in the South, slowly intensified. And as his position on this major issue clarified, he sensed in himself a growing urgency, almost a new calling, to champion the causes of human and civil rights: he would begin in his own home state of Mississippi.

For all its arguably negative residual effects on the fiction Faulkner wrote during the final fifteen years of his career, Hollywood did leave him with two salutary legacies: a desire to espouse causes and the technical skills necessary to effectively address those issues. In fact, writing for Hollywood had allowed him to absorb, assimilate, and articulate many of the actual refrains, catchwords, and formulas current among fellow practitioners. One poignant example of Faulkner's acculturation might be seen in the voice-over that accompanies the main title, musical theme, and head-on shot of a locomotive pulling a troop train across the screen in the opening scene of the final version of "Battle Cry":

> Battle cry is that which rises out of man's spirit when those things are threatened which he has lived by and held above price and which have made his life worth the having and the holding: the integrity of his land, the dignity of his home, the honor of his women and the happiness of his children;—that he and they be not cast into slavery which to a man who has once known freedom is worse than death. . . . When these things are threatened, there rises from the throats of free men everywhere, even from beneath oppression's very heel, a defiance, an affirmation and a challenge against which lust and fury shall not stand and before which tyrant and oppressor each in his ephemeral and bloody turn shall vanish from the earth.[40]

In this unmistakably Faulknerian refrain, there are clear echoes of words and phrases, even cadences, which would reappear in Faulkner's Nobel Prize and "Never Be Afraid" University High School speeches of December 1950 and May 1951, respectively. However, even more remarkable is the fact that this voice-over, introducing the most advanced version of the 270-page screenplay written almost exclusively by Faulkner, was not from the pen of William Faulkner but rather, apparently, the single written contribution of the movie's producer, William Bacher.

Already Faulkner had realized that to reach larger audiences he would have to articulate in the "national voice," not through the myriad voices of his novels. But that "national voice," Hollywood's voice, was also not providing him with fulfilling incentives. Certainly, filmland's overriding issue, Freedom versus Oppression, was relevant to him personally, but the stage and its characters were unfamiliar ones and not very stimulating. "Buzz" Bezzerides has noted how Faulkner's work on "The De Gaulle Story" was weakened by a lack of personal knowledge about French customs and events.[41]

The Mississippi setting to which Faulkner returned in mid-September 1945, marking the unofficial end of his servitude at Warner Bros., required no systematic research. Characters and dilemmas were vivid in his memory, and in his imagination they were gasping to be given their freedom. Too soon, Oxford and Lafayette County would become extensions of those imaginary battlefields on which he had done his recent, vicarious soldiering. Enthusiastically, Faulkner would transform Hollywood's back-lot war fronts, beachheads, bunkers, airstrips, military headquarters, trenches, and Underground hideouts into his own familiar Jefferson and Yoknapatawpha County beats and streets, judge's chambers, jails, and quicksand graves.

The writers' compound at Warner Bros., with its cramped cubicles and typing pool "sweatshop" accommodating all Jack Warner's "schmucks with Underwoods" at the end of an endless hall, would be transformed into Faulkner's newly constructed writing "office" at Rowan Oak where he would compose most of his remaining novels. And in transmogrifying the theaters of war, he would also disregard all armistices and formal surren-ders except for the "real" ones proclaimed by V-E Day and the September 2, 1945, signing between the defeated Japanese delegation and General Douglas MacArthur aboard the USS *Missouri*.

In fact, Faulkner would subject the world, the literary world at least, to his own blitzkrieg against inhumane values and mores to which the tradi-tional South, his mid-South specifically, yet owed its obsolete allegiance. He would name his first major offensive *Intruder in the Dust*. And as an ironic footnote, if by bolting Faulkner had abrogated his contract with Warner Bros., vowing never, if possible, to return to Hollywood as a scriptwriter, three years later he would contract Hollywood to come to Oxford, and on his own terms. One month before its publication, Faulk-ner executed with M-G-M a $50,000 sale of the movie rights to *Intruder in the Dust*. Early in 1949, Director Clarence Brown and his California-based crew would ensconce themselves in Oxford and its environs to make the film whose premiere Faulkner would attend at the Lyric Theater just off the Square in downtown Oxford later that same year.

In the spring of 1948, just months prior to publication of *Intruder in the Dust,* addressing a question put to him by a member of the select group gathered at the "confidential" interview on the Ole Miss campus, Faulkner expressed the following prophetic impression about the significance of his region, the South: "The fate of the South is the fate of the Nation."[42] Cer-tainly not by accident, Faulkner had struck upon what would become the central controversial issue of his place and time in American history: the conditions and civil rights of Negroes in Mississippi, Georgia, Alabama, and across America. In fact, Faulkner's motives for writing *Intruder in the Dust* might almost be best described by applying to its composition words that Faulkner had used sixteen years earlier in his introduction to the 1932 Modern Library edition of *Sanctuary:* "I began to think of books in terms of possible money. I decided I might just as well make some of it myself. I took a little time out, and speculated what a person in Mississippi would believe to be current trends, chose what I thought was the right answer and invented the most horrific tale I could imagine and wrote it in about three weeks."[43] *Intruder in the Dust* would be proof positive that Faulkner had mastered his voice lessons. By fusing Hollywood rhetoric and intricate surface plot with his own best aesthetic intentions from the past, he succeeded in producing a novel that would attract a wide audience and that would also lend itself directly to filmic adaptation; he had really taught himself to speak in the "national voice" on the most-listened-to frequency.

The gestation period for *Intruder in the Dust* lasted at least eight years,[44] and elements of its conception can be traced back to "Delta Autumn," published in 1940. In this short story, Ike McCaslin, ostensibly as Faulkner's mouthpiece, or "voice" of moral authority, articulates rigid attitudes about the "wrong and shame" his forebears and their contemporaries promulgated by practicing chattel slavery while permitting to go unchecked violations of their own pious strictures against miscegenation. Although well intentioned, Ike himself is shown to be incapable of resolving his ambivalent dilemma; he is a man whose failure is one of omission. Of Ike, Faulkner says, "at fourteen when he learned of it [he] had believed he could do both [cure the wrong and eradicate the shame] when he became competent and when at twenty-one he became competent he knew that he could do neither but at least he could repudiate the wrong and shame, at least in principle."[45] Unable to commit himself personally to positive actions that might redress the present inferior conditions and inequities suffered by Negroes (which his own recent ancestors helped perpetuate), Ike becomes a recluse from society. In this story, as in section IV of "The Bear," Faulkner makes a subtle, forceful indictment against Isaac McCaslin for his unwillingness to speak out against the wrongs he perceives and feels himself helpless to reverse. At the climactic moment in "Delta Autumn," when Ike realizes that his nephew Roth's mistress, with whom Roth has fathered an illegitimate child, is not a white woman, he cries out, "You're a nigger!" In that same moment, envisioning the old curse come back around on him, he thinks: *"Maybe in a thousand or two thousand years in America. . . . But not now! Not now!"*[46] That Faulkner finds Ike sadly wanting courage is certainly clearly implied; so too is his unspoken condemnation.

By 1948, with publication of *Intruder in the Dust*, Faulkner's message had become much more direct, far less subtly enunciated by his newest mouthpiece, Gavin Stevens, a lawyer with a penchant for bombast and high, flatulent rhetoric. Although considerably more articulate than Ike McCaslin, Stevens is his kindred spirit: a man of high-sounding principle, not action. And yet, as Faulkner related to Malcolm Cowley in 1948, Stevens was "speaking . . . for the best type of liberal Southerners." [47] And, in truth, perhaps Stevens does do more than just perpetuate a pessimistic attitude toward change. Possibly, he contributes in small measure to the solution by proposing actions others might take to help "cure the wrong and eradicate the shame" that Faulkner alludes to in "Delta Autumn." In the following excerpt from *Intruder in the Dust,* Gavin Stevens reveals the dilemma of Southern nationalism, the conflict between mutually held beliefs in equal opportunity and justice for all people and in the maintenance of Southern independence or identity: "The postulate [is] that Sambo is a human being living in a free country and hence must be free. That's what we are really defending: the privilege of setting him free ourselves: which we will have to do for the reason that nobody else can since going on a century ago now the North tried it and have been admitting for seventy-five years now that they failed. So it will have to be us. . . . But it wont be next Tuesday." [48]

Compared with Ike's outraged exclamation, *"Maybe in a thousand or two thousand years in America. . . . But not now! Not now!"* Gavin Stevens' "But it won't be next Tuesday" takes on a slightly more immediate, hopeful ring, albeit somewhat vague. Despite the immediate public success of *Intruder in the Dust,* Faulkner, nonetheless, must have recognized that it was a hybrid: straddling Hollywood and early Faulkner, it fell short of being great fiction. Furthermore, he must have sensed that the attitudes, emotions, and passions expressed by Ike McCaslin and Gavin Stevens were only expostulations of characters in novels: fictive, inner voices whose ultimate persuasiveness depended on successfully rising to the surface through multiple layers of style in order to be heard.

Within another two years, Faulkner would be catapulted into international prominence, and winning the Nobel Prize for Literature would allow him to assume new roles. As elder statesman of American letters, social and philosophical humanitarian, distinguished cultural emissary, political moderate, part-time pedagogue, and conscience for the South, Faulkner would avail himself of public podiums as though each were "a pinnacle from which [he] might be listened to." [49]

Perhaps creating other new Isaac McCaslins and Gavin Stevenses was no longer necessarily the best way he might spend his creative energies. Indeed, throughout the fifties his public voice would grow audibly more strident, his press for social compromise and legislative reform to guarantee personal liberties and equality of opportunity to all citizens increasingly urgent, even desperate. And in February, March, and April 1956, he would dispense altogether with artistic tropes, layers of subtlety, inferential messages, stylistic suspensions of action and character development.

Instead, he would speak directly to the nation through one of its most widely circulated magazines on a subject that by then had consumed him emotionally.

The following two excerpts from Faulkner's essay "A Letter to the North," published in the March 5, 1956, issue of *Life*, essentially reiterate what Gavin Stevens says in the previously quoted speech from *Intruder in the Dust* eight years prior, with one salient exception. Now William Faulkner actually had seized center stage from Stevens. By taking his stand, Faulkner was vindicating himself of having to remain subservient to Ike McCaslin's defeatist resignation and Gavin Stevens' pomposity and arrogance. Unlike his stymied characters, Faulkner was proving to himself, the nation, and the world that he had enough moral courage not to retreat from crucial issues, no matter how ambivalent his own feelings might be or how tenuous his position:

> The Northerner is not even aware yet of what that war really proved. He assumes that it merely proved to the Southerner that he was wrong. It didn't do that because the Southerner already knew he was wrong and accepted that gambit even when he knew it was the fatal one. What that war should have done, but failed to do, was to prove to the North that the South will go to any length, even that fatal and already doomed one, before it will accept alteration of its racial condition by mere force of law or economic threat.[50]

> So I would say to all the organizations and groups which would force integration on the South by legal process: 'Stop now for a moment. You have shown the Southerner what you can do and what you will do if necessary; give him a space in which to get his breath and assimilate that knowledge; to look about and see that (1) Nobody is going to force integration on him from the outside; (2) That he himself faces an obsolescence in his own land which only he can cure; a moral condition which not only must be cured but a physical condition which has got to be cured if he, the white Southerner, is to have any peace, is not to be faced with another legal process or maneuver every year, year after year, for the rest of his life.'[51]

A few months earlier, fearing for the life of a young black student, Autherine Lucy, who was attempting to enroll in the all-white University of Alabama, and trying to bring her plight before the public, Faulkner, with reluctance masked by considerable inebriation, granted an interview to Russell Warren Howe, New York correspondent to the London *Sunday Times*. In an otherwise relatively effective attempt to outline his moderate position regarding the need for vast change while allowing the South time to make changes without fear of court jurisdictions or harassment from federal intervention, Faulkner sounded two regrettably shameful gaffes, which Howe excerpted without their surrounding texts: "As long as there's a middle road, all right, I'll be on it. But if it came to fighting I'd fight for Mississippi against the United States even if it meant going out into the street and shooting Negroes. . . . I will go on saying that the Southerners are wrong and that their position is untenable, but if I have to make the same choice Robert E. Lee made then I'll make it."[52]

The results were traumatic for Faulkner, and despite his attempts to retract his remarks, he had weakened his position by casting doubt on himself as a logical thinker on the subject of race relations. He submitted recantatory letters to the editor of the *Reporter* and to *Time* in an abortive effort to excuse the embarrassing passages Howe cited as "contain[ing] opinions which I have never held, and statements which no sober man would make and, it seems to me, no sane man believe."[53] He further insisted that he would have caught and rectified any inaccuracies or misquotations "if I had seen it [the interview] before it went into print."[54]

Curious indeed is the remarkable similarity between this situation and Faulkner's attempts to excuse his complicity in the Hemingway flap he had stirred up nine years earlier on the Ole Miss campus when his comment denigrating Hemingway's "courage" was quoted out of context in the national media. At that time, he had written directly to Hemingway his apology for "this damn stupid thing," saying, "I was just making $250.00, I thought informally, not for publication, or I would have insisted on looking at the stuff before it was released."[55] This time Faulkner submitted his apologies to the nation, but both responses were similar and after the fact; neither had much effect on silencing the repercussions of his original words. Clearly, in both cases, Faulkner was the loser.

Yet, in hindsight, it seems fair to say that to the end of his days Faulkner never learned to cure himself of "the curse of human speech,"[56] or to have "broken [himself] of talking."[57] But equally, it should be emphasized that to the very end he also refused to "break the pencil,"[58] quit writing, as so often during the last decade of his life he threatened to do when becoming aware of his own deteriorating capacities as an artist. In fact, *The Reivers* was published just six weeks before he died on July 6, 1962.

Even though during the last fifteen years of his life Faulkner's most urgent requirements for self-expression seem to have changed from writing innovative fiction to voicing his opinions publicly, to his great credit he proved that he possessed indefatigable courage to take risks. More explicitly, what Faulkner had written to General Lanham in 1948 in defending and praising Thomas Wolfe's "failure"—"he had the most courage: to risk being guilty of bad taste, clumsiness, mawkishness, dullness; to shoot the works win or lose and damn the torpedoes"[59]—he arrogated to himself also by placing his accomplishment second to Wolfe's. When Malcolm Cowley asked him about writing, Faulkner had said, "Get it down. Take chances. It may be bad, but that's the only way you can do anything really good."[60] Had he been asked about public speaking, doubtless he would have responded with a similar assertion: Get it out. Take chances!

SIX

SORTING THE MAIL

"To live anywhere in the world today and be against equality because of race or color, is like living in Alaska and being against snow."
—William Faulkner, "On Fear: Deep South in Labor: Mississippi" [1]

"Because you escape nothing, you flee nothing; the pursuer is what is doing the running and tomorrow night is nothing but one long sleepless wrestle with yesterday's omissions and regrets."
—William Faulkner, *Intruder in the Dust* [2]

On December 10, 1950, in Stockholm, Sweden, William Faulkner received the 1949 Nobel Prize for Literature. This occasion would mark his emergence from a long and well-guarded privacy into the realm of public celebrity, and although he would continue to produce fiction, publishing five novels and three major compilations between 1950 and his death in July 1962,[3] he would involve himself directly in activities that would reinforce his unofficial role as a cultural emissary of the United States, humanitarian to the world.

By 1956, the most significant of these involvements, his position on civil rights in the South, had come to flash point. Like one of his favorite fictional characters, Don Quixote, Faulkner would sally forth to tilt lances with foes imaginary and very real; and at times reminiscent of the Don, he too might have been inclined to dub himself with the literal nom de plume, Knight of the Doleful Countenance. Yet, for all his disillusionments and rebuffs from family and a faceless public, he was decidedly, like Don Quixote, "hijo de sus obras," son of his own self-motivated labors and consequences.

During these years, one manifestation of Faulkner's celebrity was the actual mail he had become accustomed to receiving, letters from every conceivable source presuming humbly or arrogantly to impose on his time and energies. There is no way of quantifying the ratio of mail received to responses made, but even if he allowed it to accumulate, there is little doubt that he read his mail. In the case of letters coming in to him during periods when his essays and open letters on civil rights were appearing in national and international publications, there is yet greater certainty that he was attentive and inclined to keep up with it. After all, Faulkner had calculated his essays to provoke just this kind of stir from the public. Actually, in many essays and letters to the editor during 1956, Faulkner made specific reference to the fact that he was quite aware of responses to his public appeals, especially in the form of incoming letters that, he conceded, were not generally supportive of his convictions and principles.

During a visit I made with Victoria Fielden Johnson in her home in Cape Coral, Florida, May 20–24, 1985, she and I discovered among family artifacts a packet containing forty-three letters addressed to William Faulkner, some mailed directly to Oxford, Mississippi, others to the offices of Time-Life in New York and Chicago or to the headquarters of the *Reporter* magazine in New York.[4] Mrs. Johnson had no difficulty recalling the circumstances surrounding the seemingly anomalous letters she had inherited from her father, William, and mother, Victoria Franklin Fielden, Faulkner's stepdaughter. During my stay, Mrs. Johnson related to me how Kate Baker, an Oxford neighbor and close friend of William and Estelle Faulkner, had driven over to her mother's house in Oxford in 1973 to return the packet to Mrs. Fielden. Kate Baker told her then that Faulkner had given her this group of letters shortly after he had read them. Like Faulkner, Kate Baker had been keenly sensitive to the civil rights agitation that was then straining Oxford and the entire South, and she was highly sympathetic toward Faulkner's outspoken convictions on the subject. Apparently, during Faulkner's many comings and goings between Oxford and the world, Kate Baker had been unable to return the letters to him, then had misplaced them amidst her own household effects. They had gone unnoticed by her for seventeen years. Now, housecleaning, she had discovered them and wished Mrs. Fielden to have them.

The forty-three letters cover a period of approximately six weeks, the earliest being dated March 7, 1956, and the latest April 19, 1956. By far the most significant letters, representing about two-thirds of the entire group, are those containing direct or indirect responses to two specific publications that occurred just prior to and during this time period: Faulkner's controversial interview with Russell Warren Howe, published in the United States on March 22, 1956, in the *Reporter,* and "A Letter to the North," which *Life* printed on March 5, 1956.

The remaining one-third of the letters, not bearing directly on civil

rights, reveal a diffuse spectrum, which makes possible an overview of the
kind and caliber of requests to which Faulkner's ubiquitous celebrity had
made him vulnerable. One came from his Italian publisher, Alberto Mon-
dadori, concerning hope that Faulkner might help secure permission to
translate *Sartoris* to complete the full run of titles to appear in Italian. It
contained the following remark: "It is a real present we make to the Italian
readers, for I know they are keenly interested in following your production, which is for them very difficult to understand in the original text,
both for language and form." Other requests included three invitations to
speak. One came from the William Faulkner Chapter of a Memphis high
school Quill and Scroll Society. A second, from a woman's college in
North Carolina, reads in part:

> The students here are deeply concerned about the integration imbroglio. At
> our last student government assembly, a student introduced a resolution stat-
> ing that we, the Students of the Women's College of Duke University, believe
> in equal educational opportunities for all people, regardless of race and reli-
> gion, and that these principles should be incorporated in our admissions pol-
> icy. We, the Student Forum Committee, would like to have a Southerner of
> your stature and with your sentiments speak to the students concerning this
> problem.

A third invitation came from an Eastern Arts Festival whose board of gov-
ernors "has recommended an invitation for yourselves to be . . . the Festival's guests for the entire week . . . Mrs. Faulkner and yourself . . . each
speaker delivering one brief, informal chat after luncheon; any day during
your week's stay . . . Our Annual Audience Poll has indicated their eager-
ness in listening to and meeting you."

In a different vein, a letter from a New York correspondent reads: "Will
Mr. Faulkner kindly favor me with a few lines of his handwriting and his
signature on the enclosed card, to add to a very notable collection of autograph letters." Another far more direct and less discreet letter states: "We,
the Junior Chamber of Commerce of Bethlehem, Pennsylvania, would like
to impose upon your great appeal to the American Public and request that
you donate some item . . . The item may be inconsequential in value but,
because of its association with you, we hope to realize substantially more
than its real value."

Seven other letters from this group might be categorized loosely as literary in scope. One from a Pennsylvania high school senior requests assistance on the conclusion of her term paper about Faulkner's literature; one
is from a University of Southern California graduate student doing research on "pro-slavery poets who wrote and published during the years

1850–1861." Having found only "two poets and three poems," he asks of Faulkner, "Could you, as the greatest living voice of the American South, possibly suggest a few other names of poets who might fall within the framework of my topic?" Another letter, from a Viennese journalist, asks Faulkner to help him clarify the implications of the title, *Requiem for a Nun,* as he fears its current translation into German will create "resentment [that] might mount high among the narrow-minded." Yet another letter, from an art cooperative in Buenos Aires, Argentina, asks permission to stage *Requiem for a Nun.* One letter, bearing the AP Newsfeatures letterhead, states: "We're wondering if you would be interested in writing a special article for the Associated Press pointing out the ways in which you believe American Literature stands on its own, what it has contributed to American culture and what its objectives and shortcomings are." A similar letter from a New York intellectual concludes: "How I would like to gain your reaction to the word 'humanist'! In what I hope will be a definitive study of the word, I should greatly appreciate a brief response which may be included. Having read most of your work, I should imagine you might have something to say whether about theistic or naturalistic humanism . . . but I am not sure and the tangled-fire explanations of your thought are of little help."

Two of the three letters that arrived from France during this period ran a remarkable gamut: one was from a Parisian asking Faulkner to lend his name in support of an "International Jazz Club"; the other solicits Faulkner, as a member of the Nobel Academy, to vote for a particular candidate for the "Grand Prix De Littérature 1956." Finally, from the "Brown-Forman Distillers Corporation at Louisville in Kentucky," Faulkner received an invitation to attend their "22 Annual Derby Party at the Distillery" on May 3, 1956. The previous year he had traveled to Louisville on the cuff of *Sports Illustrated* to write an article on the Derby.[5] Evidently, he had not worn thin his welcome!

Obviously, this pastiche of incoming mail can only hint at the actual quantity and the almost inconceivable variety of requests Faulkner was getting during this stage in his career. Yet, it seems to me, to be privy even to this sampling gives us certain distinct advantages: most singularly, having the privilege of sorting through some of Faulkner's mail allows us to participate vicariously in his experience, which, no matter how ephemeral and tangential, nonetheless makes for a potentially closer, more textured approximation of the *Weltanshauung* that Faulkner himself must have been perceiving during the twilight of his life. Having access to this group of letters makes Faulkner's oft-quoted exhortations against strangers intruding on his privacy seem far less calculatedly cynical or even misanthropic. We hope we shall be forgiven for being history's intruders, especially since the majority of these letters render an expanded context in which to view William Faulkner operating during the mid-fifties. Indeed, those dealing explicitly with the race problem help sharpen hindsight's focus and, as such, allow us to make even less partial, more palpably objective judgments regarding Faulkner's courageous stand in support of the central issue of his time and place: civil rights for Negroes.

Faulkner's position on civil rights was most elaborately postulated in his manifesto entitled "A Letter to the North." In this essay he asserted:

> From the beginning of this present phase of the race problem in the South, I have been on record as opposing the forces in my native country which would keep the condition out of which this present evil and trouble has grown. Now I must go on record as opposing the forces outside the South which would use legal or police compulsion to eradicate that evil overnight. I was against compulsory segregation. I am just as strongly against compulsory integration. . . .
>
> So I would say to the NAACP and all the organizations who would compel immediate and unconditional integration 'Go slow now. Stop now for a time, a moment. . . .'[6]

Regarding his own personal position within the matrix, Faulkner saw himself foremost as a son of the South, a liberally enlightened son whose most pressing responsibility as its spokesman was to help convert those still crusading for obsolete ideologies by proselytizing for change—moderate, gradual change, to be sure. He envisioned himself and a relatively few other Southerners in his milieu as occupying a middle ground, "still being Southerners, yet not being a part of the general majority Southern point of view; by being present yet detached, committed and attainted neither by Citizens' Council nor NAACP; by being in the middle, being in position to say to any incipient irrevocability: 'Wait, wait now, stop and consider first.'"[7]

However, Faulkner's greatest anxiety arose from fear of being compelled to accept outside intervention, federal legislation enforced by troops and national guardsmen, because then he would have "to vacate that middle where [he] could have worked to help the Negro improve his condition";[8] he would then be forced to side with one group or the other. For aesthetic reasons, when writing about this approach-avoidance complex, Faulkner conveniently could avoid defining this alternative. In "A Letter to the North," he would say simply that, given no other choices, he and his fellow advocates of moderate change "will have to make a new choice."[9] Nor was it necessary to stipulate a precise time frame in which the changes leading to a fully integrated society would take effect.

The actual situation that provoked Faulkner to write "A Letter to the North," the court-ordered admission of Autherine Lucy to the all-white University of Alabama and the dire problem of her safety, also gave rise to two even more urgent attempts to bring Miss Lucy's plight to the public's attention. On February 21, 1956, just after Faulkner learned that the Supreme Court had overruled the high court of Alabama and made mandatory Autherine Lucy's admission on March 5, 1956, and on being notified that *Life* could not publish his "Letter to the North" until the week of March 5, he desperately acquiesced to what unwittingly became the highly controversial interview with Russell Warren Howe, of the London *Sunday Times*.[10]

Having steadily increased his intake of alcohol for nearly three weeks, Faulkner allowed himself to be more garrulous and explicitly volatile on one specific point than he had been in his essays. Possibly, Howe had antagonized or subtly taken advantage of Faulkner's vulnerable condition. Regardless, Faulkner punctuated his otherwise relatively coherent, consistent, and effective interview (subsequently published in the London *Sunday Times* on March 4, 1956, and in the *Reporter* on March 22, 1956) with the aforementioned unforgettable statements: "As long as there's a middle road, all right, I'll be on it. But if it came to fighting I'd fight for Mississippi against the United States even if it meant going out into the street and shooting Negroes. . . . I will go on saying that the Southerners are wrong and that their position is untenable, but if I have to make the same choice Robert E. Lee made then I'll make it." Whether isolated from or read in their contexts, these damaging remarks cast for some, perhaps many, an irrevocably ambiguous and unsettling shadow on Faulkner's credibility as a spokesman for racial equality.

Unfortunately, the interview does not record Howe's questions or conceivably baiting remarks, which might have provoked Faulkner's instantly attributable comments about "going out into the street and shooting Negroes." In "A Letter to the North," Faulkner had addressed the possibility of being preempted from his position by federal intervention with the veiled allowance that under such circumstances he and his fellow workers on the Negroes' behalf necessarily would "have to make a new choice." Always in his prose he had time to ponder and select the best possible choice of words to make his points effectively; obviously, this had not been the case with Howe, whose "verbatim shorthand notes" of Faulkner's comments had seemingly been etched in stone.

On February 24, 1956, three days after the Howe interview, and even more visibly inebriated, Faulkner went on live radio as a guest celebrity of "The Tex and Jinx Show" and made yet another set of infelicitous remarks trying to promote integration.[11] This time, when again forced to answer directly, without the safety net of his own revisable prose, he suggested that the racial situation in the South might fare better were the policy of maintaining separate schools for blacks and whites to continue. Obviously, to anyone who had read Faulkner's April 3, 1955, letter to the editor in the Memphis *Commercial Appeal,* this statement would have sounded a patently flat note. In that letter, he had called for one school system for "white and Negro both." [12] For Faulkner, the lingering stalemate seemed to center on the notion of "forced integration." He believed that if the Negro were exposed to superior education he would advance on his own merit to full equality of opportunity for jobs, housing, political positions, and all the fundamental freedoms and amenities denied blacks. Indeed, at the outset of his essay "On Fear: The South in Labor" in the June 1956 issue of *Harper's,* seemingly articulating an explicitly apologetic corrective to the slip he had made about segregated schooling on "The Tex and Jinx Show," Faulkner would clarify and reinforce his insistence on integrated schooling. [13]

A letter from the editors of *Time,* dated April 13, 1956, addressed to "Mr. William Faulkner / Box 124 / Oxford, Mississippi," began: "Thank you for writing to us at length concerning the statement about Mississippi attributed to you in our March 26 cover story on Senator Eastland. We also want to take this opportunity to acknowledge Mrs. Faulkner's wire concerning it." While concluding with a formal confirmation of the forthcoming publication of his letter with only "a few slight deletions," this letter from *Time* could have done little to assuage what by that time must have been extreme disillusionment occasioned by the importunate comments he had made in his interview with Howe.

As the *Time* letter promised, Faulkner's recantatory disclaimer was published in the April 23 issue. In it, Faulkner attempted to distance, if not completely disassociate, himself from obviously irresponsible remarks "imputed" to him, reasoning that the specifically cited passages from the interview "contain opinions which I have never held, and statements which no sober man would make and, it seems to me, no sane man believe." [14] Also, as promised in *Time*'s letter to Faulkner, his statements were followed by a terse rejoinder from Howe. Actually, four days earlier, a similar letter to the editor had appeared in the *Reporter;* [15] it also was accompanied by Howe's rebuttal, though in that instance Howe's remarks were more emphatic than those *Time*'s editors had printed. Howe wrote: "All the statements attributed to Mr. Faulkner were directly transcribed by me from verbatim shorthand notes of the interview. If the more Dixiecrat remarks misconstrue his thoughts, I, as an admirer of Mr. Faulkner's, am glad to know it. But what I set down is what he said." [16]

A textual comparison of Faulkner's two letters to the editor reveals few dissimilarities, even in phraseology; however, in the earlier letter Faulkner submitted to the *Reporter*, he mentions having seen a quotation of his "shooting Negroes in the street" statement in *Newsweek* as well as in *Time*. More significantly, he suggests that, although he has not seen the interview "as printed," his conclusion that "some parts of the interview with me . . . are not correct" is based on insights derived from firsthand evidence, namely, "from letters I have received." There is no way of knowing how many letters Faulkner got in direct response to his *Reporter* interview with Howe, but four extant letters that once were in his possession attest to the fact that, despite his most dire anxieties and insecurities about the ensuing scandal he had precipitated, public perception of his pronouncements ranged from cynical and vitriolic outrage to praiseworthy confirmation, all with varying degrees of qualification.

The first of these, dated March 16, 1956, postmarked Paris, France, and subscribed by thirty-four Members of the National Union of Family Allocations, was written as a direct outcry against the "go[ing] out into the street and shoot blacks" comment from the interview's appearance in the *Reporter*. Translated into English, it reads: "Considering, whatever may be your position with regard to the segregation problem, that these words reflect a total absence of humanity on your part, we are proceeding to rise up vigorously against your attitude which, because of your fame, risks having a momentous repercussion. We uniformly advise you that as of today, we are asking our library personnel to refrain from the acquisition of works bearing your name."

Conversely, excerpts from the following two letters demonstrate essentially affirmative and complimentary approval of Faulkner's position as expressed in the *Reporter* interview:

> Dear Mr. Faulkner:
>
> A few days ago the interview you gave the London Times man, as reproduced in THE REPORTER, came to my attention. As one born down in Texas, I want to thank you from the bottom of my heart. And, as an SAE, I wish to say that I am proud of you. . . .
>
> Your words are very apt: "There is no such thing as an Anglo-Saxon heritage and an African heritage. There is the heritage of man." Those are great words.
>
> I wish the hotheads in the north would read what you have to say.

> Dear Mr. Faulkner:
>
> I want to write to you, and tell you how much I appreciate your interview in *The Reporter*. It is a strong note of real wisdom and courage and understanding, so badly and quickly needed now. . . .

I think—and I have many friends here in Princeton who take the extreme liberal position—that your position is the difficult position, and that it takes real greatness to advocate calm and patience and understanding of such widespread ignorance. . . .

Also, I would like to say, that I appreciate very much that you speak out in your great understanding and feeling for human beings. Not only do you write it down in your magnificent *Light in August*. I don't demand this of artists, but I'm always glad when they do it.

Thank you again—perhaps you have saved Miss Lucy's life. What a perfect name—Autherine Juanita Lucy.

The final letter in this sequence, displaying a brand of arrogance, was written by a New York author and lecturer:

Dear Mr. Faulkner:

Your Negroes come to New York, just as the Irish came from the potato blight, and the East-European Jew after the pograms [*sic*]. Your Negroes come for similar reasons: to find decency and build a better life.

If you care for the Negro, advise him to come here. New York is impersonal and hard, and grumbles at all the new refugees, but New York is civilized and will not turn the Negro away. Those that are strong, and well-advised, will educate themselves at the public schools and colleges here, and get—free and with respect—a better education than they could get anywhere in the South. Once they have that, their battle will be half won.

The other half to be won is the bitter memory that less than a century ago a dark skin meant slavery to a whiter skin. In your South the Negro is never allowed to forget it. But in New York he grows in our streets, along side the Puerto-Rican, the Jew and the Mediterraneans who treat him as just another guy. This is worth more to a refugee Negro than all the pious mouthings about how happy he is in "his place" in the South. If he wishes to avoid the Southern Hospitality which spits on him, robs him and then calls him "Nigger," tell him to get on a train and come here.

There is a saying in Harlem; "better a lamp post on Lenox Avenue, than the govenor [*sic*] of Georgia."

The author of this letter placed in the bottom left margin the following postscript: "I was fascinated by the 3 novels of yours that I read. If only *you* had grown up in N.Y.!"

There can be little question that while Faulkner, as writer of essays and letters to the editor, had complete mastery over his conscience and its conscious expression, as public speaker, he had less control. After all, in the first medium he had the luxury of proofreading to ensure the efficacy and correctness of every syllable as well as each weighty implication. By contrast, when venturing out of his special province, either to make a "public" statement through person-to-person interviews or when asked to respond to unrehearsed questions on live radio, frequently he might confuse his well-intentioned emotions with the facts and say flagrant things. In both letters to the *Reporter* and *Time* of April 19 and 23, respectively, Faulkner implied he would have caught any tactless or factually incorrect statement "if I had seen it [the interview] before it went into print."

Fundamentally, Faulkner's position on civil rights was of a whole; it was ethical and universally humanitarian in its Gandhian nonviolent posture. Only by focusing on singular lapses, lifting them from the large contextual body of Faulkner's pronouncements on civil rights issues, thereby clouding with ambiguity his otherwise bold humanitarianism, might one conclude that his essential formulations for dealing with the endemic malaise of race relations in the South and in the United States were hypocritical or disingenuous. Indeed, it might be easier to excuse Faulkner's few public lapses, or at least put them in proper perspective, if one were aware of his physical condition and emotional state during that brief period between February and early March 1956, when he was in New York anticipating publication of "A Letter to the North" and making himself available at any cost to promote whatever immediate reconciliatory and ameliorative actions he could to help avert threats or actual danger to Autherine Lucy.

In a reflective letter to Joan Williams ten months later, Faulkner apologized for having failed to meet her for an engagement they had made during that period of personal turmoil:

> At that time, the Lucy girl had been expelled from the University of Alabama. The next step would be for the NAACP to return her by compulsion, force. If they did that, I believed she would be killed. I had been rushing here and there, trying to get air time before they sent her back. I dont know why I thought then that drinking could help, but that's what I was doing, a lot of it. I woke up that morning in an apartment not mine with just sense enough to tell you I couldn't make the luncheon, collapsed. Came to Friday and friends resuscitated me just in time to make a presentable appearance on the Tex Something, Tex and somebody like a Frankie and Johnny team on the air from the Waldorf and make my plea.[17]

If nothing else, this document makes possible a more insightful appreciation of the calculated strategy Faulkner employed in couching the apologies he sent to the editors of the *Reporter* and *Time* magazines in which he totally disclaimed apparently false quotations "imputed" to him, relegating them to "statements which no sober man would make and, it seems to me, no sane man believe." Arguably, Faulkner could have considered himself during that period in a state of inebriated non compos mentis.

What Faulkner did not relate in his letter to Joan Williams was that a week and a half after arriving in Oxford from New York he had collapsed from severe alcoholic intoxication and on March 18, 1956, had been confined to Baptist Memorial Hospital in Memphis. However, on March 23, the national wire services did report that Faulkner was "convalescing satisfactorily" from an unidentified illness.[18] But at least one young writer, Terry Southern, was aware of Faulkner's condition and on March 28 did respond, wishing Faulkner a "quick and entire recovery." He went on to say: "I suppose I was either always too awed by your actual presence to properly say how much I like your writing, or else perhaps felt the saying it would have been (from my standpoint) too superfluous—if not even more tediously useless (from your own). Anyway, it will always be an inspiration to me, and I want to express my thanks for the opportunity of being with you."

On that same day, William Eastlake, a novelist from New Mexico, wrote Faulkner. Quite possibly reading "A Letter to the North" had stirred memories of an acquaintanceship that may have occurred evanescently around the time Faulkner was fleeing from Hollywood in late September 1945. In their hyperbolic tone, the following excerpts from Eastlake's tongue-in-cheek letter almost seem to have been mined from the same vein as the Al Jackson letters Faulkner and Sherwood Anderson had exchanged thirty years earlier:[19]

Dear Bill Faulkner:
I got nothing but horses now on the ranch. The damn Indians eat cows, brand and all. My neighbors are fixin' to get ready to take their stuff up on the mountain. But I am fed up with cattle. It's about time the Indians earned their own living. The Indians have been exploiting us since they discovered us— egged the first covered wagons on. I will try a few more Angus and that's the end. How are your animals doing? . . .
When do you think you might make it? It seems to me you should get shut of writing for a while (you write better than anyone in the damn world now) and do something serious like buying one of my horses.

Between March 7, when Faulkner settled in at Rowan Oak to unwind from his New York trip, and March 18, when he was hospitalized, and again between March 24, evidently having recuperated sufficiently from acute alcoholic incapacitation, and early April, when he briefly traveled to

Charlottesville to see his first grandchild before continuing on again to New York, he attended to accumulated correspondence. Already, responses to the March 4 London *Sunday Times* interview with Howe and the March 5 *Life* essay, "A Letter to the North," had begun to pour into offices of the *Reporter* and Time-Life in New York and Chicago, respectively, and were being forwarded directly on to Oxford. Sometime soon after his arrival in Oxford on March 7, 1956, Faulkner wrote to the editors of *Life* magazine. His open letter began: "Since *Life* printed my 'Letter to the North' I have received many replies from outside the South. Many of them criticized the reasoning *in* the letter but so far none of them seem to have divined the reason *behind* the letter [which was] the attempt of an individual to save the South and the whole United States too from the blot of Miss Autherine Lucy's death."[20]

This letter to the editor appeared in the March 26 issue of *Life*. In some ways it is similar to the twin disclaimers of the Howe interview that Faulkner would place in the *Reporter* and *Time* almost a month later; however, this time his need to make qualifications would result from his not having been explicit enough, rather than overly so. In fact, in "A Letter to the North," Faulkner had only once mentioned by name Autherine Lucy or alluded to her plight at the University of Alabama. Also, in this letter, Faulkner reaffirmed what he had already stated in his "Letter to the North," namely, that "since I went on record as being opposed to compulsory racial inequality, I have received many letters." Indeed, his March 26 letter in *Life* was accompanied by four ostensibly random samples the editors had chosen to supplement Faulkner's contribution. Both letters "from outside the South" are strident; both are written by Negroes with grievances. The two samples from within the South are from presumably white Alabamians, natives of the abusive state where the demonstrations had been occurring; both these letters are sympathetic to Faulkner's moderate views. Obviously, *Life's* editorial staff was attempting to add support to Faulkner's contention in "A Letter to the North" that "the rest of the United States knows next to nothing about the South."

Regarding Faulkner's qualification, it might be argued that he may have greatly exaggerated the actual significance of the Lucy incident, at least in real, physical terms. As a symbolic event, surely he was correct in employing it as a pivot for his expressions. And yet, rereading his last brief paragraph, one can hardly fail to evoke with poignant irony the situation that developed in Faulkner's hometown of Oxford, Mississippi, just three months after his death in July 1962, when James Meredith made his stand as the first Negro to gain admittance to the University of Mississippi. Faulkner had concluded his March 26 letter to the editor of *Life:* "She was not sent back, so the letter ["A Letter to the North"] was not needed for that purpose. I hope it never will be. But if a similar situation bearing the seed of a similar tragedy should arise again, maybe the letter will help to serve."[21]

In hindsight, it appears, perhaps, that Faulkner underestimated the clarity of his "reasoning *in* the letter," that it may have been far more significant than the "reason *behind* the letter." Portions extracted from the five following letters written from outside the South, which Faulkner received in Oxford, manifest reactions laudatory rather than critical of his reasoning in "A Letter to the North."

Dear Mr. Faulkner,

Let's hope the transformation is achieved with sound common sense and in the absence of violence and bloodshed. Don't desert your position in the middle of this issue. The South needs wisdom and reason now far more than it needs patriotism.

Toronto, Canada

Sir:

After reading your masterly article in LIFE, I am taking the liberty of enclosing herewith a typewritten copy of one of my articles which appeared in the Los Angeles Times of April 2nd. . . .

I am not sending this with the object of comparing your story and mine on the same level (I have not yet "arrived") but it might give you an additional idea and also assure you that many others are thinking along your lines—maybe enough to get officials to reconsider or at least to move slowly.

Los Angeles, California

Dear Mr. Faulkner—

First may we suggest that you make a mistake in thinking of northerners as a massive heap of ignorance when it comes to thinking about the South and its problems. Granted we may not know—and keep an open mind—since who knows what your reactions would be were the situation reversed.

Secondly—we agree with the Supreme Court decision—and we agree with you wholeheartedly that now is the time to stop—and go slow. We have been pleased by the progress made in the past ten years in race relations and we are pained at the strife and furor of the past months since the decision was made.

Northville, New York

Dear Sir,

I was rather surprised to read in *Life* Magazine that you had received many critical letters from the North concerning your letter on integration. Actually,

I believe there are a great many more "moderates" up North than many
Southerners think, partly due to the fact that the moderates do not tend to
write letters on the subject so readily. Many of us are very sympathetic with
your problems in the South & are urging sympathy and moderation, as we
realize we are far from free from prejudice ourselves.

Menlo Park, California

Dear Mr. William Faulkner,

In this country nobody is able to understand that civilized people can treat
negroes as many Americans do at present. Autherine Lucy's fate can make us
hate these stupid unfeeling people who are not able to place themselves in the
same situation (in their imagination). USA loses a lot of reputation on account of such conditions. Of course it is not *all* Americans who show such
bad behavior, but however few they are (and I hope they are few) this abomi-
nable behavior reduces the reputation. At first I did not understand your
words the other day, but now I see that the purpose was as could be expected
from you, and of course the progress must come gradually, but *please* help the
negroes and accelerate progress as much as possible, for conditions now are a
disgrace for civilized people—and heartless for the poor innocent.

Copenhagen, Denmark

Regardless of the essay's relatively unambivalent and nonprejudicial
tone, there were those who read "A Letter to the North" and found in it
just the tinder they needed to reignite their own bigoted animosities. Mis-
construing Faulkner's attitudes, convictions, and purposes, the authors of
the following two letters wasted little time in communicating with the person in whom, mistakenly, they felt they had discovered a kindred spirit:

Dear Mr. Faulkner,

I live in a small southern city—perhaps thirty-thousand population. . . .
The primary reason for segregation here is to keep the white race white, so far
as I can see. But you see so many half-whites. Which race do they belong?
None of the white women I know want integration. No southern woman
wants integration, because she has been taught to fear negro men. Cant that
be understood by anyone. Fear is a strong thing and we are panic-stricken.
What shall we teach our daughters? Mine is eleven.

Dear Mr. Faulkner,

Countless LIFE readers must have been deeply stirred by your searching
article of March 5th. It is to be hoped that you will use other avenues to
broadcast this just and worthy viewpoint. Heretofore, mostly only one side of
the situation has been presented, and then not without prejudice. How then

are men, even in high places to judge? In judging a matter righteously, should they not actually KNOW the facts concerning the segregation question?

Are they not aware that segregation is practiced in every phase of human existence? The Negro students at Tuskeegee [*sic*] Institute of Alabama practice segregation according to color. Negroes as well as all other nationalities are happier when they are with those most like themselves. They feel normal and natural and not "thrown away" as in the presence of mixed groups. Negroes especially have a natural good humor and are always happy when among themselves, as evidenced by the town down South which is inhabited by Negroes only. They are so happy among themselves there is no need for a jail.

Do the thinking peoples in high places actually know about the terrible atrocities committed every hour of every day in the mixed sections of their cities where mixed romances turn into ghastly murders? Have they weighed their decision through experience among the Negroes in these crimeridden areas where the whites and the Negroes are forced economically to live next door to one another? Do they know anything at all about the deep devotion that exists between the Southern Negro and his White Folks?

Search the hearts of every Negro in America. Surely he will tell you that he wants to remain as God created him. Booker T. Washington was a great Negro, a great American. He was also an humble man. George Washington Carver was a great humanitarian. Who could enumerate those who have thought first of others? Truly they have their reward.

Like yourself, Mr. Faulkner, we are proud of the illuminating article you have written, and we want to thank you from the bottom of our hearts.

We, like all peoples, are for a world with a clear and concise understanding. And having that understanding, may we practice the dictates of an understanding heart and there will be no inner rebellion. No prejudice. No resentment. But rather peace, good will, harmony, and brotherly love for all peoples everywhere.

The next two letters exemplify attitudes remarkably similar to two strident selections from black writers "from outside the South," which the editors of *Life* had included with Faulkner's letter in their March 26 issue.

Dear Sir:

The present unrest is not of northern design. It cannot be denied that the Supreme Court decision gave heart to the colored peoples of the south, but having taken heart they seem determined to go forward. Many of the young men have tasted a different sort of life when they have been transported to the armed forces. Some through the GI Bill have been educated in the north. The cry of Moses to "Let my people go" has always held a place in the hearts of colored Christians. The unity of the participants in the bus boycott continued to amaze your neighbors who were convinced that most Negroes preferred "peace to equality."

"Wait, wait now, stop and consider first." This is not a revolutionary statement and after 98 years it would seem we have waited long enough. "You cannot force integration by legal edict," this we hear over and over, "These things have to be done gradually." There is such a thing as moving so slowly that you are going backward.

Mr. William Faulkner

Your main theme is understanding of the southern white man and his situation.

What makes him hate the Black man to the point of utter madness?

What causes him to let his hate degenerate his soul and turn his insides as black as the very pits of hell.

Segregation creates an economic stale-mate and yet the white southern man choose to live with it, why?

This hatred causes him to murder innocent women and children, to lie and steal, rape and pillage, why?

When a black man commits a crime or some one says he has, he is shot down like a dog or lynched, why?

A person or group of people who would do these things, would you say was sane and rational, just how would you classify such people Mr Faulkner? You have asked for understanding Mr Faulkner, we are trying to understand Mr Faulkner, and have been trying for one hundred years.

You want the forces of decency and equality to stop so that the forces of evil and corruption can lick their wounds. Have they been wounded Mr Faulkner?

Peace! you say. At this point you go so far as to quote an old colored southern woman whose education came from Bilbo, Rankin and Eastland, education of fear and mistrust.

You speak of personal crimes, since when do a racial issue become a personal crime? The south do not raise its voice against any injustices that occur in the north against colored people, because that would be like casting the first stone. And only he who is without sin has that distinction. And our Supreme court has that distinction and have thrown the first stone Mr Faulkner.

You speak of personal crimes of race against race, when a southern white man forces his intention on a colored woman and she conceives and give birth to his children is that a personal crime race against race? When a southern white man demands that a negro rise and give him his seat on a public bus or train is that a personal crime race against race Mr Faulkner? When the negro work from sunrise to sunset without proper compensation, ill housed, ill fed

and not given equal opportunity to vote and to obtain a proper education, is
that a personal crime race against race Mr Faulkner?

Trying to Understand

On April 15, 1956, Faulkner also received the following teletype from
California news analyst Sidney Roger. Like the preceding letters, this one
was in direct response to Faulkner's "A Letter to the North."

WILLIAM FAULKNER
DOCTOR W. E. B. DUBOIS—88 YEAR OLD NEGRO CO-FOUNDER OF NAACP,
CHALLENGES YOU TO DEBATE ON STEPS OF COURT HOUSE SUMNER, MISSIS-
SIPPI WHERE EMMETT TILL CASE WAS TRIED, ON SUBJECT OF YOUR "GO
SLOW NOW" ADVICE TO NEGROS
   REQUEST FOR PUBLIC DISCUSSION WITH YOU WAS MADE BY DR DUBOIS IN
RECORDED INTERVIEW WITH NEWS ANALYST SIDNEY ROGER ON RADIO STA-
TION KROW, OAKLAND, CALIFORNIA SUNDAY APRIL 15TH AT 8 PM
   URGENTLY REQUEST YOUR EARLIEST REPLY TO DR DUBOIS CARE SIDNEY
ROGER PROGRAM RADIO STATION KROW, 19 AND BROADWAY OAKLAND
CALIFORNIA

And on April 17, Faulkner responded to this request by means of an
open telegram sent to the *New York Times* with the following message: "I
DO NOT BELIEVE THERE IS A DEBATABLE POINT BETWEEN US. WE BOTH
AGREE IN ADVANCE THAT THE POSITION YOU WILL TAKE IS RIGHT MOR-
ALLY LEGALLY AND ETHICALLY. IF IT IS NOT EVIDENT TO YOU THAT THE
POSITION I TAKE IN ASKING FOR MODERATION AND PATIENCE IS RIGHT
PRACTICALLY THEN WE WILL BOTH WASTE OUR BREATH IN DEBATE.
WILLIAM FAULKNER"

A week and a half earlier, Faulkner had received the following solicita-
tion from the Morehouse College Personnel Office on behalf of Norfleet
Strother. Strother had served as a butler at Rowan Oak, and with Faulkner's intellectual example and encouragement, Strother had decided to
pursue a college education:

Dear Mr. Faulkner:
   One of your former employees, Mr. Norfleet Strother, who, currently, is
enrolled at Morehouse College, is in dire need of financial assistance. He
needs a minimum of $135 to carry him through the second semester of the
current academic year.
   He is to [*sic*] proud to make known his needs, and, yet, he is so deserving
that I feel that the least that I, his counselor, can do, is to apprise you of his
situation.

Norfleet is a gentleman. He is honest, reliable, deserving. He is lifting him-self up by his bootstraps. All he needs is a little financial assistance.

I've done what I can for him. So have others here at the College. However, it is now necessary and imperative that we seek additional outside help.

Are you willing—able—to help him?

To this request Faulkner would respond readily and would continue doing so throughout the span of Strother's studies. Faulkner would meet this ob-ligation with funds generated from interest earned on a portion of his No-bel Prize stipend specifically set aside for educating Negroes he deemed worthy of his sponsorship.

In December 1955, William Faulkner began writing *The Town*. Despite many distractions and interruptions caused by his highly committed in-volvement in the public debate raging over civil rights, he continued to gain momentum on the novel, and by the end of August 1956, he had com-pleted the manuscript. One month later, possibly as a way of debating W. E. B. Du Bois after all, Faulkner published in *Ebony* magazine an article entitled "If I Were a Negro." He began this essay with what amounted to a third public apology for faux pas he had made in his interview with Russell Warren Howe earlier in the year; then, from a Negro stance, he went on to advocate those same humanitarian principles he had been espousing po-lemically from his own white perspective since the late forties. Published in September 1956, "If I Were a Negro" postulated moderation. Faulkner urged his "fellow blacks" to continue peacefully applying to white schools, saying:

> This was Ghandi's [*sic*] way. If I were a Negro, I would advise our elders and leaders to make this our undeviating and inflexible course—a course of inflexible and unviolent flexibility directed against not just the schools but against all the public institutions from which we are interdict, as is being done against the Montgomery, Alabama, bus lines. . . . The white man has devoted three hundred years to teaching us to be patient; that is one thing at least in which we are his superiors. Let us turn it into a weapon against him. Let us use this patience not as a passive quality, but as an active weapon.[22]

Now, as then, it would seem difficult to misconstrue Faulkner's "gradual-ist" position on the central issue of human rights. Certainly, he had given his detractors—northern liberals, Negro activists, and segregationist South-erners—all they needed to vilify and discredit him. Yet, he had taken his stand and would continue to hold his ground tenaciously and with pas-sionate courage, prescience, and an unabashed humanitarianism few have demonstrated so persistently.

SEVEN

"WHITE BEACHES"

"And now I realise for the first time what an amazing gift I had: uneducated in every formal sense, without even very literate, let alone literary, companions, yet to have made the things I made."
—William Faulkner, letter to Joan Williams, April 29, 1953[1]

"Don't ever disbelieve!"
—A legacy from Estelle and William Faulkner to "Vicki" Fielden[2]

Originally, major portions of the following interview were recorded during a five-day visit I made with Victoria Fielden Johnson and her daughter, Gillian, in their home in Cape Coral, Florida, May 20–24, 1985. Two additional interviews were conducted in 1986 and 1987.

By nature, Mrs. Johnson, whom I first met in 1978 while she was still residing in Oxford, Mississippi, is a proud, very modest, and private person who cautiously guards her feelings about the Faulkners of Mississippi. For this reason, I am especially grateful to her for sharing her insights and candid perceptions, her accurate and poignant memories of seasons, days, and moments shared with Estelle and William Faulkner over three decades as their eldest grandchild.

This edited version of taped conversations consists of sections I have rearranged to create an approximately chronologically structured narrative. Except for necessary grammatical and stylistic refinements silently imposed, I have not altered the dialogue.

LDB: How do you think William Faulkner felt toward the Oldhams and Franklins after he married Estelle Oldham Franklin in 1929?[3]

VFJ: He had respect for my grandfather, Cornell Franklin. I doubt he felt much love for my great-grandparents, Lem and Lida Oldham. After all, they had resisted Pappy's marriage to my grandmother from the outset, and even after she had returned to Oxford from Shanghai with two children, a divorcee, they still balked at the notion of their daughter marrying Billy Faulkner. Certainly through the years he showed his love for the Franklin children, Victoria and Malcolm, and accepted them as his own.

LDB: The Oldhams had made a European-style match based on money and position and old-line family name.

VFJ: Yes, exactly.

LDB: When William and Estelle finally got married in 1929 and took up permanent residence at Rowan Oak in 1930, didn't both of Estelle's children from her former marriage with Cornell Franklin move in with them?

VFJ: Well, that was one of the things that Pappy held against the Oldhams. By keeping Malcolm with them in their home on South Lamar, acting as guardians for the frail child, they became recipients of Cornell's child support checks. Pappy realized that the Oldhams were depending on that money themselves, claiming to use it to support both children. In fact, my mother's portion never came to Pappy and Grandmama. Instead, my great-grandparents used that income to support themselves. Pappy resented them for this and for the fact that they never reimbursed Pappy for any of my mother's expenses.

LDB: What a paradox! Faulkner bore no resentment toward his wife's former husband and his family, but rather toward Estelle's family, his own in-laws.

VFJ: Yes, that's so. Pappy realized early on that Cornell Franklin was not at fault for having whisked his sweetheart away. He was almost as much of a victim of the arrangement as Estelle was.

LDB: More so, the Oldhams continued to warrant Faulkner's disrespect; they actively discouraged their daughter from marrying him, arguing that he was Count-No-Count, even a decade after they had first canceled him from her list of eligible suitors.

VFJ: People have said that Grandmama was a weak person all her life. She had succumbed at twenty-one to her parents' dictatorial demands, but at thirty-two, after she had divorced Cornell Franklin and come back to Oxford with two children, she did assert herself and, against their wishes, married Pappy. Now that required a great deal of courage. She bucked everybody to marry him. I'm not sure, but I think Estelle and the two children returned from Shanghai in 1926. I would imagine, as a divorcée in the mid-twenties, she was greeted with a leer, perhaps even shunned by the "uprights" in the town. Pappy convinced her that marriage to him would be good for her *and* for the children, but it took him at least a year and a half to do it. He wrote *The Wishing Tree* for my mother in early February 1927,[4] but he and Grandmama didn't marry until June of 1929. Her divorce from Cornell Franklin took a long while simply because communication between Oxford, Mississippi, and Shanghai, China, took months in those days. And Pappy must have done a good sales job, too.

LDB: As a young man, Faulkner doesn't seem to have been very successful in courting ladies. Even after Estelle Franklin left the United States and his love interests turned elsewhere during the interim, he failed to make lasting relationships with Gertrude Stegbauer, Helen Baird, or Sally Kirkwood. Doubtless there were others as well in Greenville, Holly Springs, Clarksdale, Memphis, and New Orleans.

VFJ: I think if he had been as persuasive with others as he must have been to get Grandmama to finally marry him, he might have ended up with somebody else. And it wasn't necessarily that Pappy had been a failure with my grandmother. Remember, she had already been promised to another man; their mutual fates had been wrested from their control.

LDB: He wasn't responsible for that failure, was he?

VFJ: No! Even after her marriage to Cornell Franklin, I strongly believe that Pappy was still very much in love with Grandmama. He realized that it hadn't been her fault either. I don't think he blamed her for that, not even in the beginning.

LDB: It seems that Faulkner's love for Estelle matured and ripened during the eleven years that lapsed between her marriage to Cornell Franklin and her wedding to him. Somehow, wasn't their relationship destined to last, to mature? Also, wasn't there something inherently doomed about it? After all those years of separation, why was Faulkner compelled to marry Estelle Franklin, already a mother of two children and no longer the romantic vision of his adolescent idealization of Southern womanhood?

VFJ: Obviously he still worshipped her. And even though many sad years would come after they married, he never stopped loving her.

LDB: Did the fact that Estelle had two children make her even more attractive to him, excite a vague and undefined sense of himself as Don Quixote coming to the rescue of his beloved maiden in distress?

VFJ: He adored the children, Malcolm and my mother, Victoria, and I know he loved Grandmama.

LDB: That Billy Faulkner remained an ardent admirer of Estelle during her eleven-year marriage to Cornell Franklin is evident when you assemble surviving gifts he gave her, persuasions to love: an inscribed book of Swinburne's poems [1919]; a copy of the hand-lettered and hand-bound one-act play *The Marionettes* [1920]; a handmade book of his own poetry, which Faulkner dedicated to Estelle and titled *Vision in Spring* [1921]; a copy of *The Marble Faun*, inscribed in 1924; the hand-lettered and -bound single-impression copy of *Royal Street: New Orleans* [1926]; and in 1927 both an inscribed copy of his second novel, *Mosquitoes,* and the handmade child's fantasy, *The Wishing Tree,* which he wrote for and presented to Estelle's daughter, your mother, Cho-Cho [Victoria] on the occasion of her eighth birthday.

VFJ: Most of these gifts were given to Grandmama on her various trips back and forth between Honolulu or Shanghai and Oxford, when she and Pappy would see each other. During the entire time of her marriage, Grandmama was homesick for her parents and friends and Pappy, too. She told me this herself. I think my Grandfather Franklin was extremely understanding and kind to keep sending Grandmama back. But it had been an arranged marriage for him, too, and probably he wasn't in love with Grandmama either. They hardly knew each other at the time of their marriage. When Grandmama left my Grandfather Franklin for the last time, he grieved—but I'm quite sure the grief was more for the loss of his children than for his wife.

LDB: It must have been obvious to Cornell Franklin during those years they shared that his wife had never lost her affections for William Faulkner. Nor did he feel rancor toward Faulkner when Estelle married him in 1929.

VFJ: Quite the contrary. My Grandfather Franklin was grateful to Pappy for his care and concern for Malcolm and my mother.

LDB: In those early years of Estelle's marriage to Faulkner, did Cornell and Estelle keep in touch?

VFJ: They did to some extent, but Cornell corresponded more with Lida, his ex-mother-in-law, mainly with regard to the children's well-being. And, of course, he would send the Oldhams monthly child support checks.

LDB: But did Faulkner and Estelle maintain ties with the Franklins?

VFJ: Later they did. In Columbus, Mississippi, in Shanghai, China, and, coincidentally, during the fifties and sixties in Charlottesville, Virginia.

LDB: What about during the early stages of their divorce? Was theirs a rude severing?

VFJ: Not at all. I recall Mama telling me how Grandmama and Pappy took her to Columbus, Mississippi, to stay with her grandmother who was Grandmama's ex-mother-in-law. About three weeks later, Mrs. Hairston brought Mama down to Pascagoula where Pappy and Grandmama were honeymooning, and she stayed with them, too, for a short while.

LDB: And when they returned and moved temporarily into Miss Elma Meek's house before purchasing and settling into Rowan Oak on Garfield Avenue, did Malcolm and your mother take up quarters with them, too?

VFJ: Actually, both Mama and Malcolm stayed at the Oldhams' until Pappy bought Rowan Oak. Then my mother moved down there and sort of "became" a Faulkner. But Malcolm, who was quite frail and very young, stayed on at the Oldhams'.

LDB: In the beginning, that had to have been an exciting, happy time for William and Estelle. Yet it must have come as quite a shock to her. After all, she had been used to a more lavish life in Shanghai. For that matter, her parents' home on South Lamar was sumptuous. At first, Rowan Oak had no electricity and no bathroom.

VFJ: It was a shabby place. My mother told me how when they arrived, she sat on the front steps and cried. And I'm sure it must have been a shock to Grandmama as well. However, you must understand, she was very much in love with Pappy, so I don't think it was as bad to her as it appeared to have been for my mother. Mama was embarrassed to have her friends—

she was only eleven then, remember—come to such a horrible, shabby place that was now her new home.

LDB: Estelle's excitement over finally consummating her childhood dream of being married to Billy Faulkner, already a successful, if unappreciated, novelist, must have softened the starkness of the place for her. She must have sensed in it a challenge, sensed the romance of possibilities that Rowan Oak presented to them both. Faulkner, too, must have seen it as a challenge in which they could both participate and share and as something more: he was a landowner for the first time.

VFJ: Absolutely! Count-No-Count had just become landlord of one of Oxford's most stately, if ramshackle, homes.

LDB: Rowan Oak provided solitude away from the city and proximity to it. Also, for Faulkner, there must have been a certain sense of snob appeal inherent in his new surroundings.

VFJ: I know Grandmama also loved the solitude of this new home; she had not been able to handle the intense social world of Shanghai, though she had tried and had found it diverting for a few years when she had first gone out there. In truth, the gambling and drinking had been too much for her. The fast pace had proved to be too much for her stamina. She welcomed this quiet place, perhaps even as Pappy did, because it was on the fringes of Oxford. She had visions of raising her family there. And a year later Pappy and Grandmama had their first child, Alabama, who tragically died after only nine days. Of course, that was a major calamity to both of them. Then, two years later, they succeeded in having Jill. This was a good time—in the beginning—and Rowan Oak was a place where Pappy would accomplish much of his very best, most significant writing.

LDB: Tell me again about the Franklins. If in those early years there was little contact between the Faulkners and the Franklins, how about later?

VFJ: Before we get to that, let me just say that there were a number of very eerie coincidences that occurred between the Franklins and the Faulkners in the thirties and fifties. For example, after Cornell Franklin and Grandmama got divorced, Cornell, like Grandmama, remarried in 1929—he to Dallas Lee, she to Pappy. Both couples had children who died very, very prematurely. Both had another child in 1933, the only child for both couples: Jill for Pappy and Grandmama, and Corney (Cornell, Jr.) for Cornell and

Dallas. Also, Dallas had two children from a previous marriage; her daughter came with her, much as Victoria had with Estelle. Dallas' son, Peter, remained with his father, and Malcolm was left at the Oldhams' to grow up. And in 1951, when Cornell and Dallas were finally allowed by the Chinese communists to leave Shanghai, they moved to, of all places, Charlottesville, Virginia—actually close by in Keswick.

LDB: And that's where Jill was living.

VFJ: No, not yet. In 1954, Jill married Paul Summers, who was in law school at the University of Virginia. They took up residence then. I remember one Christmas vacation traveling by train from Boston to Memphis where Pappy picked me up and took me to Oxford. I had stopped off first in Virginia to see Jill for a few days. We were invited by my Grandfather Cornell for dinner at his home one of those evenings I was there. And I know that later when Pappy was at the University of Virginia as writer-in-residence, he and Grandmama were often invited to parties at the Franklin home.

LDB: So Faulkner actually saw Cornell when he came to Charlottesville?

VFJ: Yes. Judge Franklin was a highly regarded lawyer, and Paul, Jill's husband, was in the University of Virginia law school. So they had that in common as well as the family connection. Furthermore, as I said, Cornell and Dallas had a son, Corney, who was the same age as Jill. He spent a number of summers with us in Oxford at Rowan Oak during the war. The Faulkner hospitality from those years was fully reciprocated by the Franklins during the fifties. In fact, today Corney is a lawyer in New York; Tad, Jill's eldest son, was a seaman. Before shipping out from New York, he would always arrive a few days early and stay with Corney. And in recent years, Corney has visited them, too, in Charlottesville.

LDB: To me, one remarkable thing is how at one time at Rowan Oak during the war, Faulkner was actually hosting Malcolm and Victoria, Cornell's children from his first marriage with Estelle, Corney, Cornell's son from his second marriage, as well as Jill, the daughter from his marriage to Estelle. What a fusion that must have been!

VFJ: Oh, and don't forget my father. During the forties and early fifties, he spent much time at Rowan Oak.

LDB: If you can, tell me about your mother's feelings toward her new father, William Faulkner.

VFJ: I think by the time they married—Mama was ten—she felt Pappy was her special friend. Billy, she called him. And he had written for her eighth birthday, for her especially, a wonderful, fabulous children's story called *The Wishing Tree,* which he typed and bound by hand. He even watercolored the front and back papers that covered the little volume, and hand-lettered in ink the title on a tiny label he glued to the front, and dedicated it to her: "For his dear friend / Victoria / on her eighth birthday / Bill he made / this Book."[5] It was not until after Jill was born in 1933 that Billy became "Pappy"—which was not until Mama was fourteen. Billy was Mama's special friend, and I think she felt that Grandmama was an interloper in that relationship. There was a certain jealousy and then later, with Grandmama's drinking, Mama felt alienation and disgust. Then the children came: first, Alabama, who died, then Jill, and they decided to send Mama to a boarding school in Holly Springs. That shoved her right out of the nest and her place with Pappy. Then, in 1936, she experienced another shattering thing: Grandmama and Pappy picked up, taking Jill, and left her alone in Oxford while they went to California.[6] Suddenly Mama had nothing where she had had it all. She had had a beautiful, loving relationship with Pappy—Billy—her father; suddenly she had nothing.

LDB: Already your mother had been split off from Malcolm after Estelle's divorce from Cornell Franklin. Now she found herself split off again, this time from her new father.

VFJ: I know my mother felt abandoned and, most likely, somewhat betrayed.

LDB: Knowing this certainly helps explain how your mother might have become infatuated with the first handsome young man that came into her life.

VFJ: Yes. Also, I think Pappy felt he had been taken advantage of by my mother, by her elopement, and getting pregnant while Pappy was in California made him feel as though she had completely betrayed him, his trust in her.

LDB: Faulkner felt strong fatherly love for your mother, didn't he? When away, he would address his letter envelopes to her "Miss Victoria Faulkner." And many of the books he inscribed to her during the thirties carried such entries as "For my daughter, Victoria, / her book with love, from Billy" or "For my daughter, Victoria."[7]

VFJ: I think Mama resented having been sent off to boarding school, being pushed out to make room for Jill. Perhaps she also felt that Pappy really had no more use for her now that he had his own flesh-and-blood daughter.

LDB: Did your mother ever give you any indications of her resentment?

VFJ: Well, she could be a very jealous, possessive person, and I think she was terribly envious of the new baby, Jill, and for many years. She adored Pappy, worshipped him, and to her, both Grandmama and Jill were intruders into her sacred relationship with him.

LDB: Did your mother blame Faulkner or Estelle for Jill's existence?

VFJ: She didn't like Grandmama at all—her own mother! Just before Mama died in 1975, she disposed of more than two hundred letters Grandmama had written to her over the years. She didn't want anyone to see them, to get to know Grandmama as a lovely human being, a lady who cared deeply about her children, her husband, and who was proud of the simplest pleasures in life.

LDB: Your mother disliked Estelle because she had given birth to Jill?

VFJ: No. I think it was the drinking that really ripped it, sundered the relationship between my mother and Grandmama. And also, she never quite forgave Grandmama for having divorced her father, Cornell Franklin.

LDB: Whom she had also loved.

VFJ: Right! Adored! My mother adored men; she didn't like women. She did not like me, she didn't like her mother, and she did not like Jill.

LDB: And apparently your mother carried this animosity toward Estelle Faulkner with her all her life.

VFJ: I would say if she loved Grandmama at all, it was because she was her mother and duty demanded it. One day when I was fourteen or fifteen, my mother said, "I don't like Grandmama," and I thought, "How can you not like and love your own mother?" It was a shock to me.

LDB: You said that when your grandmother and Jill went out to join Faulkner in Hollywood in 1936 where he was doing script work for Twentieth Century-Fox, your mother, home in Oxford, met a man whom she would soon marry.

VFJ: Yes. She was just a freshman at Ole Miss. She had graduated from high school at seventeen.

LDB: What was his name, and where was he from?

VFJ: Claude Selby—he was from Vicksburg, and he was in law school at Ole Miss.

LDB: After Estelle learned that your mother was pregnant, she and Jill returned from California?

VFJ: Yes, they came back to Oxford in late May of 1937, I believe.

LDB: When they left, Faulkner was very lonely, at least for Jill. Actually, he may even have feared for his young daughter's safety. I believe he distrusted Estelle's ability to handle herself. Her drinking had reached an almost uncontrollable pitch, in part because she had learned of Faulkner's affair with Howard Hawks' secretary, Meta Carpenter, and she was also aggravated by anxiety over her own daughter's marriage to a young man she did not know. I have read a few letters from Faulkner to your mother from that period in which he pines for his daughter Jill, imploring your mother to protect her. The following is the ending to one such letter he wrote to your mother, probably shortly after Estelle and Jill left Hollywood in late May 1937: "Take care of my little baby for me, Sister. Claude is there, dependable, and you have been my sweet pride and companion ever since our lives came together. So I know I dont even have to ask this, I just need to repeat, because she is little and helpless and wants little save to be happy and loved and looked after, 'Take care of my little baby.'"[8]

VFJ: Well, my mother was very strong. She had been a very strong-willed child.

LDB: So in a manner of speaking, Faulkner regarded your mother, rather than his wife, Estelle, as a surrogate mother for his daughter Jill. Therefore, when your seventeen-year-old mother married Claude Selby, Faulkner must have been hurt, disappointed, and felt left with a helpless situation in having neither his wife nor stepdaughter to look after Jill while he was away.

VFJ: Well, perhaps in the beginning, especially because Mama had gotten pregnant within months after she had married Claude Selby. Fortunately, Pappy had returned home from California just about the time of my birth in late September 1937, because while I was still in the hospital, my father deserted my mother and me.

LDB: And Faulkner must have quickly realized that now he had another weighty responsibility. There was another fatherless child, another daughter, in his family. Just the previous year he had virtually inherited his dead brother Dean's daughter and his widow, at least responsibility for their financial support.

VFJ: And don't forget his own mother, Miss Maud. When Pappy's father died in 1932, automatically he assumed the role of head of the household, a house full of women.

LDB: What do you know about your father's desertion of your mother and you?

VFJ: I recall Mama telling me how my father came to the hospital right after I was born and that five days later he was gone, disappeared without any word.

LDB: How did Faulkner respond to this? Was he angry?

VFJ: I believe his emotions were mixed and confused. He felt heartbroken for my mother because she was suffering, because obviously she loved the man. At the same time, Pappy was incensed that his daughter had gotten herself into such a mess. Now he was going to have to be the guardian for one more child.

LDB: Did your father really disappear?

VFJ: For awhile my mother couldn't locate him. Finally she discovered he had gone to the upper peninsula of Michigan. She took off after him with me and worked as a waitress in various lumber camps trying to find him, get him back. She finally found him, but he would have none of her entreaties to return with her to Oxford and take up life as a married couple with a child.

LDB: This almost sounds like a reprise of Faulkner's Lena Grove story from *Light in August* written less than five years earlier. Almost a prophecy in reverse. What's more, it must have seemed ironic to Faulkner to have had this come to pass, especially had he recalled the phrase in the letter I quoted for you in which he had written your mother, saying "Claude is there, dependable, . . ."

VFJ: Well, I do know that Pappy got on a bus, came all the way up to Michigan, and accompanied us back. That was in early winter of 1937. Not long after that, Pappy got in touch with my Grandfather Franklin in China and said that my mother was going through a hellish time in Oxford and suggested it might be good if she came out there for a while. My grandfather readily agreed. He had pretty well stayed out of the picture with regard to Grandmama and Pappy, except for financial support of the children. But as soon as Pappy indicated that my deserted mother was in trouble and that a time away from Oxford would be a positive thing, he said, "By all means." I am quite sure that he paid our fares for the trip, too, not Pappy.

LDB: Do you feel Faulkner's importunity derived from his awareness that the town of Oxford was talking about your mother, that not only was the whole affair a scandal but also his stepdaughter, Victoria, and her new child would be adversely affected by the notoriety?

VFJ: Of course. Just read Pappy's "A Rose for Emily" if you really want to know how the town reacted to anything and everything even slightly out of the ordinary. And my mother's dilemma was not at all ordinary at that time. That was fifty years ago, remember, and values were a lot different then.

LDB: Cornell Franklin arranged for your mother and you to travel to Shanghai.

VFJ: I feel certain he did. We went out there when I was about one year old, and we stayed with my Grandfather Cornell and his wife, Dallas, until 1940. We were evacuated when the threat of war with the Japanese grew imminent.

LDB: And it was between 1938 and 1940 that your mother met, fell in love with, and married William Fielden.

VFJ: Yes. She fell madly in love with him. My father was a self-made man. I had tremendous admiration for him. He had a high school education; that was it. His father had deserted his mother when he was about fourteen or so, and he had become the breadwinner for his family. He had a brother and two sisters, and one, the youngest sister, was a baby. My father wanted to be a professional baseball player and got into the minor leagues. But he realized he couldn't afford to spend his life doing that. He had to get a job that would allow him to support his family. He had an uncle who had connections out in China who helped him get hired as a trainee by a tobacco company.

LDB: How old was he when he met your mother?

VFJ: He was twenty-four. And as far as my mother was concerned, he was the most handsome man in the world, the sweetest man I have ever known. Not a mean bone in his body! I have never heard anyone say an unkind word about him in business, social, or any other kinds of dealings. Never! He indulged Mama, spoiled her rotten.

LDB: They got married in Shanghai in 1940. Then you and your mother came back to Oxford when you were about three years old.

VFJ: Yes, all women and children had been advised to leave China.

LDB: And your new father stayed behind in Shanghai. Was he on good terms with Cornell Franklin?

VFJ: Of course. And it was he and Dallas who gave Mama away in marriage. My father and grandfather were very close, and Cornell Franklin felt good knowing Mama was now in very kind and caring hands. My father stayed on with the tobacco company until November 1941. Anyway, in 1940, Mama and I returned to Rowan Oak, and it was awful because nobody believed that we had been evacuated. They thought Victoria Franklin Selby Fielden had just been dumped by another man.

LDB: That was the "Rose for Emily" scuttlebutt around Oxford, right?

VFJ: Exactly! And they couldn't imagine that we were actually almost at war. I mean people didn't accept divorce that readily in those days. My grandmother was a branded woman for having divorced, and my mother already had one divorce under her belt. To many people it looked like she might be getting another. She had to put up with the gossip.

LDB: William Faulkner and his family were a constant source of ridicule and slander in Oxford, weren't they?

VFJ: Yes, we were, but I never knew quite why we were treated differently. I didn't regard Pappy as a famous writer; he was simply Pappy; he was my grandfather, and I didn't say, "What do you do for a living?" I didn't inquire about things like that. Sure, I heard him pecking away on the typewriter every morning, but it just didn't register. But in Oxford, somehow, we were all made to feel we were different. There was a subtle shunning, I felt.

LDB: It must have been difficult for his fellow townspeople to imagine his doing his "work" in his own living room or sitting outdoors sipping coffee at a table positioned on the lawn or porch, sitting there with just paper and a typewriter and a few fountain pens, especially when all of them had to go to jobs with routine schedules. And to them he must have seemed profligate, without any constant patterns to his life. Certainly, they must have noticed Faulkner's inconsistent church-going and the string of broken marriages that characterized his family.

VFJ: Yes, we did frustrate their traditional expectations, that's for sure!

LDB: All right, perhaps the Faulkners were unconventional, even amoral, if you will. But they weren't immoral. Estelle's marriage to Cornell Franklin had been star-crossed from the outset, and your mother's brief marriage to Claude Selby had been a tragic miscue.

VFJ: Yes, my mother was very hurt and very disillusioned, but at least Claude hadn't run off with another woman or anything like that.

LDB: So, in 1940 you and your mother came back to Rowan Oak, and Malcolm was still at the Oldhams'. Faulkner and Estelle were at home with seven-year-old Jill. There Faulkner was with four women around him, and he himself homebound.

VFJ: And his own mother not far away with his brother Dean's wife, Louise, and her daughter, Dean, living with his mother, and all of them depending on Pappy.

LDB: His dependents were all women! And don't forget Callie Barr, his second mother, the black lady he memorialized in his 1942 dedication to *Go Down, Moses* two years after her death.

VFJ: Yes, most of Pappy's dependents were female, but don't forget the major responsibility he also assumed in inventing work for his brother John and his wife, Lucille, out at Greenfield Farm. And don't forget their two sons, Jimmy and Chooky. You mentioned Mammy Callie, but Pappy also felt totally responsible for all of his "black family." His financial obligations had to be very distracting and disconcerting to him and for his writing in those years.

LDB: With the exception of his brother John, one might almost consider Faulkner's world consisting of a kind of matriarchy with him at the center and on the peripheries simultaneously.

VFJ: Right!

LDB: This had to have been very stressful to him; not so much the matrix of the extended family beholden to him as his own inability to make his writing support himself and them.

VFJ: He was pulled in so many different directions by all who had come to depend on him. Notwithstanding, I can understand how Jill remained the object of all his awe and love. She was his flesh and blood, his one great hope at that point.

LDB: Yet Faulkner didn't seem to show favoritism or admit distinctions between the Faulkner and Franklin families.

VFJ: No, he didn't. We were all treated with equal importance. And for all of us, the same restrictions and not unpleasant deprivations prevailed. None of us minded the austerity in which we lived because there was a love for each other all felt. To me, as a young child, Rowan Oak was an enchanted place, a cocoon that protected us all, thanks to Pappy.

LDB: When did your father, Bill Fielden, come back to the United States?

VFJ: He got out of China in 1941, and he headed directly for Oxford. He was due in shortly before Christmas. Of course Pearl Harbor took place on the seventh of December, so his ship was diverted to Port Moresby, New Guinea, and he sent a wire, which my mother received when she arrived in San Francisco. All it said after the censors had done with it was, "Love

You, Bill." She didn't know where in the hell he was. So she and Dutch Silver,[9] who had accompanied her from Oxford, headed back to Mississippi in the car, picking up soldiers on the sides of the road who were trying to get to their bases to go to war. Finally, Daddy did make it to San Francisco and got a train to St. Louis where Mama and Malcolm met him. They drove back, and I remember very well the night they got back from St. Louis. Of course, I hardly knew my father at that point. They had been married for four months when Mama and I left, and suddenly a whole year had passed, so I really didn't know him. I was excited because this was my Daddy coming home. They came in that night and walked into the living room of Rowan Oak, and there was a very awkward, awkward silence; everybody just sort of looked him up and down.

LDB: And perhaps that silence was filled with a bit of trembling, too.

VFJ: Oh, sure. For Pappy, Grandmama, me, and Jill, certainly for Mama . . . but Jill broke the ice. My father was terribly ticklish and so was Jill. She walked up to Daddy and said, "Brother Bill, I'm Sister Jill. If you won't tickle me, I won't tickle you." And he got down and just hugged her, and that did it for everybody. We all broke out laughing. There was constant chatter from that moment on, lots of hugs and love, and Pappy and my father became immediate friends, and they stayed close friends for the rest of Pappy's life. In fact, my father became the son that Pappy never had and Malcolm never did become for Pappy, despite Malcolm's unceasing efforts to live up to that role in Pappy's estimation.

LDB: How old was your father?

VFJ: He was twenty-seven; Pappy was forty-four. But there didn't seem to be any age difference between them at all.

LDB: And your dad moved into Rowan Oak at that time?

VFJ: Oh, yes, until he could find work. There was never any question that my family would share living quarters at Rowan Oak until we could get our lives in order.

LDB: Your mother and dad had their own bedroom; Jill had hers, I guess?

VFJ: I slept with Jill. By that time, Grandmama and Pappy had separate rooms. He slept in the middle room upstairs; Grandmama took the far back one for hers.

LDB: Do you think this suggested a total rift between Faulkner and his wife?

VFJ: No, nor do I think occupying separate bedrooms was really a sign of frigidity on Grandmama's part. Contraceptives were largely unknown then, and I think Grandmama probably said, at the age of thirty-six or so, "Enough is enough." Her first-born, my mother, had been delivered with forceps, which damaged her head; Alabama had died prematurely, and I don't know how difficult the births of Malcolm and Jill were—but after Jill was born when Grandmama was thirty-six, I'm not surprised (in fact, I can empathize) that separate bedrooms were in order. She was a tired, sick lady by then.

LDB: Between 1940 and mid-1942 there seemed to be a full house at Rowan Oak, much bustle and excitement. Faulkner was doing some of his best writing. Whether this could be attributed to a desperate need to offset his paltry finances with new royalty-yielding fiction or whether he was motivated by a sense of his own mortality in the face of being called into service cannot be known. Regardless, he was busy, almost frantic, composing or rewriting older stories for incorporation into new novels, principally for *The Hamlet* and *Go Down, Moses,* which included his magnificent novella "The Bear." But by July 1942, Rowan Oak was empty again except for the blacks and Estelle and Jill, almost like Scarlett at Tara after the war.

VFJ: Right, and Grandmama ran the place. And she did a damn good job of it! Almost single-handedly she maintained Rowan Oak. She made repairs, grew and worked the "Victory garden," made it produce; she canned vegetables and made jams and jellies.

LDB: To backtrack, did your father enlist in the armed services?

VFJ: He tried enlisting in every branch but was turned down by them all. I don't know why.

LDB: Faulkner had a similar dilemma; he wanted desperately to go off to that war and fight, but his age must have been a deciding factor against him. Actually, he was offered a desk job in Washington, provided he could pass an extensive physical. But in the final analysis, he never was requested to take the exam, and probably he realized he needed more income anyway; that's why in late July 1942 he ended up taking the train out to California to begin his seven-year contract as a Warner Bros. screenwriter.

VFJ: It does seem strange that both men who so much wanted to fight for their country were denied the opportunity. I never did learn why my father was not accepted.

LDB: What did your father do in Oxford?

VFJ: He began at once trying to find a job. All he knew was the tobacco business, so he landed a job in North Carolina with which he soon became dissatisfied. I believe he felt he should be fighting instead of working with tobacco, so he changed jobs, went to work for Proctor & Gamble in their munitions plant at Wolf Creek, near Milan, Tennessee. Daddy commuted from Jackson for a year until housing became available at the plant early in 1944. We lived there until 1945.

LDB: Both Faulkner and Bill Fielden were unable to enter the armed services, yet both engaged patriotically in war-related jobs. Faulkner even convinced himself he was furthering the cause of freedom and his country's hopes of winning the war by writing morale-boosting propaganda scripts for Warner Bros. In fact, his first project in Burbank was an original screenplay entitled "The De Gaulle Story."

VFJ: I remember in one of his letters home, Pappy wrote Mama about that screenplay. It was a highly secretive project and he implored her not to mention a word of it. Pappy really believed he was going to make some difference in the war and that that film, which he was writing by himself, a very long one, was going to have a major impact on the public.[10]

LDB: During the period from 1942 through September 1945, Faulkner spent most of his time in Hollywood. He would return home for Christmas and spend three-month periods the studio termed "suspensions" back in Oxford.

VFJ: Most of those "suspensions," I believe, were in the winter. Pappy was always home for Christmas, and he had to be there to butcher at least one hog a year so we'd have meat for the next year.[11] Those winter nights were spent upstairs in Grandmama's room. She suffered from the cold, so we'd have a fire in the fireplace, and she'd read in bed while we played cards— Pappy, Jill, and I. Grandmama read all the time. She liked some of the Russian writers, particularly Dostoyevsky and Gogol, and I remember her reading Henry James and H. P. Lovecraft. I'd say her tastes were pretty eclectic. Pappy, Jill, and I would play a card game he had imported from Hollywood—he called it "Skombiel." I don't know where he got the word, but when he won (as he usually did, and with a vengeance) he'd shout it out just as if he'd shot the ass off some Nazi fighter pilot! I played my last game of Skombiel in March 1946. When I returned to Rowan Oak to go to school in 1949, we'd moved up to Canasta.

LDB: I believe most of Faulkner's productive time during those war years was spent elsewhere and with others than his immediate family. In fact, in Los Angeles Faulkner had resumed his relationship with Meta Carpenter, who in late 1941 conveniently divorced her husband, Wolfgang Rebner. When he did return from Hollywood in September 1945, for the last time, where were you and your mother and father? Where was Malcolm? What was the matrix that existed between all of you and Estelle and William Faulkner?

VFJ: First, let me back up a little and tell you about Malcolm. When my mother and I returned to Oxford, to Rowan Oak, from Shanghai in 1940, Malcolm was still living with the Oldhams. He was seventeen and already doing research at the University of Mississippi in Oxford. He had a brilliant mind. He was a herpetologist doing work in med school. He was doing phenomenal work on tropical diseases, so where did they send him when he went into the Army? Instead of the Pacific, they sent him to Europe. That's the good old military for you!

LDB: He enlisted?

VFJ: He enlisted on Pappy's advice.

LDB: I've read one very poignant letter Faulkner wrote from Hollywood to Malcolm in early December 1942 in which he advises Malcolm to enlist because becoming a soldier, fighting for his country, will be "public proof of his masculinity: his courage and endurance, his willingness to sacrifice himself for the land which shaped his ancestors." [12]

VFJ: But Malcolm did ask Pappy for his advice. I mean, it wasn't just gratuitous advice, and Pappy said he thought it would do Malcolm good.

LDB: And it was something he really did espouse, almost as though he were imploring himself to enlist, knowing that his participation was going to have to be vicarious.

VFJ: Yes, Pappy was as eager as my father to enlist. I think he was simply too old—older than he wanted to admit—and it was better anyway, because literally there was no one else in the Faulkner family at that time to support all its members.

LDB: Also, if Malcolm needed an example from his own immediate contemporaries, Jimmy Faulkner, his step-cousin, had just enlisted. Faulkner was very proud, especially because Jimmy was training to be a Marine pilot, and this was the highest, most glorious status William Faulkner could imagine a soldier attaining. For Malcolm, was this the first time he had left home, left Oxford?

VFJ: Yes . . . and no. In some respects, he had always been "away" from home.

LDB: Malcolm must have had considerable difficulty leaving his mother. Hundreds of extant letters attest to his attachment to Estelle, letters written almost on a daily basis from various stations and camps in Europe as well as training posts in the United States over a three-year period.[13] He seemed inordinately tied to his mother. What is your memory of that? Your mother, you have said, was disdainful of your grandmother. Was Malcolm?

VFJ: I think Grandmama was the only parent Malcolm really did feel he had, and yet he lived all those years at the Oldhams'. So that was the crutch he used. He didn't know his natural father at all, and he wasn't allowed to live with his mother and stepfather, so he grew up with doting grandparents and an aunt [Dorothy Oldham]. He was a physically weak child, and the Oldhams, having lost a boy themselves, Ned, bowed to his every whim. He learned to use them to get his way, and they spoiled him. As a minor, he inherited the estate of his Uncle Malcolm—I know the Oldhams used the liquid assets to keep their own household going, but Malcolm himself squandered the rest later on. Since he was the eldest son, and believing totally in Salic law, he felt he should have inherited *all* of Cornell Franklin's estate *and* all of William Faulkner's when they died. He felt gypped when the other children on either side got anything at all.

LDB: Lem and Lida Oldham must have lavished everything on Malcolm.

VFJ: Oh, yes, they spoiled him rotten.

LDB: From what Malcolm wrote in his book of recollections, *Bitterweeds: Life with William Faulkner at Rowan Oak*,[14] it appears he had enormous respect and love for Faulkner.

VFJ: He did, and he wanted desperately to be accepted by Pappy, treated like a son, and the fact that he wasn't living at Rowan Oak made it all the more difficult.

LDB: Did Malcolm bear resentment toward his mother or stepfather or sister because your mother had grown up there at Rowan Oak and he had not?

VFJ: I don't think there's much doubt he felt excluded, though I don't believe he blamed this on anyone in particular. However, I do know that Malcolm regretted not knowing his own father.

LDB: Malcolm had been bereft of both his fathers, hadn't he?

VFJ: Yes, and this created a terrible, terrible insecurity, horrible insecurity. He didn't know where he belonged, which father was really his, and I think the potential for greatness was there in him but that he never reached it. At a certain point he actually became quite mentally unstable, and he had problems for the rest of his life.

LDB: In the early years, what were some of the manifestations of psychological imbalance or instability? Did Malcolm begin drinking heavily, and, if so, was it in emulation of his mother and stepfather?

VFJ: I don't recall it in those years. When he went off to war, my memory is of a brilliant young man with a marvelous life ahead of him, with no significant problems. He was a dear, loving, all-American kid who also had this really wonderful mind . . . otherwise, he was rather average in appearance and demeanor. Of course, he did have an upset and screwed-up life living with his grandparents and spinster aunt, rather than with his mother and stepfather or with his real father, but . . .

LDB: Why didn't Estelle ever insist on having Malcolm come live with them out at Rowan Oak?

VFJ: Malcolm was a frail child. I believe Grandmama was concerned that life at Rowan Oak in those early years of no indoor plumbing, etc., might be too rigorous for him. Then, after Jill was born and I, a few years later, there simply wasn't room for him at Rowan Oak.

LDB: Would Faulkner have brooked that, found that arrangement acceptable?

VFJ: I don't think the Oldhams would have brooked it. They were the ones who were hanging on, and not just because of the money from Cornell, but because they doted on Malcolm. Malcolm sort of replaced the son, Ned, they had had who had died as a child. Yet, I can also remember how on Christmas, after we would have our opening of presents at Rowan Oak, we would always go up to South Lamar, and Pappy would drop us off at the Oldham house, and we would have another Christmas celebration there with Malcolm and the Oldhams.

LDB: And Faulkner would never go in?

VFJ: No. He never went into the house. He would take that time to go up and visit with his mother, Miss Maud.

LDB: He was not on speaking terms with Lem and Lida Oldham?

VFJ: No, I wouldn't say that, because Christmas dinner was always held back at Rowan Oak, and my great-grandparents would come down there for that.

LDB: He would invite the Oldhams?

VFJ: Oh, yes. He always made them feel welcome in *his* home.

LDB: But he wouldn't go into their house—ever!

VFJ: That's right, because they had so heartily disapproved of his marriage to their daughter in 1918 and again in 1929. That was Pappy's way of showing his pride: "No, you are welcome in my home because you are the parents of my wife and deserve respect as such, but I will never go into your house, never!" And I can remember begging Pappy to come in and enjoy the festivities.

LDB: Will you focus your thoughts on Malcolm, again? Tell me what happened when he enlisted.

VFJ: The war really messed Malcolm up. He was with the Medical Corps, right behind Patton as they opened up the death camps, and the horrors that he saw really screwed up his mind.

LDB: What makes you privy to that insight?

VFJ: I remember when Malcolm got back after the war in Europe was over, he moved in again with the Oldhams. I was eight years old and very much aware of what was going on then. My father had left for China in late September 1945, but my mother and I didn't leave until April of '46, so during those eight months or so in Oxford, I was with Malcolm enough to recognize the traumatic effects the war had had on him. I can recall my mother holding him while he sobbed over the horrors he had seen firsthand. He cried all the time; he had horrible nightmares.

LDB: Faulkner was home from Hollywood when Malcolm returned from the war. I know that he was very sympathetic toward Malcolm and considered him his loving son. A number of books he gave Malcolm during that period carry inscriptions that confirm Faulkner's love for "my son" in very touching, compassionate terms.[15]

VFJ: I think that was one of the few times in Malcolm's life when he felt Pappy had actually taken pride in him for doing what he had done, for going to war, for volunteering, wanting to go; and, let's face it, Malcolm was a very young man.

LDB: Also, Faulkner was being very protective, very nurturing during this time, doubtless because of the incipient instability coupled with increased drinking he must have detected.

VFJ: Yes. By then, after the war was over, all of us were aware of the horror of the Holocaust, the atrocities of war, which unfortunately Malcolm had witnessed.

LDB: Once back in Oxford again after the war, what became of Malcolm?

VFJ: Well, he went to the university. He resumed working on a degree, which he never did get. He fell in love with Gloria Moss in 1947. I think maybe Pappy had an inkling that it was not going to work out as a marriage because he sent Malcolm out to China, and once again he communicated with Cornell Franklin, saying, "I think it would be a good idea for Malcolm to get away from here and for him to see you."

LDB: Faulkner was concerned about that. He didn't think it was a proper match, and he sent Malcolm out to visit Cornell Franklin in Shanghai, China.

VFJ: Yes. My Grandfather Franklin had a very beautiful home there, and Corney was in school in the States, so there was plenty of room.

LDB: Is that where you were living?

VFJ: No, my father and mother and I lived in an apartment in Shanghai, but Malcolm stayed with my grandfather. And he became totally morose and literally would cry in his beer over Gloria. Finally my grandfather couldn't stand it anymore, and he called Pappy and said, "Can you get the damn woman over here so they can marry?" I mean Malcolm was an embarrassment. All he did was cry, even in front of perfect strangers. Granddaddy had no patience with that kind of behavior. He was a very strong, domineering, athletic man, and he considered it unmanly to cry. So Malcolm wasn't getting any sympathy from him, and at times even my mother was disgusted by his actions.

LDB: Was your mother weak like her brother?

VFJ: No! Definitely not!

LDB: Do you feel, perhaps, this strain that Malcolm exhibited came from your grandmother, or . . . ?

VFJ: I do, but I give Grandmama a lot of credit, too, more than most do, because I have seen her be very strong and so unselfish and so giving. One has to have immense courage to be that giving of oneself. But I'd have to say also that there was a strain of weakness in Grandmama genetically that Malcolm inherited and perhaps even exploited to get his way with her. It should be said, as well, that Malcolm's visit to Shanghai with his father was pretty scary. Since leaving there as a baby in 1925 or 1926, he had seen his father only two or three brief times: once in late '42 when Cornell, Dallas, and Corney had been repatriated—before Malcolm went to Europe as a soldier—and maybe a couple of times after the war was over. He didn't know his father, and Cornell could be an intimidating man—poor Malcolm didn't stand a chance.

LDB: Needless to say, your grandmother had to be very concerned, worried, and overly protective of Malcolm at that time.

VFJ: Naturally. I mean that was part of the problem from the beginning. He had been such a sickly child, and the Oldhams convinced Grandmama that he was better off staying there than with Pappy and her at Rowan Oak in the unheated house with no bathroom, etc. But I think Grandmama always felt guilty about not keeping Malcolm closer to her while he was growing up.

LDB: So, in the later years she spent a great deal of time with Malcolm.

VFJ: Yes, coddling him, which he did *not* need. He needed a swift kick in the ass! Malcolm's problems arose from *over*nurturing, I think. There were the grandparents and an indulgent aunt, and my mother, too, was very protective of Malcolm, her brother. Over the years I think she was the only one who really *liked* him. They had a rapport that no one could shake. Even when Mac [Malcolm] attacked me once later on, my mother refused to believe it and reduced it all to an overly active imagination on my part. Finally, during his divorce from Gloria he had a complete breakdown, and Pappy brought him up to Virginia, thinking it might help to get him away from Oxford. But he got crazier and crazier, so Pappy took him to a hospital in Richmond. When my mother found out, she was furious and wanted to get him out right away. She refused to believe that her little Mac was mentally ill.

LDB: Faulkner had recognized all along that Malcolm's slow undoing was the coddling, hadn't he, that his own sense of manhood was being stifled?

VFJ: Yes, but unfortunately Pappy has gotten a lot of criticism for having tried to offset that by treating Malcolm more sternly and for having tried to instill in him more sense of discipline and responsibility toward his own person, other persons, and personal objectives. In fact, Pappy was attempting to make Malcolm a more self-reliant, independent person. I really feel that the contempt some have had for Pappy for his rough treatment of Malcolm was unwarranted and certainly undeserved.

LDB: Let me shift the focus a little by underscoring the fact that generally, with the exception of Malcolm's problems, the years between Faulkner's return from Hollywood in 1945 and late 1947 were relatively peaceful and tranquil, if artistically unfertile ones for him. However, by 1948 he got an idea, which perhaps Phil Stone, his good friend and lawyer in Oxford, had suggested to him and which may have spawned the book-length novella *Intruder in the Dust*. Although Faulkner could not have realized it, soon his solitude would dissolve. Its diminishment would coincide with publication of *Intruder* and the attendant publicity it would generate.

VFJ: Also, *Intruder in the Dust* was an easier book to read than earlier novels Pappy had written. And probably it was an easier book for him to write. Basically it was a mystery story.

LDB: Earlier you mentioned you were sent back from Shanghai to attend school in Oxford in 1949. Can you recall the time early in 1949 when M-G-M sent Clarence Brown and his film crew to Oxford to do on-location shooting of *Intruder*?

VFJ: I remember the crew scouting around for outdoor locations. In town they found the house they wanted to use pretty quickly, but I think it was Pappy himself who suggested Pea Ridge Road for one of the early scenes where Claude Jarman is going across the log and falls into the creek below. And my father and Pappy and Jill and I would go out there and watch them shoot—pouring paraffin on the water to make it look like an icy stream. You know, it was kind of hokum but a helluva lot of fun. One of Jill's classmates was Claude's stand-in, and he fell off that log into the cold water five or six times so that Clarence Brown could get the cameras located properly. Then Claude did it, and they cut a take immediately.

LDB: What did Faulkner think of all that?

VFJ: Oh, he was fascinated, spellbound, and amused. That paraffin could look so much like ice was intriguing.

LDB: Although, earlier that same decade, Faulkner had spent nearly four years in Hollywood and doubtless visited many on-location sets, he probably never dreamed then that someday, and soon, he would actually bring Hollywood to Oxford. That just *had* to touch his sense of the ironic. In some bemused sense, it must have seemed like poetic justice.

VFJ: I think so, and he seemed pleased. He seemed rather excited, animated, about it.

LDB: Did he intermingle, socialize with the crew and actors?

VFJ: More than I would have thought he might have.

LDB: Was there anyone in particular to whom he was most drawn?

VFJ: Oh, well, Miss Patterson he adored. Elizabeth Patterson. She was

Miss Habersham in the movie. And he was taken by Juano Hernandez who was a fine gentleman. He played the role of Lucas.

LDB: In those days, Oxford was a very segregated, closed society, wasn't it?

VFJ: Absolutely!

LDB: What were conditions like for Juano Hernandez in Oxford during the filming of *Intruder*?

VFJ: Well, Grandmama and Pappy wanted to entertain everyone, and of course his was the leading role in the film. But they were told in no uncertain terms that to have Mr. Hernandez to their home would cause such a brouhaha that they did not dare.

LDB: You're talking about entertaining him at Rowan Oak?

VFJ: Yes.

LDB: And they did not invite him?

VFJ: They did not invite *anyone*! Pappy was furious but managed to stifle his anger. Instead, they had a small party for Claude with the teenagers—Jill's friends mainly, who, of course, were all white at that time—1949.

LDB: And that's because . . .

VFJ: Because they were told it couldn't be done without causing trouble. They intended to go ahead anyway until a relative, Bob Williams—Sally Murry Williams' husband and the mayor of Oxford at the time—came and begged Pappy not to do it for the sake of peace in the town.

LDB: So Juano Hernandez himself actually became the "intruder." And they found a home for him in a black family's residence in Oxford.

VFJ: Yes, he stayed with a black family the whole time and socialized with no one when not on the set.

LDB: After the movie was finished, the premiere was held at the Lyric Theater in town—Bob Williams' theater, if I recall—on October 12, 1949.

VFJ: There was tremendous excitement: Oxford put on a parade. There had been parades before, but we'd never had *three* marching bands and *three* floats. I mean, it was something for that little town. Talk about a high! I mean everybody really put on the dog! Grandmama made a dress for me with taffeta I'd brought back from Hong Kong.

LDB: And was Faulkner excited or frightened by all the celebration?

VFJ: Initially he was pleased, but then he backed off. I think he had gotten a little too close.

LDB: He realized he had stirred something up that wasn't . . .

VFJ: Yes, he was upset and disappointed about the Hernandez incident, for one thing, how it reflected badly on his hometown and on his state, and also just the inevitability of facing that movie on the giant screen where everybody would have the opportunity to criticize it got to him. He had to back off and rebuild his defenses in case it did not go well. I believe Pappy was quite aware that his views were not commonly held and that now they were also going to be on parade.

LDB: Among other acknowledgments and addresses preliminary to the showing of the movie for the first time in public, the Lyric "Premiere Program" for *Intruder in the Dust* announced that the novel's author, William Faulkner, would make a speech to the audience in attendance.

VFJ: Pappy made a very insignificant speech. In fact, his remarks were more just an inaudible mumbling of words, very quick and very short.

LDB: Was there a problem getting him to the function that evening?

VFJ: Yes, there was. The whole town went all out for the cast and crew members who returned for the premiere. The university gave a formal ball, and Pappy refused to go to that.

LDB: Did Juano Hernandez return to Oxford for the premiere?

VFJ: No, he did not.

LDB: Claude Jarman did, didn't he?

VFJ: No, he couldn't either; he was shooting on location somewhere else.

LDB: What was the nature of the difficulty getting Faulkner to make an appearance that evening of the premiere?

VFJ: Well, he dug in his heels and said, "No," he wasn't going.

LDB: Specifically, what did he do?

VFJ: He stayed up in his room in his pajamas and refused to get dressed to go out. He was like a child throwing a tantrum, digging in heels and saying, "No, no, no." Physically he was stronger than any of us women—Jill, Dean, me, and Grandmama. There was no way that we could force him to go, so we just stood there entreating him. We were all dressed to the nines, you know. Thinking back on it now, it was pretty hilarious, but it wasn't funny then.

LDB: Luckily, there was one woman who finally did convince him.

VFJ: Yes. Aunt Bama McLean. She was a very formidable woman and one of Pappy's favorites. She was the Old Colonel's daughter from Memphis—the only surviving member of that part of the family. In her grand-nephew's eyes she was indomitable. And that evening, fortunately for all of us, she prevailed.

LDB: Who had contacted her?

VFJ: Everyone had known about the premiere for weeks and weeks, and she wouldn't have missed it for the world. But Pappy would not have invited her. Probably Grandmama extended the invitation and likely with the notion that she might have to be the one to coerce the "stubborn mule."

LDB: So Aunt Bama was going to be in Oxford anyway. But it was only with her coaxing that Faulkner consented to go. How did she do it?

VFJ: Well, she came down to the house so that all of us could go to the theater together.

LDB: You mean it had gotten that late; it was that close to the time for the ceremonies to begin, and he was still refusing?

VFJ: Yes, there was to be a cocktail-reception at The Mansion [restaurant] just before the showing of the film, and he was the only man in our midst, and Aunt Bama darn well just said, "We need an escort, Billy, and you're going to be it," and he didn't, couldn't, refuse her.

LDB: And he got dressed up in his best duds, I suppose.

VFJ: Yes. Yes, he got all gussied up, like a peacock strutting around, almost, but it was Aunt Bama who made him do it. We had to take two cars there were so many of us.

LDB: That had to have been quite a scene, too: six women and William Faulkner pulling up in front of the Lyric Theater.

VFJ: There were Grandmama, Jill, Dean, Aunt Bama, Miss Maud, and me. With the klieglight spots out front it was so funny. I mean, this dingy, rat-ridden theater with all the sweeping lights in the sky and Pappy in his formal attire escorting a pack of six formally dressed ladies. The whole spectacle was something Oxford had never seen.

LDB: Although he couldn't have realized it then, digging in his heels in the upstairs bedroom of Rowan Oak may have been the last time he would find sanctuary there.

VFJ: Well, I think with this premiere showing and the fame and everything, suddenly he was scared again, and he wanted to retreat. He wanted his privacy again, wanted it back very badly. He wasn't too sure he wanted that celebrity, after all. It was even worse when he got the Nobel Prize about a year later—at least this time he didn't go on a binge.

LDB: But now he had stirred it up; actually, he had begun making it worse.

VFJ: Yes, he had definitely gone too far. He couldn't stop it.

LDB: The sorcerer's apprentice had supplanted the sorcerer. Indeed, he had gone quite far. Civil rights legislation was very close at hand and would come to flash point in 1954 with *Brown* v. *The Board of Education.* His very timely book, *Intruder in the Dust,* had isolated and addressed a social malaise. Just as twenty years earlier he had proclaimed in his introduction to the 1932 Modern Library edition of *Sanctuary,* again he had begun "to think of books in terms of possible money . . . and speculated what a person in Mississippi would believe to be current trends . . ."[16] In this case, the "most horrific tale" he could imagine wasn't about Temple Drake and

Popeye Vitelli but Lucas Beauchamp and the Gowries of Beat Four, Jefferson, Yoknapatawpha County, Mississippi, the South, U.S.A.

VFJ: Pappy certainly hit upon the right trend, didn't he?

LDB: Yes, he did. But in doing so, he also began surrendering his cherished solitude and privacy. Rowan Oak itself would cease being the real sanctuary it had been for him during the thirties.

VFJ: True. Not even there would he be able to have peace again, and this would be very difficult for him to come to terms with.

LDB: At least the movie version of *Intruder* made the public aware of William Faulkner, Mississippi, Oxford, and the seemingly typical Southern plight of the white-Negro problem in the South.

VFJ: The movie was not just a good one, it also was true to Pappy's book.

LDB: Through it Faulkner had made the public take notice of his home state and its racial dilemma. But how about the very immediate public reaction of Oxford?

VFJ: Before the book and movie appeared, Oxford had regarded Pappy pretty much as an eccentric failure. Suddenly, though, he had brought fame and glamour to the town, to Oxford. But along with it they did not agree with that film, certainly not with the implication of its conclusion. They could not and would not accept as viable his stand about the Negro and civil rights, so there was tremendous resentment, rancor, controversy, and open hostility toward him and the Faulkner family—toward all of us.

LDB: Specifically, who in the family resented him?

VFJ: His brother John and his wife, Lucille, and that whole side of the family. I don't know that they ever had words, but perhaps it was jealousy on John's part, because he would never accomplish much with his own writing. They were avowed segregationists, and they went out and joined the Citizens' Council right away to thwart progress. That was their reaction.

LDB: How about debates or scenes within the family? Miss Maud's reaction? Were there heated arguments, vindictiveness, unhealed wounds? Was Miss Maud embarrassed, ashamed, angry?

VFJ: I never talked with Miss Maud directly about civil rights. I don't know if she shared John's cynical, negative views, but she probably thought that Billy had gone a little too far in his liberal attitude. Whether she discussed or argued such issues with Pappy, I just don't know.

LDB: My impression from letters I've read between Miss Maud and Phil Stone is that she also was a strong segregationist, as you put it.[17] Regardless, Faulkner had caused considerable animosity and hostility within the family, as well as from without.

VFJ: Oh, yes. There is no doubt about that!

LDB: In the minds of people in his hometown and in his state.

VFJ: A lot of his own former close friends. There were many who did not want to associate with him anymore.

LDB: Or did not dare to for political or commercial reasons. William Faulkner had become a dangerous agent, someone espousing seditious views that, if sided with, could completely ruin one's business or chances of succeeding in gaining political office. Worse, after he received the 1949 Nobel Prize for Literature in December 1950, he became extremely vocal and began submitting open letters to the editors of important national newspapers.

VFJ: Also, the Nobel Prize made him more powerful. The town really feared him. He had access to the world. And now the world would know all about Oxford, Mississippi, and its prejudices and mores and cultural biases and attitudes.

LDB: Indeed, he was in a position to expose bigotry and prejudice, which had been an influential part of his heritage.

VFJ: Right. But I think he always did this with mixed feelings. I don't think there was ever a time when he didn't realize that this was his own background, his own native land, his heritage, and that by exposing these inherent evils, he was simultaneously indicting himself as well. He never wanted to be thought of as a traitor. He felt a deep love for Mississippi, but he also knew that the route Mississippi had taken was wrong, basically, humanly wrong, and he could not help speaking out. Pappy was not a political animal, but here he was involved in political aspects of the civil rights movement in the South, and he was a moderate. But being a moderate in Mississippi in those days meant being considered a flaming liberal.

LDB: As you suggested, he was a moderate, but in America, especially in the South, there was a place for moderates. Northern moderates were liberals; Southern moderates were lukewarm conservatives, segregationists at heart. Soon enough, Faulkner himself realized there was no room for him on the middle ground, despite the fact that, ideologically, it was on this middle ground that he had firmly entrenched himself.

VFJ: You're right. He became embroiled in politics, which was not his milieu, and he was being badgered constantly for opinions. Many people wanted him to be more liberal, and he retreated. He was a moderate, and he didn't want to offend his own place or people anymore.

LDB: Frequently his public statements were misread, depending upon who was interpreting them. Some saw him as holding to the middle ground, which indeed was what he was espousing: namely, that changes had to be made now—but *now,* for Faulkner, didn't mean today or next week. The moderate in him refused to abandon his belief that basic inequalities or at least differences of skin color, religious faith, economic status would forever differentiate people.

VFJ: All too often he was misunderstood by both liberals and radicals. Yes, you are correct. Some people were reading him as a segregationist; others, the desegregationists, were pushing him to take a hard-line stance, and he was begging for more time from everyone: "Give us time and we'll correct this." And when the Supreme Court decision came down in 1954, Pappy contended that there was no way you could *legislate* attitudes; you had to *educate* people to them. There's no doubt that almost all of Pappy's associates, friends, and many who didn't know him at all found him traitorous and his public sentiments reprehensible.

LDB: By the mid-fifties, Faulkner and his wife realized the course they were on was not a viable one. The celebrity he had achieved within the last six or eight years was empty and did not consist of the stuff he had dreamed as a youth it would. Estelle would begin to correct her problem by attending Alcoholics Anonymous meetings, but Faulkner would suffer extremely debilitating consequences during this time. By 1956, it would seem to come to a head in the form of a disastrous interview he gave to Russell Warren Howe for the *Reporter* magazine in which he proclaimed that, if it came down to it, he would be forced to go out in the streets of Mississippi and shoot Negroes.[18]

VFJ: He would fight against the federal government.

LDB: Right! And I believe that, when he awakened from the living nightmare the outcries arising from that interview caused around the world, he was stunned. Without openly admitting it, he implied that he had been irresponsibly inebriated during the interview, impassioned, well intentioned, but drunk nonetheless. This was a rude awakening for him. Introspectively he recognized just how far he had veered. Politics was too treacherous a vocation for him, too Medusa-like.

VFJ: He wasn't temperamentally suited to be a politician.

LDB: In his fiction, ambiguity and ambivalence were appropriate. But he was shattered and disillusioned because it seemed that each time he tried to express himself openly in public his words and his thoughts invariably were misinterpreted, misconstrued. It wasn't that the message he was presenting was wrong or even fundamentally distinct from that which he had been subtly propounding in his fiction all those years but that the medium was not conducive to his gifts for expression. Foremost, he was a writer, a fictionist, not a polemicist. And if he were to be a propagandist at all, one who did care about changing the world, it would have to be of a much more subtle, less didactic persuasion—the stuff of metaphor: understated, implied, evocative. All his finest fiction had been woven of these qualities. In fact, what Faulkner suddenly discovered was that he *was* a propagandist, a politician, and . . .

VFJ: He was frightened about it, terrified at finding out just how far away he had gotten from that which he did best.

LDB: By mid-decade he was suffering severe stress exacerbated by acute drinking and distractions from all corners: the State Department, extramarital affairs, and anonymous citizens in and out of Mississippi confronting and challenging him on racial issues. He realized it was time for him to attempt to realign his priorities, among which were the need to get back to his writing, bring to completion *A Fable* and the anecdotes comprising the Snopes cycle he had envisioned occupying two books beyond the already written *The Hamlet*. Also, the need to deal directly with his deteriorated marriage to Estelle must have preoccupied his thoughts. His drinking problem had to be addressed because ever more frequently it was causing him embarrassments like the Howe affair, and it was threatening his health. Less pressing, but still of substance, he had to come to terms with what should be his role as cultural representative for President Dwight D. Eisenhower's government.

VFJ: As spokesman for the United States of America.

LDB: All these issues were closing in, forcing him to re-evaluate himself as a writer, patriotic citizen, Southerner, liberal humanitarian, politician. Essentially, his life was far too occupied with activities and visions that were counterproductive to writing fiction.

VFJ: Writing fiction *at home*!

LDB: Right. From 1950 through 1955 Faulkner had been very much away from home, uprooted, dislocated.

VFJ: Both geographically and spiritually. I think he was lost, losing it in those years. We left Mississippi in June 1952. Already he was very much involved with Joan Williams. I think even Pappy realized the hopelessness of that. Joan was saying no. But, of course, there were other women as well, as we now know. He was a pitiful man at that point. He was lost. He didn't seem to know where to go. And he was traveling. He was a celebrity, meeting people, influential people, and he was also meeting women. And most of all, Pappy was away from his family. His country had turned against him. I mean his country in terms of Mississippi and Oxford. I think he sank into a despair and that was the cause of his excessive drinking. His health was just going to pot because of it.

LDB: In letters Estelle wrote to Saxe and Dorothy Commins, she confirmed that Faulkner virtually hadn't been home at all between 1950 through 1954.[19] He really was at odds. Rowan Oak had been invaded; it had ceased providing him with that refugelike state of contentment and tranquility it once had. To make it worse, at one point during the early fifties he was having affairs with Else Jonsson in Stockholm, Joan Williams, Meta Rebner, and within another year, 1953, he would become smitten by a teenager, Jean Stein.

VFJ: I think these women were just poor substitutes for more substantial rewards he was searching so hard for to fulfill his life. He wasn't gaining rewards from his writing despite the numerous awards his writing was residually receiving. *A Fable* had not come out as he had wanted. That was his biggest disappointment during those years.

LDB: And *Requiem for a Nun* had not really been the great experimental novel some critics considered it to be.

VFJ: I don't think he cared as much about *Requiem*. I really don't! Frankly, Ruth Ford had bothered him for years to do that one because she wanted to be a star, and she thought it was a good story. Sure, Pappy had it as a story before he actually started a play, dialogue, and Ruth pushed and pushed him. It was not one of the things he really wanted to do, because he knew that his forte was not straight dialogue.

LDB: Other than for *Requiem for a Nun* and *A Fable*, both of which were derivative legacies from earlier conceptions, Faulkner's publications between 1949 and 1957 consisted of collections and compilations of rewritten stories, almost all of which had appeared years earlier. These included *Knight's Gambit* [1949], *Collected Stories* [1950], *The Faulkner Reader* [1954], and *Big Woods* [1955], books fabricated as sales ploys to follow up on Faulkner's Nobel Prize publicity and mostly done under the fatherly guidance of his editor and trusted confidant, Saxe Commins.

VFJ: Thank God for Saxe! And for Dorothy, his wife. Pappy said she was one of the kindest women he had ever known. I believe the Comminses saved Pappy's life during the fifties—literally.

LDB: Even with Saxe's assistance, the writing was not very consequential, that is, other than with the exceptions of the three prose prologues to *Requiem*, a short biographical story entitled "Mississippi," his Nobel Prize speech (which had been heard like a shot fired around the world), and perhaps his foreword to *The Faulkner Reader*, a spectacular raison d'être of his most explicitly profound thoughts about himself as a writer, and *The Reivers*, a wonderfully funny book.

VFJ: You're right. Very little of it seemed consequential and even less that he was particularly fond of. He had had such high hopes that *A Fable* would be his greatest novel. He dedicated it to Jill because he thought it was going to be his *chef d'oeuvre*, but he was not satisfied when it went to print—it wasn't good. And that was another source of depression. Things really hit an all-time low, I think, in '54. And to make matters worse, Jill got married that year.

LDB: That had to be very depressing.

VFJ: Certainly. Pappy went on a binge as soon as she got married, right after the wedding. And so did Grandmama, but that was her last one as far as I know.

LDB: In many respects, 1954 seems to have marked the nadir in the lives of Estelle and William Faulkner.

VFJ: Indeed, I agree. That was an extremely bleak period in their relationship. Grandmama had not yet really decided to lick her drinking problem, but she was beginning to see the necessity of doing so—if for no other reason than for Jill's well-being. And Jill herself was actually playing a role in Grandmama's change. She had insisted that Pappy make an agreement with Grandmama to provide her with adequate funds to allow her some freedom. After all, Pappy had been traveling, leaving for months at a time without providing Grandmama with enough money to keep up Rowan Oak. He was taking off around the world, going to Egypt, to Europe; he was doing all these things while expecting her to sit home alone at Rowan Oak, and that was immediately after Jill got married. Grandmama was very lonely. Nobody was there. That's when my parents suggested she come to the Philippines. She protested all the way to the airplane, but she did get on the plane and go, much to Pappy's amazement. He was surprised at her independence in doing that, that she got a visa, the papers done, had her inoculations, and went. And she was gone for three months. On her flight back home she came to visit me in Switzerland where I was attending school. She even spent a week in Paris and some time in Rome on the way—all by herself.

LDB: And it was shortly after this that Estelle determined to commit herself to the AA program.

VFJ: Yes, I think so; though she may have already started getting help some months before, because she was wonderfully herself during those days in Switzerland.

LDB: From that point forth, there seemed to be a different relationship between William and Estelle Faulkner.

VFJ: It certainly didn't happen overnight, though. I don't think Pappy trusted her for a couple of years. He kept watching to see if she would relapse into her drinking.

LDB: Yet Faulkner maintained his own double standard, didn't he? She could attempt to cure herself, but there was no way he was going to quit. He continued to deteriorate.

VFJ: No. Pappy was not the same kind of alcoholic Grandmama was. He could control his drinking if he wanted to, and I guess he couldn't understand why Grandmama couldn't do the same thing. My grandmother was the classic alcoholic—a glass of wine at dinner was enough to set her off. Once she started, she couldn't stop and wouldn't until she passed out. That was it. I mean, she was a *real* alcoholic. It had an allergic effect on her. On the other hand, Pappy could drink socially and not get drunk. He could have a few drinks, wine at dinner, and that would be that. But when he was under a great deal of stress, he might decide, "I'm going on a binge," and he would make the decision consciously and soberly.

LDB: That strikes me as a very selfish act.

VJF: Without a doubt. But Pappy would do that. Often he struck me as a willful child who merely wants his own way. I remember one incident that occurred after Jill married Paul that August of 1954. Grandmama drank at the wedding and that started her off. Dorothy and Saxe left, and my parents had to go on elsewhere. I was left after the wedding at Rowan Oak with Grandmama and Pappy. I had just learned to drive that summer, and I didn't drive too well, and I didn't have a license yet. Grandmama went off the deep end and was in bed, immobile, out! She had lost her baby. Her Jill was gone.

LDB: That summer Estelle suffered severe hemorrhaging and had to be hospitalized; that could have been a few months earlier.

VFJ: Yes, she did have ulcers, I'm sure from keeping everything inside her. She never burdened anyone with the knowledge of Pappy's affairs, except in her letters to Saxe and Dorothy Commins, because they were the only people she confided in. And she never, never told her children; she never let out all this agony, so she got ulcers, and it was exacerbated by the drinking, of course. Pappy also realized his baby had gotten married and gone away, and he sort of looked around, and you could almost see the wheels working: "Stelle's gone and done it, I might as well, too." He went on a binge of binges. I was there by myself. Finally, after two days or so of my trying to keep at least the beds clean of vomit and excrement and everything else, Pappy somehow, in his drunken stupor, realized I couldn't take it anymore, couldn't handle it. I was too immature. I really couldn't drive;

I couldn't go to the bootlegger for them or do anything, really. Pappy kept mumbling in his stupor, "Get Malcolm! Get Malcolm to take me to Byhalia." Two days later, having gone to the grocery store to get something to put into Grandmama so she could sober up, I drove into the driveway, and Pappy was sitting out on the front porch in his favorite rocking chair like he had never been away, and I said, "Pappy, I'm so glad to see you," and he said, "Yessum, I knew you were in trouble." Even in his drunken state he realized I couldn't cope with the situation, and he'd gone to "dry out." Grandmama took a while longer.

LDB: Fundamentally, Faulkner was a very conscious drinker, and even in that drunken state you described, he knew what was going on.

VFJ: True, but my grandmother, no! She was blotto; she passed out. When she woke up from bouts like that one, she never knew anything that was going on or what had gone on. She would just take another drink and pass out again.

LDB: Faulkner used alcohol to balance his tension, didn't he?

VFJ: Yes, he did.

LDB: Buzz Bezzerides has told me similar tales that occurred during the time Faulkner worked in the early-to-mid-forties at Warner Bros. Yet I have not encountered one person who has ever expressed the notion that Faulkner drank heavily, if at all, during periods when he was writing.[20]

VFJ: The question of Pappy's drinking has been asked of me often: "Did Faulkner drink while he was writing his fiction?" Also, "Was his writing affected by his drinking?" I have always said, "Absolutely not, because when he drank, or when he was drunk anyway, he couldn't get down the stairs to the typewriter to write." I mean, he would be in bed ranting and raving, hollering for me to play Mozart—which reminds me, Pappy had no knowledge of music that I'm aware of, but knowing that the Oldham side of the family was musically oriented, he somehow decided that Mozart was the great guru, and Mozart was what he yelled for when he was drunk. Many years after the big Nobel Prize binge, I was practicing a Handel piece when he came in one afternoon; knowing his aversion to "noise," I stopped—but he said I could keep on playing because he liked Mozart so much. I never told him it was Handel because I figured that if he didn't know the difference *sober,* I could slip in some Handel the next time he got drunk and demanded Mozart. That was in 1960, though, and I never had the chance to fool him.

LDB: At any given time, Faulkner's condition was a response to his own volition. He could determine his own state, could willfully impose the condition on himself.

VFJ: I remember when he had been out drinking with his hunting buddies for a week, and he hadn't gotten drunk. He had been drinking socially, but he was not drunk. But when he got home and learned that he had been selected to receive the Nobel Prize within a month or so in Stockholm and realized that he was going to have to face that audience, make that trip, submit himself to protocol, suddenly he said, "I can't handle it! I ain't going!" His only response was to start hitting the bottle. And I'm telling you, we had a time getting him to Sweden at all.

LDB: Shades of the premiere of *Intruder in the Dust*.

VFJ: That occasion had been child's play compared to this spectacle. Talk about tantrums and displays!

LDB: And he got very sick on that trip. But let's focus on that period a little more closely. We discussed Faulkner's passage from the forties through the mid-fifties, suggesting that 1954 might be considered a catastrophic low-water mark in his life. Perhaps that period gave Faulkner sufficient alarm and caused him to reassess himself as a family man and as a public figure.

VFJ: Yes, indeed. And as a *writer*. Yes, I believe the change started about the time Pappy went to Charlottesville as writer-in-residence at the university. You see, Jill had settled there with Paul, and their first child, Tad, was born in the spring of 1956.

LDB: This may have been the beginning of a new life together for Estelle and William Faulkner.

VFJ: Yes, I believe so. They became very close friends again. At times they even looked and seemed like they were a newly married couple. There was a joy they shared, and Pappy took pride in Grandmama's having licked her alcoholism. He was very proud of her. I don't think he felt she ever would have had the guts to do it, but she did quit and without too damn much help from him, either.

LDB: Would it be a fair assessment to suggest that when it came down to those last six years of Faulkner's life, 1956 to 1962, he came full circle, that in his mature years, the image, the vision that as a young man he had possessed of Estelle Oldham, the one who had married away from him, caused him so much heartache, actually returned to him absolved, vindicated, redeemed?

VFJ: Oh, I think so. Definitely! Actually, despite all his other affairs, I believe that Grandmama always had been at the center of Pappy's emotional life.

LDB: I've been told there was a new tenderness between them.

VFJ: Yes, there was. And it was lovely to see.

LDB: In 1956, Faulkner started working on new fiction. *The Town* would embody his attempt to tie up major loose ends he had been contemplating since the early twenties when he and Phil Stone had idled away days concocting humorous anecdotes about the Snopes clan of Yoknapatawpha County. By 1957, the book was published. In 1959, he followed *The Town* with the concluding volume of his Snopes trilogy, *The Mansion*. If these novels didn't seem to have the same force as their predecessor, *The Hamlet,* at least they were proof positive that Faulkner still had the capacity to invent entertaining narrative fiction.

VFJ: I think those books reflect the new peace of mind that had come to Pappy because Grandmama had licked her alcoholism and he suddenly saw her as a completely different and new and appealing woman. He tremendously admired her fortitude, and it showed in his work as a mellowing force.

LDB: Estelle admired his writing, didn't she?

VFJ: She did. Yes! And whenever Pappy would finish a new novel, type it out, he would ask her to read it. This was a consistent routine for him throughout the years. I remember being at Rowan Oak one afternoon toward the end. Grandmama and I were sitting and talking in the kitchen. It was in the early spring, sort of a chilly day, and Pappy came in from the barn, and Grandmama said, "Billy, I think now is the time to tell her. Don't you want to tell Vicki something?" And he looked rather smug, with a little smile, just as proud of himself as he could be, and he said, "Vic-Pic, I've got a new book coming out," and I said, "Oh, Pappy, that's great! What's it about?" And he said, "No, you're going to have to read it," and I said, "What is it called?" He replied, "*The Reivers*," and I said, "What does that mean? I've never heard that word before." He said, "It's 'The Thieves'; it's a Scottish word I found and liked," and he told me about how he had debated its spelling. He said, "Vic-Pic, the best part is that it's dedicated to you and to my other grandchildren, and you head the list." I just wanted to cry, I mean, it pleased me so much. I just kept on saying, "What's it all about, what's it all about?" He said, "Vic-Pic, it's the funniest story I've ever read"—not *written,* but ever *read.* And he was just smiling all over himself, and he was happy, and you could see Grandmama was happy; she was sharing it with him right there. They didn't hold hands or touch or anything like that, but they were together in his happiness, their happiness.

LDB: And in what respect did you head Faulkner's list?

VFJ: Well, I was the eldest. But, I mean, I was a *step*grandchild.

LDB: Were you really a *step*grandchild?

VFJ: I guess not to Pappy. He considered me his grandchild, and that's what pleased me so much. He could have dedicated *The Reivers* just to Jill's children—Tad, Will, and Bok—but he did include me and Mark, Malcolm's son. And he did it according to age. I was at the top. I was the firstborn of Pappy's grandchildren.

LDB: Although Faulkner never legally adopted Estelle Franklin's two children, Victoria and Malcolm, there was never any question of his fatherly sentiments; they were unequivocally his daughter and son. His dedication to *The Reivers* proclaimed and celebrated his steadfast love and devotion to his son and two daughters by commemorating their five children.

VFJ: Sadly, Pappy died before he could autograph a copy of *The Reivers* for me. Actually, he did inscribe one for my parents the first of June. He and Grandmama had come back to Oxford from Charlottesville especially to attend my graduation from Ole Miss. But I was not staying at Rowan Oak, rather at Jim and Dutch Silver's house on campus. Then everything got rushed, and I was gone. When I did return in late August or early September with Mama and my fiancé to discuss possibilities of having my wedding at Rowan Oak, Grandmama gave me the copy of *The Reivers* Pappy had saved to inscribe for me; and Jill wrote in it: "For Vicki, because Pappy would have—if he'd had the time before July."[21]

LDB: Let's backtrack once again. When William and Estelle Faulkner were in Charlottesville, did they rent a house or buy one?

VFJ: When he assumed the position of writer-in-residence, they rented. I recall they rented one place on Ivy Road (where I stayed once), then a second place at 917 Rugby Road, which they ended up purchasing.

LDB: But they still made an effort to keep ties with Rowan Oak, with Oxford, with Mississippi, didn't they?

VFJ: Oh, yes. They were always there at Christmas, at least through 1956 while I was in college. After that I think they may have celebrated Christmas in Charlottesville. And usually they returned in the spring so that Pappy could get in some jumping and Grandmama could tend to her rose garden. They made three or four trips a year going back and forth. They never flew. Grandmama and Pappy shared the long drive back to Oxford and then the return to Charlottesville. And even though their hearts were now with Jill and her growing family, Rowan Oak remained very important.

LDB: Yet, in Virginia he had found a new home, and he was very flattered to count as friends the sophisticated horse and hunting crowds, flattered that they would admit him into their circles. I can understand how in his mellowing he might have considered their acceptance of him and his family a sign that he had "arrived." After all, his whole life he had set up their manner of living as a standard of the highest order to be sought after and emulated.

VFJ: Well, yes and no. Don't forget, there was a great deal of snobbism in Pappy, and that society was rife with snobs. Actually, only a very small part of Pappy's life touched theirs.

LDB: Faulkner was never willing to abandon completely his roots.

VFJ: Nor could he have, even if that had been his choice.

LDB: When Faulkner died in early July 1962, he and Estelle were in Oxford.

VFJ: Yes. As I said, they had come for my graduation from Ole Miss.

LDB: Did Jill return to Oxford with them to attend your graduation?

VFJ: No. She had three little children. But Grandmama and Pappy gave me a wonderful party at Rowan Oak.

LDB: Your grandfather died less than a month later, didn't he?

VFJ: Yes. It was a shock.

LDB: Did Estelle go into a depression when Faulkner died?

VFJ: She was devastated, utterly devastated, but I wouldn't call it a depression where she let herself go, and she certainly didn't resort to drinking. She hadn't touched a drop since 1955. Not a drop!

LDB: It was Faulkner's wish that one-half interest in Rowan Oak should go to your mother and one-half to Jill.

VFJ: Well, he had deeded Rowan Oak to Jill in 1954 when she was twenty-one to avoid future inheritance tax problems. But he thought my mother had always gotten the short end of the stick with regard to her own father, Cornell, who had left her practically nothing, so what he did, and Jill and Grandmama agreed, was to see that one-half of Jill's share should be transferred to Grandmama, then have Grandmama deed that share to my mother. My mother would inherit one-half interest in Rowan Oak when both were gone.

LDB: Was that how it worked out?

VFJ: Yes and no. Since Jill as executrix had the burden of estate taxes on her shoulders, Mama relinquished her right to the property so that Jill could sell it and pay the taxes.

LDB: All right, but it was certainly understood that Faulkner's hope was that your mother and father would eventually occupy Rowan Oak.

VFJ: Yes. They would retire there, keep it intact, always as a place for any member of the family. It would always be home for the Faulkners and the Franklins and the Fieldens.

LDB: But shortly after her father died, Jill realized his original intention was not feasible. Instead, she attempted to interest the state of Mississippi and the university in taking it over and preserving it as a memorial.

VFJ: Not at that point! Jill was the executrix of Pappy's estate; yet she was having severe problems because apparently Pappy hadn't gotten the best legal and financial advice about his will. Jill was really stuck with paying the taxes since most of the royalties from Pappy's books were tied up at Random House. Essentially, what my father agreed to do at the time he could retire was to assume my mother's half share in Rowan Oak and buy Jill's share. But my father became ill with cancer, and it was obvious that he would not be able to maintain Rowan Oak. He died in 1970 and Jill was strapped with the taxes. Her only recourse was to sell Rowan Oak. My mother realized that Jill was bearing all the burden, and she agreed to the sale to Ole Miss, which was effected in 1973.

LDB: There would have been no way Estelle would have considered moving back to Oxford and occupying Rowan Oak, living there alone, would there?

VFJ: No way at all. As I said, she was devastated by Pappy's death. I remember a few months after Pappy passed away, my fiancé and my mother flew up to Mississippi from Caracas as I mentioned earlier. I couldn't think of anything more romantic than the possibility of being married in the garden at Rowan Oak, and we talked to Grandmama about it. Although she regretted it very much, she said she just couldn't bear it—a wedding at Rowan Oak at that time. It would be too painful for her to stand. Instead, I married in Caracas, and she intended to come to the wedding, but in getting her smallpox vaccination, she contracted it and ended up in the hospital. Regrettably, she missed the wedding, but Jill came and was my matron of honor.

LDB: Can you recall any specific moments when Estelle reflected on your grandfather after he was gone?

VFJ: Yes. One instance I remember happened in February. It was February the nineteenth, I recall, because it was Grandmama's seventy-fifth birthday in 1972. It was three months after my husband had died.

LDB: And shortly before she was to die.

VFJ: Yes. Just a few months. Anyway, Grandmama was living with Jill in Charlottesville. She had her own quarters in Jill and Paul's house, and it was quite separate from the rest of the house, a private area.

LDB: She had sold the house in which she and Faulkner had lived?

VFJ: Yes, the one on Rugby, I believe, and she had put the money into Jill and Paul's house to build onto it so that she could be close by in case she got ill and needed someone to care for her. She always suffered from colds, and up in Virginia, particularly, the dampness and the harsh winters were more rigorous than in Mississippi. She had a chronic case of bronchitis.

LDB: She was a heavy smoker.

VFJ: Yes, and a heavy coffee drinker, too.

LDB: Was she a frail woman?

VFJ: Yes, yes! Tiny!

LDB: Valetudinarian?

VFJ: No. No! But frail. She was always very, very small, very thin, and of course the years of drinking had not helped. Anyway, by the time of her seventy-fifth birthday, she was suffering from old age as well. She would huddle in bed most of the day. My mother, Gillian, and I had come down from New York to Virginia to be with her. I went into her room that afternoon to talk to her privately, and she asked me how I was getting along. I told her that I was still very much grieving over my husband's death but that I had had a dream in which I had seen my husband across a room full of people, and I was trying to get to him. He just smiled and nodded, and though I never could get to him, I had this feeling that everything was all right. Then she said to me that she had had the same thing happen after Pappy's death—I can't recall her saying just how long after. She'd had a dream, and she believed in ghosts, and she said she didn't know whether it, the dream, was actually a vision, whether she was waking or dreaming, but it was so vivid she thought she must be awake. She had seen Pappy come and sit on the end of her bed at Rowan Oak, and he said, "Stelle, everything is all right," and after that she had had a deep serene feeling of peace. Three months later, Grandmama died and was brought back to Oxford to be buried in St. Peters beside Pappy.

LDB: Victoria, when you think today of your grandmother, Estelle Oldham Franklin Faulkner, what is the most poignant memory that comes to mind?

VFJ: I can still hear her singing and playing her own music at the piano in the living room of Rowan Oak. I can actually hear Grandmama singing long before her image comes into focus behind my thoughts.

LDB: You had grown up listening to her music and her singing. You mentioned one song for which she had written the music and the lyrics, your favorite and hers, too. She had titled it "White Beaches." You said you had coaxed her into copying it down for you because you didn't ever want to forget it. When was that?

VFJ: That was not long after Pappy died. She made a trip to Venezuela in 1963 after I had married and I was living in Caracas. My parents were there, too, so Grandmama came down and stayed quite a long time. I had a piano and she played for me at my request. We taped her playing without her knowing it, or she never would have allowed it. She said the words rather than singing them, but the words were muffled, nearly inaudible, so I asked her to write them down for me.

LDB: Did you know that in 1927, after Estelle had separated from Cornell Franklin and left Shanghai, she presented Billy Faulkner with a novel she had written, a novel entitled "White Beaches"? And that she asked him to submit it to a publisher for her? [22]

VFJ: I had no idea Grandmama ever wrote a novel. I'm amazed, but not surprised!

LDB: Faulkner sent the novel to Scribners, who rejected it and returned it without too much delay. When Faulkner informed Estelle, she became so distraught she burned the manuscript. Faulkner's response was one of extreme anger toward her. What strikes me as most remarkably coincidental is the identical title of the novel and the song you said she played until the end of her life.

VFJ: She wrote the poem "White Beaches" [23] and set it to music before she wrote the novel. Of this I am quite certain.

LDB: To what do you imagine "White Beaches" referred?

VFJ: I can only speculate that the novel must have been set in Hawaii and that it could have been about her youth, her arranged marriage, and about the lover she left behind. I feel certain that she wrote the song "White Beaches" in Hawaii in 1919, before she moved to Shanghai with Cornell Franklin.

LDB: Can you recite the lyrics to this song?

VFJ:

> When the wanderlust comes, it is time to go
> To the place your heart calls you to.
> Mine is a place by the blue, blue sea,
> Where I'll go someday, Love, and take you.
>
> It's a bit of a cove with its bit of a beach,
> And around it the cliffs loom stark,
> But we will be sailing there soon, dear heart,
> In our strange and beautiful bark.
>
> White beaches and starlight,
> And the sea is beckoning me
> To a place that men might call lonely,
> But it means all heaven to me.
>
> To my beach with its surf and its wind-bent palms,
> And the feel of your loveliness in my arms,
> With the god of true lovers to stay all alarms,
> On my white beach 'neath the low tropic stars.

LDB: Was Hawaii the place where Estelle and Cornell Franklin honeymooned?

VFJ: No, but it was the location of their first home. And for Grandmama, all her life it remained the most romantic spot in the world.

LDB: Undoubtedly, in the song she had captured all her own most profound longings and emotions from that period. The unnamed lover in the song—obviously this was not a reference to Cornell Franklin.

VFJ: Right! Although she had married Cornell Franklin, it had been a marriage arranged by both families. He was a good match for her. He was from an exceptional, old Mississippi family, and he was a brilliant young man with an equally bright future who had just finished law school at Ole Miss. But Grandmama didn't know him. She married a stranger who took her off, away from Mississippi. She had never really been anywhere in her life, except perhaps to attend Mary Baldwin in Virginia. Well, she had been born in Texas, but Mississippi—Oxford—had been her life. Then she was taken away to this strange, almost foreign country and with a strange man. She was enchanted by the beauty of the place; she had an artist's eye. But she had left her romantic lover behind, at home, and that was Billy Falkner, Pappy. She had written her poem, her song, about a place that had struck her for its beauty, and she wanted to show it to Billy. The line is right there: "Mine is a place by the blue, blue sea, / Where I'll go someday, Love, and take you."

LDB: "To a place that men might call lonely . . ."

VFJ: "But it means all heaven to me."

LDB: And the object of her affection and her longing was Billy Falkner.

VFJ: Oh, yes! *Love,* within commas, capitalized—Yes! That's Pappy! After all, Cornell Franklin would hardly have required a description of this place; certainly, it was the secret, exotic place she would always dream of sharing for the first time, initiating it with her true love.

LDB: Estelle would play this song whenever she sat down at the piano?

VFJ: No. Not unless we specifically requested it. But it was her favorite, and it was ours, too, the entire family's: Jill's, mine, my parents' . . . and Pappy's, too!

GLIMPSES WITHIN GLIMPSES

Faulkner's cartoon for proposed eleventh-grade yearbook, ca. 1918.

Faulkner posing in Canadian RAF flier's dress uniform, ca. 1918.

VII.

Mississippi Hills : MY EPITAPH.

Far blue hills, where I have pleasured me,
Where on silver feet in dogwood cover
Spring follows, singing close the bluebird's "Lover!"
When to the road I trod an end I see,

Let this soft mouth, shaped to the rain,
Be but golden grief for grieving's sake,
And these green woods be dreaming here to wake
Within my heart when I return again.

Return I will! Where is there the death
While in these blue hills slumbrous overhead
I'm rooted like a tree? Though I be dead,
This soil that holds me fast will find me breath.

The stricken tree has no young green to weep
The golden years we spend to buy regret.
So let this be my doom, if I forget
That there's still spring to shake and break my sleep.

William Faulkner.

Signed typescript, 1924, later included in *Mississippi Poems*.

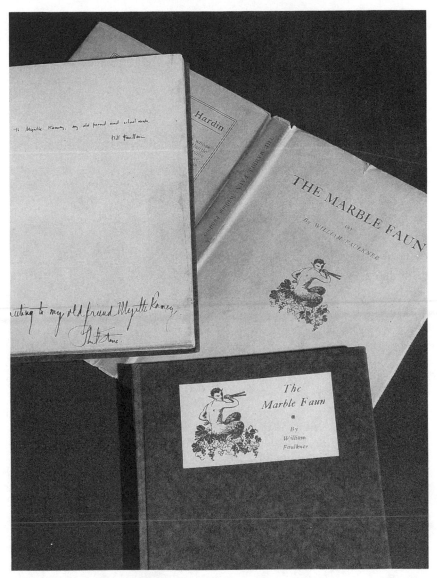

The Marble Faun, signed by Faulkner and Phil Stone, 1924.

Odiorne ——— Paris

Faulkner at Notre Dame, Paris, 1925; signed by photographer.

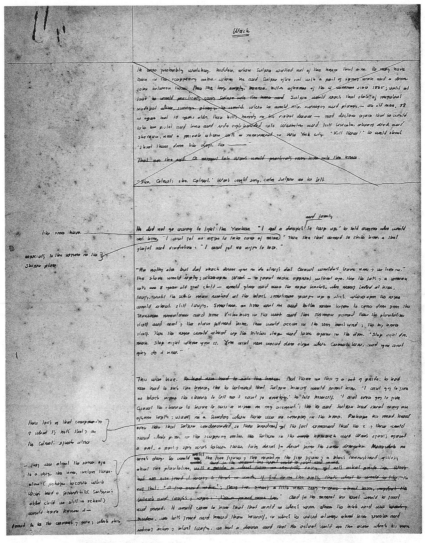

Title page of working draft of "Wash," ca. 1933.

Photograph of Faulkner, inscribed to his Aunt Bama McLean, 1933.

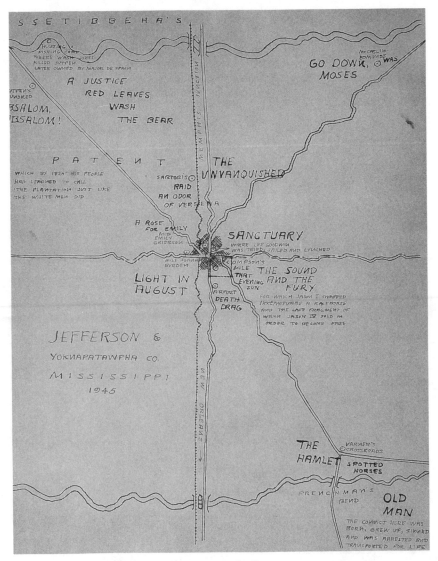

Faulkner's 1945 pen-and-ink map of Yoknapatawpha County.

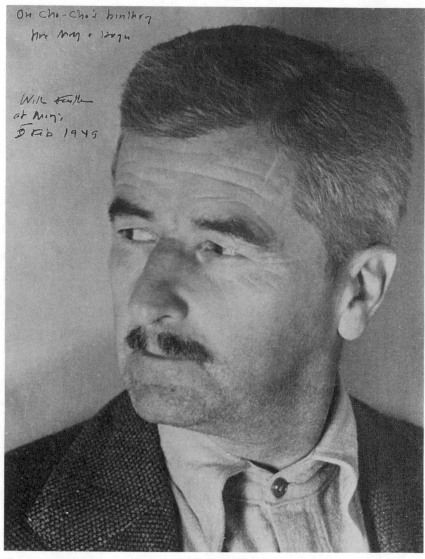

Photograph inscribed to Faulkner's stepdaughter, "Cho-Cho," 1949.

Rowan Oak, Faulkner's Oxford, Mississippi, home, ca. 1951.

  Tuesday

Dear Saxe:

            Thank you for your note. No, I dont feel
too well. My back gives me a little trouble, but not
much; mainly, for the first time in my life, I am
completely bored, fed up, my days are being wasted.
It is just possible that I shall do something quite
drastic about the matter before long. I have done no
work in a year, do not want to, yet I have work which
I must do. We talked some of my giving myself six
months of absence, getting completely away from here
and all my familiar life. I think now it will take
more than that. I think now I may, to save my soul,
something of peace, contentment, save the work at least,
quit the whole thing, give it all to them, leave and
be done with it. I can earn enough to live on, I think.
I am really sick, I think. Cant sleep too well, nervous,
idle, have to make an effort not to let the farm go to
 pot, look forward only with boredom to the next sunrise.
I dont like it. Maybe I will have to get away, for at
least a year, almost vanish. Then maybe I will get to
work again, and get well again. But I dont have enough
time left to spend it like this. That is, I still want
what I have always wanted: to be free; probably until
now I have still believed that somehow, in some way,
someday I would be free again; now at last I have begun
to realise that perhaps I will not, I have waited, hoped
too long, done nothing about it; and so now I must, or
-- in spirit -- die.

I haven't quite reached the point yet, but I dont think
I shall be much longer. There will be scorn and oppro-
brium of course, but perhaps I have already sacrificed
too much already to try to be a good artist, to boggle
at a little more in order to still try to be one.

                              Yours,

                               Bill

Letter from Faulkner to Saxe Commins, early October 1953.

Faulkner and Phil Stone in Stone's Oxford, Mississippi, law office, ca. 1952.

  Wednesday

Dear Phil:

          I haven't seen the LIFE thing yet, and wont.
I have found that my mother is furious over it, seems
to consider it inferentially lies , cancelled her sub-
scription.

          I tried for years to prevent it, refused always,
asked them to let me alone. It's too bad the individual in
this country has no protection from journalism, I suppose
they call it. But apparently he hasn't. There seems to be
in this the same spirit which permits strangers to drive
into my yard and pick up books or pipes I left in the
chair where I had been sitting, as souvenirs.

          What a commentary. Sweden gave me the Nobel
Prize. France gave me the Legion d'Honneur. All my native
land did fro me was to invade my privacy over my protest
and my plea. No wonder people in the rest of the world
dont like us, since we seem to have neither taste nor
courtesy, and know and believe in nothing but money and
it doesn't much matter how you get it.

                              Yours,

                              Bill

This time I wasn't even consulted, didn't even know it
was being done, nor did my mother. She knew she was being photographed and specifically asked the photographer
not to print the picture anywhere.

This seems to me to be a pretty sorry return for a man
who has only tried to be an artist and bring what honor
that implies to the land of his birth.

Letter from Faulkner to Phil Mullen, early October 1953.

Faulkner jumping his horse in paddock, Rowan Oak, ca. 1954.

Faulkner's impressions of "Danzas Venezuela," April 1961.

To Deb with love
Bill
21 Feb 1961

Portrait
By
Col. C.field

Inscribed photograph of Faulkner in full riding regalia, 1961.

APPENDIX A

INDIAN GIVER

The publication history of William Faulkner's *The Wishing Tree* is byzantine and highly curious. To be precise, it spans two months more than four decades from the date of its very private, officially recorded "publication" as a personally typed, hand-bound, single copy that Faulkner gave as a birthday gift on February 5, 1927,[1] to its initial magazine appearance as a short story, "The Wishing Tree," in the April 8, 1967, number of *Saturday Evening Post,* vol. 240, pp. 48 ff., followed three days later by the Random House first printing as a self-contained novella, replete with elaborate illustrations commissioned for the simultaneously issued trade and specially bound and slip-cased numbered edition entitled *The Wishing Tree.*[2]

According to definitions adopted and promulgated by the United States Copyright Office,[3] it was Faulkner who fixed the official dates of creation and, by implication, publication of *The Wishing Tree* when he typed the phrase, "single mss. impression / oxford-mississippi- / 5-february-1927" [*sic*], at the foot of the verso of the title page, then bound and presented his gift booklet to Lida Estelle Franklin's daughter, Victoria de Graffenried Franklin, presumably on that same day. Officially, this date satisfies the terms of the Copyright Office's statute that asserts that "a work is 'created' when it is fixed in a copy . . . for the first time." Understood is the fact that the text itself could not have sprung simultaneously and completely intact on February 5, 1927, rather, that its gestation and the revisionary process leading up to the typing and binding of this "single mss. impression" had seemingly culminated on that date.

Accepting the Copyright Office's statutory definition of "publication" as that date on which the first "distribution of . . . a work to the public by sale or other transfer of ownership" is made, it would appear that February 5, 1927, also should be considered the official recorded date of publication for *The Wishing Tree.* On the title page, below the title, THE WISHING

TREE, Faulkner added the following first of two dedications: "For his dear friend / Victoria / on her eighth birthday / Bill he made / this Book." Victoria Franklin, who, with the marriage of her mother to William Faulkner on June 20, 1929, would become the author's stepdaughter, had been born in Honolulu, Hawaii, on February 5, 1919. Implied in his dedication is the fact that Faulkner had made the book for the occasion of the little girl's birthday, not that he had actually made it on that day. Two additional assumptions as well may be extrapolated from Faulkner's wording: first, that on the actual day of the birthday, February 5, 1927, Faulkner would have physically given Victoria the book, and second, that in giving her the book, he would have fulfilled the dedication's promise to cause a transfer of ownership to be accomplished.

Ironically, no more than six days later, possibly even before February 5, 1927, Faulkner would either repeat the magnanimous gesture he had made to Victoria Franklin or make the first of what would become two such similar deeds by personally delivering to the house of Dr. and Mrs. Calvin S. Brown, of Oxford, Mississippi, a differently typed copy of a story he had titled, *The Wishing-Tree*.[4] Although it is impossible to date with absolute precision the exact day on which Faulkner brought to the Brown house his gift for daughter Margaret, we do know from the entry Dr. Brown made in his diary for February 11, 1927, that he "read a story by William Faulkner called *The Wishing-Tree* which he brought over to Margaret."[5] Unfortunately, the usually fastidious diarist failed to record the actual day on which Faulkner dropped off the manuscript; Dr. Brown could have been coming to the task of reading the story days after, rather than on that very day the gift arrived. Nonetheless, the fact remains that Faulkner did present Margaret Brown, who was dying of an irreversible disease, with a gift of friendship and consolation, a newly written fairy tale entitled *The Wishing-Tree* (note the hyphen), which he suggested he had composed especially for her. In the upper left portion of page 1, Faulkner had inscribed in ink what amounted to a dedication: "To Margaret Brown / from her friend, / Bill Faulkner."

Unquestionably, Faulkner's two separate gifts, *The Wishing Tree* and *The Wishing-Tree,* would go unremarked for thirty years. So, too, would the awareness, or even the slightest suspicion by any single party other than Faulkner himself, that more than one copy of *The Wishing Tree* existed. Both recipients, and, later, Margaret Brown's surviving family members, would continue to believe that the copy each possessed not only had been written exclusively for her by William Faulkner but also was uniquely hers to do with as she might see fit.

A first printing of *Intruder in the Dust,*[6] which Faulkner inscribed for Mrs. Maud Morrow Brown, Margaret Brown's mother, and dated De-

cember 10, 1948, may document the day on which the author came to the
Brown house in Oxford to borrow the typescript of *The Wishing-Tree* that
in 1927 he had originally given to the now-long-deceased Margaret. The
inscribed copy of the recently published book may have been a token of
politeness for a favor he correctly anticipated Mrs. Brown would grant
him.

Doubtless, Faulkner's reason for his request was neither exacted by
Mrs. Brown nor proffered by the borrower. In fact, Faulkner's purpose for
taking the typescript home was to type from it two copies, ribbon and
carbon, which he could give as Christmas gifts to the children of two intimate friends: Phil Stone and Ruth Ford. Presumably, when he finished his
retyping chore, Faulkner delivered to the Stone residence the recently
typed forty-four-page bound ribbon copy he had made from the forty-
seven-page Brown carbon copy. On page 1, in the upper left-hand corner,
Faulkner had inscribed in ink: "For Philip Stone II, / from his god-father.
/ William Faulkner / Oxford. / Xmas 1948."[7] The corresponding unbound
carbon copy was mailed to its recipient. Its ink inscription read: "For
Shelley Ford. / Xmas, 1948 / William Faulkner."[8]

Except for the conscious omission of the verse epigram that accompanied the copies Faulkner had made in 1927 for Victoria Franklin and for
Margaret Brown,[9] these two new copies resembled the original Brown text
he had recently borrowed from Maud Morrow Brown. In fact, except for
accidental variants caused by typographical errors and not a half-dozen
minor alterations in diction and with only one obviously mistaken transposition of two lines of dialogue with its concomitant misattribution of
speaker in one of the two lines, the text of the Philip Stone and Shelley
Ford copies remained true to the Margaret Brown copy.

Coincidentally, the previously mentioned copy of *Intruder in the Dust*
may also contain information that documents the occasion on which Faulkner returned the borrowed typescript to Mrs. Brown. The first free front
endpaper of the book not only contains the presentation inscription that
Faulkner made, "For Mrs. Calvin Brown / Bill Faulkner," with its accompanying provenance appearing on the title page, "William Faulkner /
Oxford Miss / 10 Dec 1948," but also bears beneath his first inscription a
second one to Mrs. Brown's visiting daughter, Faulkner's childhood
friend, Edith Brown Douds: "For Edith / Xmas 1948 / Bill Faulkner."
Quite possibly, on his appearance with the typescript, Mrs. Douds, a collector in her own right, could have requested of Faulkner his signature on
the book he had left with her mother a few weeks earlier.

Neither Phil Stone nor Ruth Ford imagined that their child had received a Christmas gift from William Faulkner that was anything other
than unique; certainly, they never questioned its originality. In fact, it was

not until Maud Brown saw a copy of the Princeton University catalogue[10] highlighting a copy of *The Wishing-Tree* among the entries on display for the vast Faulkner exhibition running from May 10 through August 30, 1957, that she even surmised what Faulkner's intention had been for borrowing her copy of *The Wishing-Tree* that Christmas of 1948. The exhibited copy was the one Faulkner had given to Philip Stone and had been reluctantly loaned for the occasion by Phil Stone. On July 16, 1958, expressing consternation and hurt over having become aware of the existence of a second copy of her daughter's story, Mrs. Brown wrote a letter to Faulkner imploring him to grant her permission to publish the story:

> Dear Billy,
>   You told me, I know, that The Wishing Tree was mine to do with as I pleased. Through all these years I've cherished it as something personal because Margaret loved it so much. The manuscript is yellow and dogeared from her handling of it. I have never before considered publishing it but now I believe it should be published. Since a copy was on exhibit at Princeton it has become an object of public curiosity.[11]

After numerous unsuccessful attempts on Mrs. Brown's behalf by Professor James W. Silver to interest *Life,* then Random House, in publishing *The Wishing-Tree,* Faulkner himself finally learned of the escalating attempts and with provocation wrote to his publisher, Bennett Cerf, instructing him emphatically not to proceed:

> Dear Bennett:
>   This story was written as a gesture of pity and compassion for Mrs. Brown's little girl who was dying of cancer.
>   I would be shocked if Mrs. Brown herself wanted to commercialize it. But it belongs to her. I will not forbid her to sell it, but I myself would never authorize it being published, unless perhaps, the proceeds should go to save other children from cancer.[12]

It is apparent that even at this late date Faulkner maintained his stance in having made for and given to Margaret Brown *The Wishing-Tree.* His gift had been given outright; it belonged to her, except for its copyright. Possibly at this juncture Faulkner may have realized the potential embarrassment that could arise from publication of this story, especially were it to be discovered by his stepdaughter, for whom, surely, he might have uneasily recalled, he also had made the story thirty-two years earlier.

During the fifties, Professor James W. Silver had become friends with William Faulkner; much earlier, he had nurtured an intimate friendship with Faulkner's two stepchildren, Malcolm and Victoria. As coincidence would have it, Silver, who had already become quite familiar with the Brown typescript of *The Wishing-Tree,* was shocked to discover yet another copy of the story. In a letter to John Cook Wyllie, dated September 1, 1961, Silver described this and other relevant revelations:

> For a long number of years I assumed that Mrs. Maude [*sic*] Morrow Brown (who has known "Billy" since the moment he was born) had the original copy. She had an afflicted daughter who died a couple of years after Faulkner brought to her the story . . . Faulkner borrowed it from "Miss Maude" in 1949 [*sic*] and made another copy for Phil Stone's son. . . .
>
> Anyway, in May of this year, I was talking one night with Faulkner's stepdaughter, Victoria Franklin Fielden, who accidentally remarked that she had a copy of a short story written for her by Faulkner when he was courting her mother. This was the "Wishing Tree" and was apparently given to Mrs. Fielden on her ninth [*sic*] birthday, in 1927 . . . Mrs. Fielden was shocked to discover that there was another copy in existence, and I think a bit hurt, for she had treasured this story as being hers alone. Of course, Mrs. Brown has felt about the same way, particularly after the death of Margaret and after Faulkner had told her that she could do with it as she pleased.[13]

Neither Professor Silver nor Victoria Fielden dared mention this seemingly blatant disparity to Faulkner, who died fourteen months later. Yet, in 1964, fearing that either Mrs. Brown or Phil Stone might press the issue of publication, thereby jeopardizing, possibly squandering, her own proprietary rights to "her" story, and without any opposition from her stepsister, Jill Faulkner Summers, Faulkner's literary executrix, Mrs. Fielden filed for and obtained complete copyright authority to the story, *The Wishing Tree.* Three years later, Random House published what soon became apparent was not merely just another copy of the story, but a distinct version of *The Wishing Tree:* the Victoria version.

APPENDIX B

"PAPPY'S" RECIPE FOR CURING PORK

In late December 1941, William Fielden returned from China to the United States. His destination was Oxford, Mississippi, and Rowan Oak, home of William and Estelle Faulkner. In Shanghai in July 1940, Bill Fielden had married Victoria Franklin, Estelle's daughter and Faulkner's step-daughter. Shortly after their marriage, the Japanese threat of war had increased, and in late 1940 all American women and children were advised to leave the country. Fielden's new bride and his adopted daughter, also named Victoria, were evacuated. Mother and daughter traveled unescorted to Mississippi, while Fielden remained at his job with the British American Tobacco Company.

Estelle and William and their eight-year-old daughter, Jill, eagerly awaited the appearance of the new bridegroom whom they had not met. On his arrival at Rowan Oak, an instant rapport developed between Bill Fielden and "Pappy" (as Faulkner readily instructed Fielden to call him). Fielden was unpretentious, and his gentle personality also immediately captivated Jill and her mother. The Fieldens resided with the Faulkners for several months, while Fielden alternated between job hunting, trying to enlist in the armed services, and working as a field hand at Rowan Oak. Until Faulkner's death in 1962, Rowan Oak would be home for the Fieldens whenever they visited the United States on vacation.

In January 1942, while Bill Fielden was getting acquainted with routines observed in Oxford and especially at the Faulkner residence on Garfield at the edge of town, he witnessed for the first time a pig being killed, butchered, and prepared for curing.[1] His father-in-law, William Faulkner, assisted by the black retainers Prince and Ned Barnett, was in charge of the ceremony. Fielden was so intrigued by his procedure that he asked "Pappy" to type out his own personal "recipe" (as he referred to it from that day forth) for curing pork.[2]

"Pappy" Faulkner obliged his son-in-law, as much an expedient measure as out of cordial compliance. His books had failed to provide him with financial security, and Faulkner was keenly sensitive to his own precarious situation: any day he might be forced to accept war work far from Oxford or be called away to fight for his country. In point of fact, he could imagine Bill Fielden assuming the role of provider for his household. And, indeed, by the end of July 1942, Faulkner would be behind a desk in Burbank, California, fighting for his country by writing war propaganda film scripts for Warner Bros. Although Faulkner could not predict this imminent change of circumstances in early 1942, he could and did feel compelled to instruct his son-in-law in the necessary realities of self-reliance: maintaining a Victory garden, raising poultry, keeping a milk cow, and "Curing Hams[,] Shoulders [and] Bacon."[3]

CURING HAMS SHOULDERS BACON

After the pieces are trimmed and thoroughly cooled, either by 24 hours of natural temperature or by artificial temperature NOT LOW ENOUGH TO FREEZE IT, that is, about 35 degrees F.

Lay the pieces flat, flesh side up, cover thoroughly with plain salt, about 1/4 inch deep. Work saltpeter into the bone-joints and into the ends where the feet were removed, and into any other crevices or abrasions. Do this well and carefully, to prevent 'blowing'. A slightly higher temperature will help the salt penetrate. Leave 24 hours.

After 24 hours, turn the pieces over SKIN SIDE UP, to drain. Sprinkle skin side with salt. I punch holes through the skin with an ice pick, to help draining. Leave 24 hours.

After 24 hours, turn the pieces flesh side up again, make a paste [of] 1/2 plain salt 1/2 molasses, sugar, red and black pepper just moist enough to spread over the pieces without flowing off. Leave 7 days.

After 7 days, make a paste [of] 1/4 plain salt 3/4 molasses, sugar, red and black pepper slightly more fluid than the first mixture, so that it will flow slowly over the pieces, penetrating the remains of last week's treatment, dripping down the sides. Leave 7 days.

After 7 days, make a paste WITHOUT SALT [of] molasses, sugar, red and black pepper fluid enough to cover the pieces without flowing off too much, cover the pieces and the residue of the two former treatments, leave seven days.

Hang the pieces and smoke with hickory or oak chips, keep it in smoky atmosphere for 2 to 7 days. The meat may be treated either before smoking or afterward with a preparation to prevent blow flies. Then wrap or enclose in cloth or paper bags and leave hanging until used.

APPENDIX C

FROM YOKNAPATAWPHA TO CARACAS

Part One   The Andrés Bello Award
   Three years after William Faulkner's death, Random House published in 1965 what was intended to be a complete compilation entitled *Essays, Speeches, & Public Letters by William Faulkner,* edited by James B. Meriwether. However, the volume failed to include a formal acceptance speech Faulkner had delivered on Thursday morning, April 6, 1961, in Caracas, Venezuela, a three-paragraph address acknowledging receipt of the Order of Andrés Bello, that country's most prestigious civilian award.
   This omission would go unredressed until 1974 when two separate publications would attempt to complete the record. The first of these, appearing in March 1974, was Joseph Blotner's two-volume *Faulkner: A Biography.* In his chapter containing a detailed description of Faulkner's two-week sojourn in Venezuela in April 1961 and referring to Faulkner's receipt of the Order of Andrés Bello, Blotner recorded: "[As Faulkner] began to read from a sheet of paper, the audience listened intently. He was reading a Spanish translation of his one-page acceptance speech."[1]
   Without suggesting that the Spanish translation, its words, its phraseology, might have been attributable to anyone other than William Faulkner, Blotner concluded his account with a lengthy excerpt in English of Faulkner's climactic third paragraph, the origin of this English version not being identified.[2] For a reader to assume Faulkner's authorship of the Spanish translation might be understandable since Faulkner had made a similar gesture in New Orleans when he delivered, entirely in French, his acceptance speech in November 1951 on the occasion of receiving the Legion of Honor award. In translating his Legion of Honor speech directly into French, Faulkner not only bypassed the assistance of an intermediary but, more significant, also transmitted his thoughts originally and unalterably into foreign language patterns of written speech. Indeed, al-

though only approximating competency in both written and spoken expression, Faulkner's command of French was far superior to that of Spanish for which he demonstrated no aptitude in written form and little more in verbal fluency. To accomplish in Caracas a presentation similar to that he had effected in New Orleans, Faulkner actually required a translator to take his words from English into an equivalent Spanish text that might approximate his desired expressions and from which he might read in the native language of his presenters: the ultimate goodwill gesture.

In August 1974, following Blotner's biography, James B. Meriwether added the complete English translation made by Muna Lee (from which Blotner had quoted)[3] to an otherwise exclusive gathering of essays and articles previously published in summer "Faulkner" numbers of the *Mississippi Quarterly*. This *Faulkner Miscellany*, in fact, printed on pp. 164–166 two distinct versions, one in Spanish and the other the Lee version in English. The accompanying headnote included the following information, all that was known at the time:

On April 6, 1961, in Caracas, William Faulkner received from the Venezuelan government the Order of Andres [*sic*] Bello, first class. He made his speech of acceptance in Spanish. It was published in the Caracas newspaper *El Universal* April 7, 1961, p. 5, and that text is reprinted here.[4]

Faulkner's original English version has apparently disappeared, and who translated it into Spanish is not known. However, at a later date Miss Muna Lee, a Foreign Service officer who was also a poet, made a translation back into English, which is given here.

Had it not been for my very recent recovery of Faulkner's original single-page holograph draft of his Andrés Bello acceptance speech, Faulkner's authentic words, specific turns of phrase, his measures, and sensibility itself would perhaps never have been known.

Among family effects, various documents relating to that two-week period in Faulkner's life were discovered in the home of Victoria Fielden Johnson, whose parents had been his hosts on that 1961 trip to Caracas, Venezuela. Of particular significance was a typed letter dated April 4, 1961, bearing the official seal of "The Foreign Service of the United States" on its letterhead. Written by Cultural Attaché Cecil L. Sanford to Faulkner, it accompanied a package delivered to the home of Mr. and Mrs. Fielden where Faulkner was staying. The package, as the letter stated, contained various Faulkner titles in Spanish translation, which the author might wish to present personally to Sr. Rómulo Gallegos. On the verso of this letter was Faulkner's three-paragraph pencil holograph draft of the speech he subsequently delivered two days after the date affixed to the letter.

From the six minor strikeovers and only one circled five-word phrase Faulkner had shifted slightly from the beginning of one to the end of a contiguous sentence, it would appear that the composition had given its author very little difficulty. A plausible conjecture might suggest that, having written this brief piece, Faulkner easily could have dictated from this clean draft to his interpreter, Hugh Jencks, the contents of what would become a speech translated with relative literalness into Spanish. Likewise, in a matter of a half hour, Jencks could have retyped his Spanish transcription into ribbon and multiple carbon copies and handed them over to Faulkner for study. Indeed, Jencks also might have coached Faulkner in his pronunciation prior to making his Thursday morning speech at the Ministry of Education. Having delivered his speech in Spanish, Faulkner could have passed along for publication to the *El Universal* reporter in attendance his own ribbon copy of the Spanish translation by Jencks from which he had just read. A carbon copy of this speech in Spanish was in the same group of effects containing the original Faulkner holograph, just one sheet below it in a massive stack of related documents.

A complete and accurately transcribed Spanish version of the typescript of the text Faulkner delivered in Caracas, Venezuela, on April 6, 1961, appears below. Following it, in its original English version, is William Faulkner's own acceptance speech for the Andrés Bello Award.[5] Fortunately, English-language readers need rely no longer on a twice-removed rendition of this speech. Its recovery and present publication assure a reliable text, one that its author would have delivered had he chosen to do so in English.

El artista, quiéralo o no, descubre con el tiempo que ha llegado a dedicarse a seguir un solo camino, un solo objetivo, del cual no puede desviarse. Esto es: tiene que tratar por todos los medios y con todo el talento que tenga—su imaginación, su propia experiencia y sus poderes de observación—poner en una forma más duradera que su instante de vida frágil y efímero—en la pintura, la escultura, la música o en un libro—lo que él ha experimentado durante su breve período de existencia: la pasión y la esperanza, lo bello, lo trágico, lo cómico del hombre débil y frágil, pero a la vez indómito; del hombre que lucha y sufre y triunfa en medio de los conflictos del corazón humano, de la condición humana. A él no le toca solucionar la disyuntiva ni espera sobrevivirla excepto en la forma y el significado—y las memorias que representan e invocan—del mármol, la tela, la música y las palabras ordenadas que, algún día, tendrá que dejar como su testimonio.

Esta es, sin duda, su inmortalidad, tal vez la única que le sea concedida.
Quizá el mismo impulso que le condujera a esa dedicación, no era más que el
simple deseo de dejar grabadas en la puerta del olvido, por la cual todos tene-
mos que pasar algún día, las palabras "Lalo estuvo aquí."

Así pues, estando yo aquí, en este día de hoy, siento como si hubiera ya
tocado esa inmortalidad. Porque yo, un extraño aldeano que seguía en un
lugar muy distante, esa dedicación, ese afán de intentar capturar y fijar así, por
un momento en unas páginas, la verdad de la esperanza del hombre en el
medio de las complejidades de su corazón, he recibido aquí en Venezuela la
acolada que dice, en esencia: "Su dedicación no fue en vano. Lo que buscaba y
encontró e intentó capturar fue la verdad.

The artist, whether he would have chosen so or not, finds that he has ~~become~~
been dedicated to a single course and one from which he will never escape.
This is, he tries, with every means in his possession, his imagination, experience and observation, to put into some more durable form than his own fragile and ephemeral life—in paint or music or marble or the covers of a book—
that which he has learned in his brief spell of breathing—the passion and
hope, the beauty and horror and humor, amid the conflicts of his own heart,
in the human condition. He is not to solve this dilemma nor does he even
hope to survive it save in the shape and significance, the memories of the
marble and paint and music and ordered words which ~~to~~ someday he must
leave behind him.

This of course is his immortality, perhaps the only one. Perhaps the very
drive which has compelled him to that dedication was simply the desire to
have ~~written~~ inscribed beside that final door into oblivion through which he
first must pass, the words 'Kilroy was here.'

So, as I stand here today, I have already tasted that immortality. That I, a
country-bred ~~w~~ alien ~~from thousands of miles away~~ who followed that dedication thousands of miles away, to seek and try to capture and imitate for a
moment in a handful of printed pages, the truth of man's hope in the human
dilemma, have received here in Venezuela the official accolade which says in
effect— ~~Yes. What you~~ Your ~~search~~ dedication was not spent in vain. What
you sought and found and tried to imitate, was truth.

Part Two   "Impressions" of "Danzas Venezuela"

On that same evening in April 1961, under the auspices of the Department of State, as a cultural emissary of the United States government, in
the company of Mr. and Mrs. William Fielden, and with others from the
American entourage, William Faulkner attended a performance of indigenous music and dancing at the Teatro Municipal.[6]

The performance itself was divided into various acts, one of which had its premiere and was dedicated to William Faulkner. This act, inspired by three poems composed by Andrés Eloy Blanco, consisted of three dances that had been choreographed by Mrs. Paulina Ossona. Later that evening, perhaps backstage or at the formal dinner party given by Dr. and Mrs. Arturo Uslar Pietri, the lady in charge of the production, Mrs. Isabel Aretz de Ramón y Rivera, made a request of the celebrated American author that he put in writing his impressions of their offering.[7]

Even had Faulkner considered the request that he write this occasional piece a nuisance, doubtless he would have felt a sincere obligation to give it his best effort. After all, he regarded his position as cultural representative of the United States and his presence in Venezuela as matters of national importance. Furthermore, protocol demanded of him nothing less than compliance. Possibly the following day, working from a general outline of notes most likely supplied him by his assigned interpreter, Hugh Jencks, and drawing upon felicitous impressions from the previous evening, Faulkner composed a one-paragraph, 202-word encomium celebrating the occasion. In the end, the impressions to which he did give written form, ostensibly intended to extol a specific event, became an eloquent tribute to the people of Venezuela:[8]

Notes [by Hugh Jencks] which may be of help in writing a few lines on "Danzas Venezuela."[9]

The group is sponsored and its expenses defrayed by the Cultural and Social Welfare Section of the Ministry of Labor. The dancers receive training at the School of Artistic Formation (Development), whose directress is Mrs. Isabel Aretz de Ramón y Rivera, the determined lady of stentorian voice who asked if you would "write a few lines" about your impressions of the Thursday performance.

The three poem-dances which formed one group were given their premiere in your honor. They were "Hilandera" (The Spinning Woman or Weaver), "Silencio" (Silence) and "Giraluna" (a coined name which doesn't mean anything), three poems by Andrés Eloy Blanco, Venezuelan poet who died several years ago. The choreography was done by Paulina Ossona (Mrs.), of Argentina, who has been working with the Danzas Venezuela group recently.

It is my impression that what Mrs. Ramón y Rivera would like is not necessarily something referring specifically to the individual numbers on last night's program, but rather something of a general nature on your impressions which they could proudly reproduce on programs and in literature about the group. I put down the specific data merely as background.

Faulkner's Impressions of "Danzas Venezuela"

Anyone who had received as many honors as myself since reaching Venezuela, might have supposed that there was no new honor he could be worthy of. He would have been wrong. In this performance of Danzas Venezuela I saw not merely another warm and generous honor, gesture from one American country to a visitor from another one, I saw the spirit and history of Venezuela caught and held ~~for a moment~~ in a bright and ~~happy~~ warm moment of grace and skill and happiness, by young men and women who gave one the impression that they were doing it out of love for what they were doing, to show to this stranger, this foreigner, so that he could carry back home with him the ~~remembrance of~~ fuller poetic knowledge of a country which he had already come to admire ~~and respect,~~ never to forget the gesture nor the inspiration of it from the poetry of Andres Blanco and the other Venezuelan poets whose [*sic*] ~~names~~ perhaps had no names, which senora Ossona translated into spectacular and significant ~~so wonderfully into~~ motion, nor senora Ramon y Rivera who directed it and the young men and women who performed it. He thanks them all. He will not forget ~~it nor them.~~ the experience nor those who made it possible.

APPENDIX D

GHOSTWRITING
THE GHOSTWRITER

William Faulkner delivered his last public acceptance speech in New York City on May 24, 1962, less than six weeks before his death.[1] The occasion was the awarding to him of the Gold Medal for Fiction by the American Academy of Arts and Letters and the National Academy of Arts and Letters. Recalling the ceremony, Malcolm Cowley assessed Faulkner's speech with prescient, almost prophetic intuitiveness: "Faulkner's acceptance . . . had a tone of retrospection, of lament for the dignity and freedom of the past, that was not exactly new for him, but that seemed to have a new resonance. He compared his own gold medal with those that used to be awarded to products displayed at Leipzig, St. Louis, and other world's fairs."[2]

Indeed, if Faulkner's tone, as conveyed in a prose style that by then had long become synonymous with his name, was "not exactly new for him," its "resonance" was. But at that time, neither Cowley nor any other individual except the one man who had collaborated in writing Faulkner's acceptance speech, could have known that its resonance owed a substantial measure of indebtedness to the typewritten draft from which Faulkner had drawn his thematic inspiration, a version of the speech composed at his own suggestion by Faulkner's young friend, Joseph L. Blotner, assistant professor of English at the University of Virginia during and after the academic years of 1957 and 1958 when Faulkner was writer-in-residence at that institution.

Nor, for that matter, could Blotner himself have realized, at the time he was drafting his version of the speech Faulkner would utilize, that he would be co-conspiring in a pattern to which Faulkner had resorted at least twice before. Only during the last years of the sixties, while Blotner was gathering information for *Faulkner: A Biography,* would he discover that Faulkner previously had sought the assistance of Abram Minell in

writing his October 2, 1959, speech to the 7th Annual Conference of the
U.S. National Commission for UNESCO, and that two years prior, Faulkner had coerced Duncan Emrich, cultural affairs officer for the State Department's International Education Exchange Service in Greece, into writing the speech he would deliver on March 28, 1957, upon receiving the
Silver Medal of the Athens Academy.[3]

Clearly, during the last twelve years of his life, Faulkner seemed to
regard literary, civic, and humanitarian accolades bestowed upon him as
perfunctory and ephemeral afterthoughts or footnotes to his writing career. With few exceptions, the obligatory oratory that was required for
him to win deliverance from each award ceremony would be as tediously
bothersome and uninspired to compose as it appeared painful for him to
deliver publicly. Yet, with uneasy resolve, out of a patriotic or professional
sense of duty, he repeatedly acquiesced to conventional, formal protocol.
If only a few of his public utterances, most notably his Nobel Prize, "Never
Be Afraid," and "Delta Council" speeches, achieved oratorical and rhetorical eloquence worthy of universal acclaim, the others, at least, were idio-
syncratically Faulknerian in prose style, tone, and attitude, even one like
the 1962 Gold Medal speech upon which he had unabashedly collaborated.
Faulkner predictably was here a fastidious craftsman striving to make his
prose uniquely, distinctively his own, despite the highly derivative nature
of its motifs and image clusters. Indeed, in this case, his most compelling
task was to impose his Faulknerian style on the imitation in which the
draft had been written. Accomplishing this required four revisions before
he could feel satisfied that he had adequately transmuted Blotner's original
into his own personal expression.

Actually, the document from which Faulkner initially worked, a two-
page ribbon typescript with corrections in blue ink, was Blotner's revised
draft of his own initial two-leaf, three-page, blue-ink holograph rendering.
On the verso of the second leaf of this holograph, Blotner has written the
following explanatory comments referring to the diarylike pencil notations
he had made on this same page twenty-five years before: "I made these
pencil notes after William Faulkner told me, on one of his periodic visits to
my office in the English Department in Cabell Hall at the University of
Virginia, that he had to write an acceptance speech when he received the
Gold Medal for Fiction from the National Institute of Arts and Letters.
This was April 27, 1962. When he said 'I hate to swot up a speech for that
Gold Medal,' I volunteered to write one for him. I wrote the draft version
in blue ink and then gave him the black ribbon typescript version when he
visited my office again on May 4. When he returned on May 8, he gave the
typescript back to me and the carbon typescript of his final version of the
speech. 'Here's your copy,' he said. 'Maybe you can make some money out

of it sometime.' He delivered the speech on May 24, 1962, in New York."

These three documents were acquired from Joseph Blotner in early April 1987.[4] Ms. Nancy Johnson, librarian of the American Academy and Institute of Arts and Letters, confirmed by a letter that the academy did have on file the ribbon typescript of Faulkner's Gold Medal speech for 1962.[5] The accompanying photocopy proved to be identical to the carbon typescript Faulkner had given Blotner on May 8, 1962, except that the academy's copy carried in Faulkner's hand in blue-black ink the superscription, "Speech of William Faulkner for May 24th." Regarding the speech, Ms. Johnson wrote, "I looked through the correspondence files again and there is nothing at all to indicate that there was any other version of this speech. Miss Geffen's requests for an advance copy apparently went unanswered. It seems that Mr. Faulkner brought this typescript with him and left it here following the award presentation."

In point of fact, the complete census of extant manuscripts of Faulkner's 1962 acceptance speech upon receiving the Gold Medal for Fiction numbers seven documents, of which six are textually variant. The Brodsky Collection contains Joseph Blotner's three-page holograph original draft [A] and his revised two-page, hand-corrected, ribbon typescript [B]. The one-page, blue-ink holograph manuscript that Faulkner himself drafted after reading Blotner's text and adopting it as his prototype [C] and two sequentially advancing one-page authorial ribbon typescript revisionary drafts with holograph corrections [D & E] are part of the Faulkner Collections at the University of Virginia's Alderman Library.[6] The last typescript version in this sequence, the one-page ribbon copy [F] from which Faulkner read to its attending members and then deposited there, resides in the files of the American Academy and Institute of Arts and Letters. The carbon typescript [G] of this reading version, formerly in the possession of Joseph Blotner, is located in the Brodsky Collection.

Transcribed below in order of composition are Blotner's ribbon typescript version [B] followed by the carbon typescript [G] of the final version revised from [E]. Joseph Blotner's text is presented without textual apparatus but incorporates all his intended deletions and additions as though it were a fair-typed copy. The typed final version is transcribed as delivered.

[B] Blotner's Typescript Version

This award is to me a source of double pleasure, in that it is not simply a recognition of work done over long years in a demanding craft, but also because of itself apart, by its name and nature, it recognizes, I think, qualities most worthy of the artist's striving and man's cherishing. The substance of which the tangible embodiment of this award is formed can suggest many things: a system of finance, a long-gone politician's frenetic oratory, or the self-induced catastrophe of a mad king. But in the present context it suggests to me other, utterly different things. It is redolent of the past, of those distant days of quasi-innocence when the world's fairs at which medals were awarded were rare and almost magical happenings and not giant commercial enterprises occurring more often than presidential elections. It suggests not just the faded airs and rotogravures that record the vanished splendor which briefly crowned St. Louis or Leipzig. It evokes the qualities they celebrated, immortalized thereafter on labels identifying everything from great vintages to nonpareil pickle relishes.

I think that those gold medals—and their cousin-german counterparts, the shining blue ribbons that glittered on the tables of myriad forgotten county fairs—recognized qualities which, though they are still present today when the earth is worked like a mine and the factories begin to be worked by machines, were more clearly seen and more highly honored than they are today. Apart from the old testamental virtues, venerated in colony and frontier, these qualities cluster around the idea of individuality of a kind of excellence compounded of resourcefulness, independence, and complete uniqueness.

So, today when roads get shorter and neighbors closer, needs better provided for and range more circumscribed, it seems to me a good time to remember the qualities denoted by the gold medals of the last century. And I think it is vital for them to be a part of the artist and his work—for him and for those who read it—individuality and independence, to go beside the other qualities in the hierarchy that makes up man's best virtues, the pride and pity, the honor and compassion that sustain him in his life.

[G] Faulkner's Carbon Typescript Final Version

This award has, to me, a double value. It is not only a comforting recognition of some considerable years of reasonably hard and arduous, anyway consistently dedicated, work. It also recognizes and affirms, and so preserves, a quantity in our American legend and dream well worth preserving.

I mean a quantity in our past: that past which was a happier time in the sense that we were innocent of many of the strains and anguishes and fears which these atomic days have compelled on us. This award evokes the faded airs and dimming rotogravures which record that vanished splendor still inherent in the names of Saint Louis and Leipzig, the quantity which they celebrated and signified recorded still today in the labels of wine bottles and ointment jars.

I think that those gold medals, royal and unique above the myriad spawn of their progeny which were the shining ribbons fluttering and flashing among the booths and stall[s] of forgotten county fairs in recognition and accolade of a piece of tatting or an apple pie, did much more than record a victory. They affirmed the premise that there are no degrees of best; that one man's best is the equal of any other best, no matter how asunder in time or space or comparison, and should be honored as such.

We should keep that quantity, more than ever now, when roads get shorter and easier between aim and gain and goals become less demanding and more easily attained, and there is less and less space between elbows and more and more pressure on the individual to relinquish into one faceless serration like a mouthful of teeth, simply in order to find room to breathe. We should remember those times when the idea of an individuality of excellence compounded of resourcefulness and independence and uniqueness not only deserved a blue ribbon but got one. Let the past abolish the past when—and if—it can substitute something better; not us to abolish the past simply because it was.

NOTES

1. Life Masks

1. William Faulkner, interview with Jean Stein, reprinted in James B. Meriwether and Michael Millgate, eds., *Lion in the Garden: Interviews with William Faulkner, 1926–1962* (New York: Random House, 1968), p. 255.

2. See p. 65 below.

3. William Faulkner, *Absalom, Absalom!* (New York: Modern Library, 1951), pp. 9–10.

4. William Faulkner, *Knight's Gambit* (New York: Random House, 1949), p. 141.

5. William Faulkner, *The Unvanquished* (New York: Random House, 1938), p. 262.

6. William Faulkner, *The Hamlet* (New York: Random House, 1964), p. 111.

7. Joseph Blotner, ed., *Selected Letters of William Faulkner* (New York: Vintage Books, 1978), p. 216.

8. Patrick H. Samway, S.J., *Faulkner's Intruder in the Dust: A Critical Study of the Typescripts* (Troy, N.Y.: Whitson Publishing Company, 1980), p. [ix].

9. Louis Daniel Brodsky and Robert W. Hamblin, eds., *Faulkner: A Comprehensive Guide to the Brodsky Collection, Volume II: The Letters* (Jackson: University Press of Mississippi, 1984), p. 45.

10. Ibid., p. 94.

11. James B. Meriwether, ed., *Essays, Speeches, & Public Letters by William Faulkner* (New York: Random House, 1965), p. 144.

12. Meriwether and Millgate, *Lion in the Garden*, p. 82. This interview appeared in the *New York Times Book Review* on January 30, 1955.

13. Joseph Blotner, *Faulkner: A Biography* (New York: Random House, 1974), p. 289.

14. See ibid., p. 200. William Faulkner spelled his name without the "u" until 1920 when he was 23 years old.

15. Louis Daniel Brodsky, "The Autograph Manuscripts of Faulkner's 'The Lilacs,'" *Studies in Bibliography* 36 (1983): 240–252.

16. Blotner, *Selected Letters of William Faulkner*, p. 170.

17. William Faulkner, *Country Lawyer and Other Stories for the Screen,* ed. Louis Daniel Brodsky and Robert W. Hamblin (Jackson: University Press of Mississippi, 1987), pp. 83–101.

18. Blotner, *Selected Letters of William Faulkner,* p. 159.

19. Ibid., p. 148.

20. Ibid., p. 149.

21. Ibid., p. 152.

22. Ibid., pp. 153–154.

23. Ibid., p. 155.

24. Ibid., p. 157.

25. Ibid., p. 155.

26. The complete record of Faulkner's work on this project, including his different versions of the script, has been published in *Faulkner: A Comprehensive Guide to the Brodsky Collection, Volume III: The De Gaulle Story,* ed. Louis Daniel Brodsky and Robert W. Hamblin (Jackson: University Press of Mississippi, 1984).

27. Blotner, *Selected Letters of William Faulkner,* p. 165.

28. Ibid., p. 166.

29. Ibid.

30. See Louis Daniel Brodsky and Robert W. Hamblin, eds., *Faulkner: A Comprehensive Guide to the Brodsky Collection, Volume V: Manuscripts and Documents* (Jackson: University Press of Mississippi, 1989), pp. 316, 318–319.

31. See Faulkner, *Country Lawyer and Other Stories for the Screen,* pp. 61–81.

32. Blotner, *Selected Letters of William Faulkner,* pp. 169, 167.

33. Faulkner's "First Extended Treatment" and "Second Temporary Draft" appear in *Faulkner: A Comprehensive Guide to the Brodsky Collection, Volume IV: Battle Cry,* ed. Louis Daniel Brodsky and Robert W. Hamblin (Jackson: University Press of Mississippi, 1985).

34. Blotner, *Selected Letters of William Faulkner,* pp. 173–174.

35. Ibid., p. 177.

36. Ibid., pp. 170–171.

37. Ibid., p. 180.

38. Brodsky and Hamblin, *Faulkner: A Comprehensive Guide to the Brodsky Collection, Volume V,* pp. 320–321.

39. Blotner, *Selected Letters of William Faulkner,* p. 204.

40. Ibid., p. 186.

41. Ibid., p. 205.

42. William Faulkner, *The Sound and the Fury & As I Lay Dying* (New York: Modern Library, 1946), p. 9.

43. Ibid., pp. 10–11.

44. Blotner, *Selected Letters of William Faulkner,* p. 215.

45. Ibid., p. 219.

46. Ibid., p. 220.

47. Ibid., p. 166.

48. Meriwether, *Essays, Speeches, & Public Letters,* p. 119.

49. Ibid., p. 122.

50. Ibid., pp. 122–123.

51. Brodsky and Hamblin, *Faulkner: A Comprehensive Guide to the Brodsky Collection, Volume IV,* p. 110.

52. Brodsky and Hamblin, *Faulkner: A Comprehensive Guide to the Brodsky Collection, Volume II,* p. 217.

53. Ibid., p. 219.

54. See, for example, Blotner, *Selected Letters of William Faulkner,* pp. 75, 84, 122, 123, 128.

55. Brodsky and Hamblin, *Faulkner: A Comprehensive Guide to the Brodsky Collection, Volume II,* p. 150.

56. Ibid., p. 84.

57. Ibid., pp. 84–85.

58. Ibid., p. 91.

59. Ibid., p. 96.

60. See Carl Petersen, *Each in Its Ordered Place: A Faulkner Collector's Notebook* (Ann Arbor: Ardis, 1975), p. 96, item A27b.

61. See Appendix A, "Indian Giver."

62. Brodsky and Hamblin, *Faulkner: A Comprehensive Guide to the Brodsky Collection, Volume V,* pp. 328, 330.

63. Ibid., p. 135.

64. Ibid., p. 136.

65. Ibid., p. 200.

66. Ibid., p. 138.

67. See Appendix C, "From Yoknapatawpha to Caracas."

68. See Martin J. Dain, *Faulkner's County: Yoknapatawpha* (New York: Random House, 1964), p. 151, and Ed Meek, "Spring Workout," *Mississippi Magazine,* Spring 1961, pp. 12–13.

69. Brodsky and Hamblin, *Faulkner: A Comprehensive Guide to the Brodsky Collection, Volume II,* p. 286, photograph 43.

70. Bennett Cerf, *At Random: The Reminiscences of Bennett Cerf* (New York: Random House, 1977), p. 134.

71. Carvel Collins, ed., *William Faulkner: Early Prose and Poetry* (Boston and Toronto: Little, Brown and Company, 1962), p. 12.

72. Meriwether, *Essays, Speeches, & Public Letters,* p. 193.

73. See Appendix D, "Ghostwriting the Ghostwriter."

74. See p. 77 below.

75. Meriwether, *Essays, Speeches, & Public Letters,* pp. 181–182.

2. Poet-at-Large

1. William Faulkner, *Mississippi Poems* (Oxford: Yoknapatawpha Press, 1979), pp. 39, 41.

2. Blotner, *Selected Letters of William Faulkner,* p. 182.

3. See Blotner, *Faulkner: A Biography,* pp. 161–162.

4. For a detailed account of Faulkner's work on these early volumes, see ibid., pp. 307–312, 347–350.

5. *Images Old and New,* by Richard Aldington, is one of numerous "survivors"

from Phil Stone's library acquired by William Boozer and now part of his Faulkner Collection.

6. This, and eleven other poems variously dated October through December 1924, was incorporated by Faulkner into a manuscript with the title *Mississippi Poems* (see n. 8). On December 30, 1924, Faulkner inscribed a carbon copy of this typed manuscript for an old school friend, Myrtle Ramey. Among the offerings contained in this group was the poem "Pregnacy" [*sic*]. With its unconsciously misspelled title, "Pregnacy" ended up as the final poem in the series, which one can only suppose Faulkner and Stone were preparing, possibly in the process of adding to it, for eventual publication. See Louis Daniel Brodsky and Robert W. Hamblin, eds., *Faulkner: A Comprehensive Guide to the Brodsky Collection, Volume I: The Bio-bibliography* (Jackson: University Press of Mississippi, 1982), pp. 35–40, 33, and *Volume V*, pp. 75–84.

7. On the publication of *The Marble Faun* and Faulkner's difficulties in his positions as postmaster and scoutmaster, see Blotner, *Faulkner: A Biography*, pp. 347–382.

8. Faulkner composed at least three other books of poetry either concurrent with or following *The Marble Faun*. One, consisting of fourteen typed pages, twelve poems and a title page dated "October, 1924," was called *Mississippi Poems*. A second, lettered and bound by hand and dated June 1926, contained sixteen poems variously dated June through September 1925; it was entitled *Helen: A Courtship*. The third, *A Green Bough*, published in 1933 by Smith and Haas, consisted almost entirely of poems composed before December 19, 1924, although in most cases revised. Among these was a revised version of the poem "Pregnacy," now carrying the roman numeral XXIX instead of a title.

9. Malcolm Cowley, *The Faulkner-Cowley File: Letters and Memories, 1944–1962* (New York: Viking Press, 1966), pp. 67–68. In a footnote Cowley says "moral reasons" refers to Faulkner's notoriety as the author of *Sanctuary*. *Sanctuary* was not actually published until February 9, 1931.

10. This information was supplied to me by Miss Jacquelin Jones, daughter of Mrs. Homer K. Jones, in a telephone conversation on May 14, 1982. At that time, Miss Jones still resided at the address to which Faulkner mailed his letter to Mrs. Jones dated "Dec. 2. 1924." Miss Jones also noted that her mother, having been born in 1884, would have been forty years of age at the time she and Faulkner, age twenty-seven, met in her home. Furthermore, she conjectured, Faulkner might indeed have been "taken" by her mother because the latter was a well-informed reader of modern fiction and poetry.

11. Brodsky and Hamblin, *Faulkner: A Comprehensive Guide to the Brodsky Collection, Volume II*, p. 3. Faulkner wrote his letter to Mrs. Jones and was "fired" as postmaster within a space of a few weeks. It is interesting to compare his phrase "moral charge" in the letter to the biographical note supplied to Cowley, on December 8, 1945, about being dismissed as scoutmaster for "moral reasons" (see n. 9). Faulkner clearly intends the euphemism to stand for his drinking habits.

12. One such instance appears obliquely in a letter to Saxe Commins dated December 24, 1952, in which he complains: "I should have stayed the tramp, with one shirt, which I was born to be" (see Brodsky and Hamblin, *Faulkner: A Comprehensive Guide to the Brodsky Collection, Volume II*, p. 103).

13. Years later similar revelry produced two ink-scribbled, nearly illegible quatrains approximating James Joyce's poem "Watching the Needleboats at San Sabba," which Faulkner entered on the endpaper of Anthony Buttitta's copy of *Mosquitoes* (see Petersen, *Each in Its Ordered Place,* p. 29).

14. It should be noted that the "correct copy" Faulkner sent to Mrs. Jones is actually a second carbon copy, not the manifold copy, which would have been positioned just beneath the carbon paper during typing; in fact, it is a third copy of the poem. Close study shows that this "correct copy" is an exact, though less distinct, duplicate of the carbon copy of "Pregnacy" that appeared as the last poem in the manuscript, *Mississippi Poems,* that Faulkner gave to Myrtle Ramey on December 30, 1924 (see n. 6).

3. "Elder Watson in Heaven"

1. Meriwether and Millgate, *Lion in the Garden,* p. 100.

2. Faulkner, *The Sound and the Fury & As I Lay Dying,* p. 209.

3. The sales history of *The Hamlet* is recorded in Blotner, *Faulkner: A Biography,* pp. 1050–1051, 1053, see also Blotner, *Selected Letters of William Faulkner,* pp. 132–133.

4. See Blotner, *Selected Letters of William Faulkner,* pp. 284–285.

5. Robert W. Daniel, *A Catalogue of the Writings of William Faulkner* (New Haven: Yale University Library, 1942).

6. For a complete transcription of this letter, see Brodsky and Hamblin, *Faulkner: A Comprehensive Guide to the Brodsky Collection, Volume II,* p. 21.

7. Both poems were ribbon typescripts, with typed signature on the bottom left-hand side of the last page; both poems, the former consisting of two pages, the latter of three pages, were executed on 8½-by-14-inch unwatermarked legal sheets. And at the bottom of the third page of the "Pierrot" poem, penciled in Mrs. Wasson's hand, appeared this note: "Written while visiting in the house / of Mr & Mrs Ben F. Wasson / in 1921."

8. See Brodsky and Hamblin, *Faulkner: A Comprehensive Guide to the Brodsky Collection, Volume V,* pp. 74–75.

9. Reading "Richard Cory" (1897), "Miniver Cheevy" (1910), "Cassandra" (1916), "Bewick Finzer" (1916), and especially "Flammonde" (1916), one is struck by their pervasive affinities to William Faulkner's "Elder Watson in Heaven." These poems and others by E. A. Robinson focus with irony and occasional pity on human failures; they are about ambiguous lives generally characterized by hypocrisy, though not of the religious kind. Additionally, "Richard Cory," "Bewick Finzer," and "Flammonde" are narrated by the collective, personalized first-person plural "we," the technique employed by Faulkner to achieve a similar sense of familiarity in his poem.

In Robinson's "Flammonde," it becomes evident that the initial two octaves of this poem contain phrases Faulkner actually might have borrowed for his description of Elder Watson. Robinson's first stanza describes and qualifies "the man Flammonde" as appearing "with glint of *iron* in his walk" (emphasis added). Faulkner's second quatrain reads: "Elder Watson, when *erect* / And circumscribed with moral good, / Presents the world an *iron* curve / Of dogma and of platitude" (emphasis added). Similarly, the second octave of "Flammonde" begins: "*Erect,* with his alert repose / About him, and about his clothes" (emphasis added), and concludes with a couplet that might serve as a synecdoche for Elder Watson's condition as well: "And what he needed for his fee / To live, he borrowed graciously."

In fact, under the imperious tutelage of Phil Stone during the years of his poetic apprenticeship commencing in 1916, Faulkner's reading of and interest in E. A. Robinson's poetry may have been considerably more extensive, his admiration and debt greater, than scholars have considered and appreciated. In a letter, now part of the William Boozer collection of Faulkner materials, Robinson himself may have documented this possibly not-so-obscure or fugitive interest on the parts of Stone and Faulkner when he wrote on March 7, 1922, politely discounting Stone's apparent notion that he had used Swinburne as a model for a particular poem:

My Dear Mr. Stone,
  Let me thank you for the poem by Swinburne—which I do not remember, though I must have seen it—and for your interesting comment. I should have said [?] Swinburne, if only for the line, "All the sting [?] and all the stain [?] of long delight—." On the other hand I "see what you mean" and thank you for your courtesy. I am glad to infer from your note that you and your friend have found something in my work that you remember.

Yours very sincerely
E. A. Robinson

Robinson's note provides insight not only into the reading habits and cultural predilections of Stone but those of his student as well. Confirmed by Phil Stone's widow, Emily Whitehurst Stone, there is absolutely no doubt that the "friend" to which Robinson refers in his last sentence is "Bill Faulkner."

In "Verse Old and Nascent: A Pilgrimage," dated October 1924 (apparently the only extant typescript is in the Brodsky Collection) and first published in the *Double Dealer* 7 (April 1925): 129–131, Faulkner himself reinforced this connection when he eulogized the ending of his apprenticeship to nineteenth- and twentieth-century poets and poetry with this valedictory: "That page is closed to me forever. I read Robison [*sic*] and Frost with pleasure, and Aldington; Conrad Aiken's minor music still echoes in my head; but beyond these, that period might never have been."

Over thirty years later, Faulkner recalled Robinson in substantially similar terms. Responding to a question about poets whose work he liked, Faulkner recalled, "I remember when I read more poetry I read Elinor Wylie, Conrad Aiken, E. A. Robinson, Frost" (*Faulkner in the University*, ed. Frederick W. Gwynn and Joseph L. Blotner [New York: Vintage, 1965], p. 15).

10. Faulkner, *The Sound and the Fury & As I Lay Dying*, p. 212.

11. Ibid., pp. 341–342.

12. See Brodsky and Hamblin, *Faulkner: A Comprehensive Guide to the Brodsky Collection, Volume V*, p. 324.

13. Ibid., p. 325.

14. William Faulkner, *The Mansion* (New York: Random House, 1964), p. 419.

4. Bill and Buzz: Fellow Scenarists

1. Blotner, *Selected Letters of William Faulkner*, p. 172.

2. Ibid., p. 177.

3. William Faulkner and Meta Carpenter first met in 1935, when he was working on the script of *The Road to Glory* and she was secretary to Howard Hawks. They soon became lovers, that relationship continuing until Miss Carpenter's marriage to Wolfgang Rebner, a concert pianist, in 1937. Following the Rebners' divorce in 1942, and upon Faulkner's return to Hollywood that same year, Faulkner and Meta resumed their affair. The liaison ended when Meta remarried Rebner in 1945, although Faulkner continued to correspond with Meta until his death in 1962. The story of Faulkner's relationship to Meta is recounted in Meta Carpenter Wilde and Orin Borsten, *A Loving Gentleman: The Love Story of William Faulkner and Meta Carpenter* (New York: Simon and Schuster, 1976).

4. See Appendix B, "'Pappy's' Recipe for Curing Pork."

5. This script by Bezzerides was filmed and shown nationally on the Public Broadcasting Service on December 17, 1979, and was subsequently edited by Ann Abadie and published by University Press of Mississippi in 1980.

5. From Fictionist to Polemicist

1. Blotner, *Selected Letters of William Faulkner*, p. 190.

2. Gwynn and Blotner, *Faulkner in the University*, p. 177.

3. *Proceedings of the American Academy of Arts and Letters and the National Institute of Arts and Letters* (New York: Spiral Press, 1951), p. 19.

4. Cowley, *Faulkner-Cowley File*, p. 126.

5. Ibid., p. 67.

6. Ibid., p. 96.

7. Ibid., p. 99.

8. Blotner, *Selected Letters of William Faulkner*, p. 302.

9. This document, previously unpublished, is in the Brodsky Collection.

10. W. Alton Bryant to William Faulkner, photocopy from Joseph Blotner's files, now in the Brodsky Faulkner Collection, Southeast Missouri State University.

11. Marvin M. Black press release, photocopy from Blotner files, Brodsky Collection.

12. Marvin M. Black to Harrison Smith, photocopy from Blotner files, Brodsky Collection.

13. Black press release, Brodsky Collection.

14. Harrison Smith to Marvin M. Black, photocopy from Blotner files, Brodsky Collection.

15. William Faulkner to W. Alton Bryant, photocopy from Blotner files, Brodsky Collection.

16. W. Alton Bryant to Marvin M. Black, photocopy from Blotner files, Brodsky Collection.

17. W. Alton Bryant to William Faulkner, photocopy from Blotner files, Brodsky Collection.

18. Blotner, *Selected Letters of William Faulkner*, pp. 249–250.

19. C. T. Lanham to William Faulkner, photocopy from Blotner files, Brodsky Collection.

20. Ibid.

21. William Faulkner to C. T. Lanham, photocopy from Blotner files, Brodsky Collection.

22. William Faulkner to Ernest Hemingway, photocopy supplied by Carlos Baker to Joseph Blotner, Blotner files, Brodsky Collection.

23. Cowley, *Faulkner-Cowley File,* p. 96.

24. Cleanth Brooks' copy of this mimeographed document, now in the Brodsky Collection, p. 1.

25. Ibid., pp. 3–4.

26. William Faulkner, *Go Down, Moses* (New York: Random House, 1942), pp. 294–295.

27. William Faulkner, *Intruder in the Dust* (New York: Random House, 1948), p. 155.

28. Cowley, *Faulkner-Cowley File,* pp. 110–111.

29. Ibid., p. 107.

30. Tom Dardis, *Some Time in the Sun* (New York: Charles Scribner's Sons, 1976), p. 8.

31. Blotner, *Selected Letters of William Faulkner,* p. 166.

32. Ibid.

33. Faulkner, *Country Lawyer and Other Stories for the Screen,* p. 20.

34. Ibid., p. 46.

35. Ibid., p. 47.

36. Ibid.

37. Ibid., pp. 48–49. See "Funeral Sermon for Mammy Caroline Barr," *Essays, Speeches, & Public Letters,* ed. Meriwether, pp. 117–118.

38. Budd Schulberg, "A Bell for Tarchova," *Saturday Evening Post,* October 24, 1942, pp. 12ff.

39. Brodsky and Hamblin, *Faulkner: A Comprehensive Guide to the Brodsky Collection, Volume IV,* pp. 102–103.

40. Ibid., p. 185.

41. See pp. 70–73.

42. Brooks' copy, p. 3.

43. William Faulkner, *Sanctuary* (New York: Modern Library, 1932), p. vi.

44. See Blotner, *Selected Letters of William Faulkner,* pp. 122, 128.

45. Faulkner, *Go Down, Moses,* p. 351.

46. Ibid., p. 361.

47. Cowley, *Faulkner-Cowley File,* p. 110.

48. Faulkner, *Intruder in the Dust,* pp. 154–155.

49. Meriwether, *Essays, Speeches, & Public Letters,* p. 119.

50. Ibid., p. 89.

51. Ibid., p. 91.

52. Meriwether and Millgate, *Lion in the Garden,* pp. 261–262.

53. Meriwether, *Essays, Speeches, & Public Letters,* p. 226.

54. Ibid., p. 225.

55. Faulkner to Hemingway, Brodsky Collection.

56. Cowley, *Faulkner-Cowley File,* p. 96.

57. Faulkner to Hemingway, Brodsky Collection.

58. Meriwether and Millgate, *Lion in the Garden,* p. 255.

59. See p. 95.

60. Cowley, *Faulkner-Cowley File,* p. 111.

6. Sorting the Mail

1. Meriwether, *Essays, Speeches, & Public Letters,* p. 101.

2. Faulkner, *Intruder in the Dust,* p. 195.

3. Faulkner, *Requiem for a Nun* (1951); *A Fable* (1954); *The Town* (1957); *The Mansion* (1959); *The Reivers* (1962); *Collected Stories* (1950); *The Faulkner Reader* (1954); *Big Woods* (1955).

4. The forty-three letters—which passed in succession from Faulkner to Kate Baker to Mr. and Mrs. William Fielden to Mrs. Victoria Fielden Johnson—alluded to or excerpted in this chapter are now a part of the Brodsky Faulkner Collection at Southeast Missouri State University.

5. The article, entitled "Kentucky: May: Saturday: Three Days to the Afternoon," is reprinted in Meriwether, *Essays, Speeches, & Public Letters,* pp. 52–61.

6. Meriwether, *Essays, Speeches, & Public Letters,* pp. 86–87, 91.

7. Ibid., pp. 86–87.

8. Ibid., p. 87.

9. Ibid.

10. See Meriwether and Millgate, *Lion in the Garden,* pp. 257–264.

11. For a detailed account of this incident, see Blotner, *Faulkner: A Biography,* pp. 1590–1592.

12. Meriwether, *Essays, Speeches, & Public Letters,* pp. 218–219.

13. Ibid., pp. 92–106.

14. Ibid., p. 226.

15. Ibid., p. 225.

16. Meriwether and Millgate, *Lion in the Garden,* pp. 265–266.

17. Blotner, *Faulkner: A Biography,* pp. 1591–1592.

18. Ibid., p. 1599.

19. See Blotner, *Faulkner: A Biography,* pp. 403–405.

20. Meriwether, *Essays, Speeches, & Public Letters,* p. 224.

21. Ibid.

22. Ibid., pp. 109, 111.

7. "White Beaches"

1. Blotner, *Selected Letters of William Faulkner,* p. 348.

2. Related to Louis Daniel Brodsky on May 21, 1985, in a personal interview with Victoria Fielden Johnson, Cape Coral, Florida.

3. Estelle Oldham, Faulkner's childhood sweetheart, had married Cornell Franklin on April 18, 1918. Estelle and Cornell had two children, Malcolm and Victoria, but were separated in 1926 and divorced on April 29, 1929. Estelle returned to Oxford with the children and resumed her love relationship with Faulkner. Faulkner and Estelle were married on June 20, 1929, at College Hill, Mississippi.

4. See Appendix A, "Indian Giver."

5. This copy of *The Wishing Tree* is now in the Brodsky Collection, housed at Southeast Missouri State University.

6. Faulkner was employed as a screenwriter in Hollywood for Twentieth Century-Fox during this period.

7. Faulkner entered these respective inscriptions in copies of *Pylon* (1935) and *Doctor Martino and Other Stories* (1934), both now in the Brodsky Collection.

8. Blotner, *Faulkner: A Biography,* p. 957.

9. Wife of Ole Miss history professor James W. Silver. The Silvers were close personal friends of the Faulkners and Fieldens.

10. See Blotner, *Selected Letters of William Faulkner,* pp. 163–164.

11. See Appendix B, "'Pappy's' Recipe for Curing Pork."

12. Blotner, *Selected Letters of William Faulkner,* p. 166.

13. These letters are now in the Malcolm A. Franklin archive at the University of South Carolina, Columbia.

14. Malcolm Franklin, *Bitterweeds: Life with William Faulkner at Rowan Oak* (Irving, Texas: The Society for the Study of Traditional Culture, 1977).

15. Three such books are the first British editions of *As I Lay Dying, The Wild Palms,* and *The Hamlet,* which Faulkner inscribed to Franklin on March 20, 1946, shortly upon his return from military service during World War II. These volumes are now in the Brodsky Collection at Southeast Missouri State University. See Brodsky and Hamblin, *Faulkner: A Comprehensive Guide to the Brodsky Collection, Volume I,* p. 64, #177; p. 114, #485; p. 123, #521.

16. William Faulkner, *Sanctuary* (New York: Modern Library, 1932), p. vi.

17. See, for example, Brodsky and Hamblin, *Faulkner: A Comprehensive Guide to the Brodsky Collection, Volume II,* p. 232, item 1394.

18. Meriwether and Millgate, *Lion in the Garden,* p. 261.

19. See, for example, Brodsky and Hamblin, *Faulkner: A Comprehensive Guide to the Brodsky Collection, Volume II,* pp. 133–134, item 986.

20. See pp. 63–65, 68, 77–78.

21. This copy was shown to me during my interview with Victoria Fielden Johnson on May 21, 1985; the book remains in her possession.

22. See Blotner, *Faulkner: A Biography,* p. 541 and corresponding note.

23. The manuscript version of this poem, in Estelle's holograph, formerly in the possession of Victoria Franklin Fielden, is now in the Brodsky Collection.

Appendix A

1. The booklet itself consists of front and back boards, covered in colored paper, with a blank sheet pasted down to the interior surface of each board. In addition, the front cover carries a paste-on paper label bearing in black ink Faulkner's hand-printed title, THE WISHING TREE. The pages themselves, measuring evenly with the boards, 5 1/2 × 6 3/4 inches, consist of a free-front endpaper with blank recto and verso, title page [i], verso of title page noting date, place, and number of copies [ii], dedication page [iii], blank verso of dedication page [iv], pages 1–67 [68], running in correct paginated sequence on the typed text, a blank facer to the last page of text [69], and a blank verso [70].

2. William Faulkner, *The Wishing Tree* (New York: Random House, [April 11] 1967). Illustrations by Don Bolognese. The limited and trade copies of this book are from the same printing.

3. This information has been taken from the Application for Copyright Regis-

tration for a Nondramatic Literary Work, Form TX, United States Copyright Office, Library of Congress, Jan. 1980.

4. This carbon, typed manuscript of 47 pages is located in the University of Virginia, Alderman Library, and carries the accession number 9821. The typed page numbers run: 1–37, 39 (38 has been entered in ink above the typed designation 39), 39–47. The text is sequential and unbroken throughout. For the listing of this accession number and verification of the textual sequence and pagination, as well as for the information relevant to all referred to holdings at the University of Virginia, Alderman Library, I gratefully acknowledge the assistance of Edmund Berkeley, Jr., Curator of Manuscripts.

5. For this information, I am indebted to Professor James W. Silver, who, having had made available to him during the 1950s the diary of Calvin S. Brown, recorded this data from Dr. Brown's entry of February 11, 1927, on the cover sheet of a typescript he had had copied from the Brown typescript of *The Wishing-Tree*. Dr. Silver's copy resides in the Brodsky Collection.

6. See Brodsky and Hamblin, *Faulkner: A Comprehensive Guide to the Brodsky Collection, Volume I*, p. 143.

7. Ibid., p. 146.

8. This carbon, typed manuscript of 44 consecutively numbered pages is located at the University of Virginia, Alderman Library, and carries the accession number 10,124-a.

9. Appearing on page [iii] of the Victoria typed booklet, the five-line epigram that follows is introduced by the second of two dedications: To Victoria / " . . . I have seen music, heard / Grave and windless bells; mine air / Hath verities of vernal leaf and bird. / Ah, let this fade; it doth and must; nor grieve, / Dream ever, though; she ever young and fair." Except for a variation in the number of dots that follow the initial quotation marks (twelve in the Brown version; seven in the Victoria version), and in the Victoria version the substitution of a period at the end of line 3 for four dashes at the end of the same line in the Brown text, the first four lines are identical. Only the fifth, final lines are at variance. The last line of the Brown version reads: "Wish ever, thou; nor gain, but find it fair."

10. See Brodsky and Hamblin, *Faulkner: A Comprehensive Guide to the Brodsky Collection, Volume I*, p. 271.

11. See Brodsky and Hamblin, *Faulkner: A Comprehensive Guide to the Brodsky Collection, Volume II*, p. 244.

12. Ibid., p. 266.

13. Ibid., pp. 291–292.

Appendix B

1. Six years later, Faulkner would compose a mood set piece for the opening of his new novel, *Intruder in the Dust*, which, through the eyes of twelve-year-old Chick Mallison, describes the ubiquitous occupation engaging the country populace outside Jefferson, Mississippi, at the time of "the first winter cold-snap":

> . . . from the first farmyard they passed and then again and again and again came the windless tang of woodsmoke and they could see in the back yards the black iron pots already steaming while women . . . stoked wood under them and the men . . . whetted

knives or already moved about the pens where hogs grunted and squealed, not quite startled, not alarmed but just alerted as though sensing already even though only dimly their rich and immanent [*sic*] destiny; by nightfall the whole land would be hung with their spectral intact tallowcolored empty carcasses immobilised by the heels in attitudes of frantic running as though full tilt at the center of the earth. (*Intruder in the Dust* [New York: Random House, 1948], p. 4)

2. This single-spaced, single-page manuscript, typed by Faulkner, remained in the possession of William and Victoria Fielden until 1975, when it and other family effects became the property of Victoria Fielden Johnson. In May 1985, Mrs. Johnson made legal disposition of her inherited Faulkner archive by placing it in the Brodsky Faulkner Collection at Southeast Missouri State University.

3. In a letter to me dated August 5, 1986, Victoria Fielden Johnson wrote: ". . . virtually all of the food served at Rowanoak in the forties derived from hunting, fishing, hog and chicken-raising, and vegetables and fruit grown there (and canned or preserved by Grandmama [Estelle]). Of course, some items, such as coffee, rice, sugar, etc. had to be bought at the store, but *most* came from the land and its animals."

Appendix C

1. See Blotner, *Faulkner: A Biography*. The notes accompanying pages 1779–1786 detailing Faulkner's Venezuelan trip in April 1961 appear on pages 213–214 of the Notes section of the second volume. Blotner cites "Charles Harner, American Embassy, Caracas, to Dept. of State, 27 Apr. 1961; Hugh Jencks, 'Report to the North American Association on the Visit of Mr. Faulkner'" as his sources for the description of events and the specific award ceremony. But he does not date the Jencks report (it was May 10, 1961) and, as remarked below, he does not document the source of his quotation in English from the speech.

2. In the one-volume edition in 1984 of his more comprehensive *Faulkner: A Biography,* Blotner condenses all reference to the speech in one sentence, without quotation: "After Faulkner read his short, graceful acceptance speech—in Spanish—he took from his buttonhole the prized rosette of the Legion of Honor and replaced it with that of the Order of Andrés Bello."

3. In a phone conversation I had with Joseph Blotner on June 18, 1985, he very kindly confirmed that in October 1972 he had supplied Meriwether with a photocopy of Muna Lee's two-page undated translation of Faulkner's Andrés Bello speech from the Spanish. He also quoted to me the following note that Muna Lee had penned at the end of page 2 of her translation: "This is my attempted translation. It is wholly unauthorized: Mr. Faulkner never saw it. Perhaps Mrs. Faulkner and Mrs. Summers would be willing to go over it and give it his turn of phrase. If they would not be willing to do so, and disapprove its present form, please destroy it. M. L."

4. The reprint of the Spanish translation actually created some incorrect variations in punctuation, spelling, accent marks, and pronoun correspondence from the text as printed in *El Universal;* more seriously, it allowed to go unrestored

almost half of the penultimate sentence apparently dropped by the American typesetter.

5. The important differences between the Faulkner holograph original and the Lee translation from the Spanish may be illustrated by quotation from Miss Lee's opening sentence versus Faulkner's: "The artist, whether or not he wishes it, discovers with the passage of time that he has come to pursue a single path, a single objective, from which he cannot deviate." Some of the differences derive, of course, as much from the Spanish version as from the translator, although these deviations account for very few of the major distortions attributable to Muna Lee's rendition. One such difference does occur, however, in the following version of Miss Lee's second paragraph: "This undoubtedly is his immortality; it may be, the only immortality that will be granted him. Perhaps the very impulse that led him to that dedication was nothing more than the single desire to leave carved upon the portal of forgetfulness through which *all of us must some day pass* the words 'He passed this way'" (emphasis added). The phrase in italics represents a transposition from singular to plural pronouns committed by the original translator from English into Spanish, not the reverse as is generally the case in carrying across the relatively literal Spanish translation into English. The final sentence in Miss Lee's version goes, ". . . striving to capture and thus fix for a moment on some pages the truth of man's hope amidst the complexities of his heart, have received here in Venezuela the accolade which says in essence: 'What he sought and found and tried to capture was Truth.'"

6. See note 1 for Blotner's sources for information relating to a description of events and for the specific fact that Faulkner "wrote out a short speech of thanks to the dancers." However, Blotner does not date the Jencks report (it was May 10, 1961) to which he refers, and he supplies no supporting evidence that Faulkner ever delivered a "speech." Furthermore, from the information disclosed in note 7, it would seem unlikely that Faulkner had his thoughts formulated in time to present them that night to the dancers; unlikely, in fact, that he would present them earlier than Friday, April 7, 1961.

7. From the reference to "last night's program," there seems little question that the sheet containing "Notes which may be of help in writing a few lines on 'Danzas Venezuela'" was typed out on Friday, April 7, 1961, and given to Faulkner, doubtless by Hugh Jencks, his interpreter and go-between. This sheet and the holograph manuscript of Faulkner's impressions of "Danzas Venezuela," cited in note 8, were clipped together, apparently as they had been joined and set aside by Faulkner twenty-four years before I discovered them.

8. I found both the "Notes" cited in note 7 and this holograph document while examining myriad family effects and artifacts in the possession of Victoria Fielden Johnson. I am deeply indebted to her for graciously welcoming me on my visit to her in Cape Coral, Florida, from May 20 to 24, 1985, and for letting me inspect and acquire these and various other documents, letters, manuscripts, and photographs relating to William Faulkner and his family that formerly had belonged to her parents.

9. The system of transcription is that recommended by Fredson Bowers, "Transcription of Manuscripts: The Record of Variants," *Studies in Bibliography* 29 (1976): 212–264.

Appendix D

1. Meriwether, *Essays, Speeches, & Public Letters*, pp. 168–169. This speech was originally published in *Proceedings of the American Academy of Arts and Letters and the National Institute of Arts and Letters*, second series (1963).

2. Cowley, *The Faulkner-Cowley File*, p. 149.

3. See Blotner, *Faulkner: A Biography*, pp. 1744–1745, 1649–1652.

4. These materials, along with other significant items from Blotner's Faulkner files, are now housed in the Brodsky Collection at Southeast Missouri State University.

5. Letter from Nancy Johnson to Louis D. Brodsky, April 9, 1987, signed ribbon typescript, 1 page, on letterhead of American Academy and Institute of Arts and Letters.

6. All three Faulkner manuscripts at the University of Virginia's Alderman Library bear the same accession number: 9817F. Permission to publish is gratefully acknowledged.

INDEX